COLD COMFORT

Mothers, Professionals, and
Attention Deficit Disorder

DATE DUE

Mothers ⋯⋯⋯ isorder must
inevitabl ⋯⋯⋯ osis within a
context c ⋯⋯⋯ disorder and
the legiti ⋯⋯⋯ sions within
an overri ⋯⋯⋯ *Cold Comfort*
provides ⋯⋯⋯ with/against
the 'help ⋯⋯⋯ ent for their
children.

Malaci ⋯⋯⋯ rs of ADD/
ADHD c ⋯⋯⋯ for Ritalin to
manage t ⋯⋯⋯ assumptions
of materr ⋯⋯⋯ n documents
Malacrid ⋯⋯⋯ d children in
both Car ⋯⋯⋯ ray in which
these wc ⋯⋯⋯ npares their
narrative ⋯⋯⋯ the complex
mother-c ⋯⋯⋯ of her critical
inquiry.

Drawi ⋯⋯⋯ nd feminist
standpoi ⋯⋯⋯ o qualitative
methodo ⋯⋯⋯ raphy of the
construct ⋯⋯⋯ . On a more
personal ⋯⋯⋯ d satisfying
examinat ⋯⋯⋯ e and private
challenges linked to ADD/ADHD.

CLAUDIA MALACRIDA is an assistant professor in the Department of Sociology at the University of Lethbridge.

COLD COMFORT

Mothers, Professionals, and Attention Deficit Disorder

Claudia Malacrida

UNIVERSITY OF TORONTO PRESS
Toronto Buffalo London

© University of Toronto Press Incorporated 2003
Toronto Buffalo London
Printed in Canada

ISBN 0-8020-8752-3 (cloth)
ISBN 0-8020-8558-X (paper)

Printed on acid-free paper

National Library of Canada Cataloguing in Publication

Malacrida, Claudia, 1953–
 Cold comfort : mothers, professionals, and attention deficit
 disorder / Claudia Malacrida.

 Includes bibliographical references and index.
 ISBN 0-8020-8752-3 (bound)   ISBN 0-8020-8558-X (pbk.)

 1. Attention-deficit-disordered children.   2. Mother and child.
 3. Mothers – Interviews.   4. Attention-deficit hyperactivity
 disorder – Diagnosis – Cross-cultural studies.   5. Attention-deficit
 hyperactivity disorder – Treatment – Cross-cultural studies.
 I. Title.

 RJ506.H9M34 2003   306.874'3   C2003-900681-6

This book has been published with the help of a grant from the Canadian
Federation for the Humanities and Social Sciences, through the Aid to
Scholary Publications Programme, using funds provided by the Social
Sciences and Humanities Research Council of Canada.

University of Toronto Press acknowledges the financial assistance to its
publishing program of the Canada Council for the Arts and the Ontario
Arts Council.

University of Toronto Press acknowledges the financial support for its
publishing activities of the Government of Canada through the Book
Publishing Industry Development Program (BPIDP).

For Hilary

Contents

Acknowledgments

Cold Comfort began as a doctoral dissertation, but earlier than that, it had germinated during my own chilling experiences of dealing with attention deficit disorder on behalf of my daughter Hilary. During my years of research and the writing of the book, Hilary's life as a student took a decided turn for the better when she entered Foothills Academy, a Calgary school specifically geared towards providing education to children with learning difficulties. I am more than grateful to the good folks at Foothills, and for the care and excellence they brought to my daughter's education.

During those years, my husband Carey provided emotional support and intellectual challenges. As well, he took on sole care of our home and family for protracted periods of my research and teaching time. I am blessed. My good friend Anne Hughson, whose work in the disability advocacy movement challenged me both personally and politically, provided me with ample opportunities to thrash out the details, consider the politics, and refuse the easy answers. Finally, a number of people in Canada and the U.K. were helpful in bringing participants into the project and in familiarizing me with aspects of AD(H)D in their local areas. Thanks to Monica Alcide, Andrea Bilbow, Gordon Bullivant, Allan Rimmer, and Gina Betteridge.

The academic community of the University of Alberta in Edmonton, and particularly my supervisor, Ros Sydie, provided opportunities for exploring and theorizing as the project developed. As well, Joane Martel and Jerry Kachur provided excellent critiques of project, both before and at its defence. Of course, my dear friend Arthur W. Frank of the University of Calgary provided his ongoing wisdom and insight, understanding the book's nuances in incisive ways. Finally, my thanks go to the three anonymous manuscript reviewers, who provided excellent comments and suggestions for improving the final book, to Harold Otto, whose copy-editing was superb, and to Virgil Duff who steered the entire project admirably. Of course, any omissions or errors in the final product remain solely my own.

The University of Alberta provided financial support through a University of Alberta PhD Scholarship and a Doctoral Dissertation Grant. Additional support came through a social Sciences and Humanities Research Council Doctoral Fellowship held at the University of Alberta in Edmonton, and a Social Sciences and Humanities Research Council Post-Doctoral Fellowship held at the University of Calgary. The final drafts of the book were written with the support of my current employer, the University of Lethbridge.

COLD COMFORT

Prologue

Our beautiful daughter. Straight back, round head. Sweet, smart, beanie. Standing at the bus stop every morning amid happy, laughing children. Going to school, eager to learn, eager to live, eager to be part of it all. She is seven years old.

A lovely winter morning – crisp and sunny and glistening, as only an Alberta winter morning can be. I strip the duvet off the bed and lay it on the open window's sill, to take advantage of the sun and the clean foothills air. Pausing, I breathe in the delights of the day – dazzling sunlight, sparkling snowdrifts, the chirp and flutter of myriad small birds, and – slowly it comes to me – the sound of children's voices. Chanting.

'We hate Hilary! We hate Hilary! We hate Hilary!'

My heart stops. Literally. I can tell, because my hands and my feet are suddenly cold, and my breathing has gone still. No. I feel the slow thud of my heart, as I strain to listen. I'm not wrong, I *do* hear it – 'We hate Hilary! We hate Hilary!'

Running barefoot, dressed only in slacks and a shirt, I cover the distance to the bus stop. Heart pounding, voice quaking, I address this gaggle of four-foot-tall torturers, speak to their better nature, beg for their compassion, appeal to their shame. They are sullen. The silence is deadening.

The bright yellow bus rounds the corner in the cheery morning sun, pulls up, its door swinging open. Two by two, the children board the bus. Our daughter, our beautiful, brave, daughter, gets on as well, to be taken off to a place I now no longer believe is either innocent or safe.

As I watch her ride away with them, I stand in the freezing morning, sobbing, feeling more helpless and hopeless than I have ever felt before.

And so it began. The first crack in the facade, the first inkling – no, that's not true – the first *confirmation* that something terribly bad was happening to our beautiful girl. After all, that nagging worry was what led me to volunteer in the classroom and take a job working lunch hours as a playground supervisor, so I could keep an eye on things.

But that incident at the bus stop crystallized my doubts. I could no longer resist the sense that Hilary was slowly, almost imperceptibly drifting away from us, and that she was no longer her spunky, curious, courageous, happy self. From that moment on, I have never again assumed that for our daughter things are okay, that things will be okay, or that the world in which she lives is safe.

That night, my husband and I talked until very late. We talked about how our plan to remain in student family housing while I finished my degree might have to change. We talked about how we might have to stop sending our daughter to the school she attended – a school attached to the university's faculty of education and reputed to be one of the best in town. Mostly, we talked about finding a way to improve things for Hilary, and about how this could have happened to the bright, congenial little girl we knew.

The next day, I meet the school principal, my daugher's classroom teachers, and the vice principal. I tell them of our concerns. They tell me they have none. Hilary is a good girl, no bother in the classroom. And no, there haven't really been problems at this school with bullying before, but they promise to keep an eye on things.

Hilary speaks, finally. She's become harder and harder to speak with lately – refusing to talk, to tell us what's wrong. Now, however, she speaks.

She says, 'Can I change schools?'

We talk again, and think about our finances, and in one late-night epiphany decide that we can buy a house, and that we can move, and that we will do this. Within two days, we have bought a house, and I have taken Hilary to visit her new school.

It is charming, small. It has traditional-style classrooms, unlike her present school with its open plan and team teaching. There is artwork on the walls, and the hallways smell of wax. Hilary slips her hand inside mine and tells me, 'This school feels safe, Mom.' I decide she should not wait until we have moved before she starts her new school. I can drive her there for the interim. I just want it to be okay, and the sooner the better.

Hilary is to start at her new school right after the Easter break. She is delighted, and that night she begins to tell us about the harassment she has suffered at her present school, the name-calling, the ostracism, the bullying. I guess she feels she can tell us this, now that she knows she's never going back.

The old school requires an exit interview. I sit in the little chair at the table, and the teacher sits in an adult chair across from me. She is a woman who only speaks to me with her eyes closed; I never learn what colour they are. I am here to collect Hilary's report card and to bring home her unfinished assignments. The report card is glowing. Hilary is bright, hardworking, and achieving well, it says.

I am given Hilary's portfolio – the work she has accomplished during the first seven months of the school year. The contents would fit inside a small envelope. There is nothing. She has done nothing for seven months.

I tell the teacher about the harassment. About the little boy who bullied her, called her names, and whose language and behaviour, had they not come from a seven-year-old, would have been termed sexual harassment. The teacher, through closed lids, says, 'Oh. That explains it then.' I say, 'Explains what?' She replies, 'Well, I just always suspected that Hilary might be being sexually abused.'

I say nothing. I am afraid to speak, I am so angry. How could she think this, and do nothing? I am also silenced because I am beginning to understand what this woman has been thinking about me, about my husband, and our little family. I take the small envelope of schoolwork and leave, wondering what Hilary's other file – the one that has been forwarded to her new school – says about her and about her parents in light of this teacher's suspicions.

The new school. It is better here. The Grade 2 classroom has rows of desks, and the teacher is firm and organized, and Hilary has made a couple of tentative friends within weeks. However, the teacher pulls me aside one day and says, 'We have to talk.'

It seems that Hilary is so far behind in her schoolwork that they think she might need to repeat Grade 2. I know enough to understand that failing a grade will not be good for Hilary psychologically, especially since she has had some social problems already. I make a deal with the teacher. 'Give me time,' I say, 'we'll get her caught up.' I begin to take her to a tutor for her math, and we send her to summer school so she can catch up on her writing and reading. Grade 2 and she is attending summer school. 'Oh well,' we say, and adopt a motto that, over the next years, becomes a mantra:

'Whatever it takes. Whatever it takes.'

Whatever it has taken for Hilary, in the intervening years, has proved to be quite considerable. In Grade 3 her classroom teachers (there were two teachers sharing a class in this year) still could not seem to reach her. There were endless phone calls from the teachers:

'Hilary is not doing well in Math class. Is there something wrong at home?'

'Hilary's homework has not been done. Is there something wrong at home?'

'Hilary's agenda has not been signed. Is there something wrong at home?'

'Hilary does cartwheels in the cloakroom. Is there something wrong at home?'

'Hilary doesn't seem to connect with peers. Is there something wrong at home?'

By now, my husband and I are doing upwards of two hours of homework a night with Hilary. No longer are we playing catch-up because of the first school. Now we are playing catch-up because Hilary is not learning anything at this school. By the end of each night's homework session, Hilary and I are usually both crying. I begin to feel resentment, but above all, I am worried, worried, worried.

There are endless meetings. At one crucial meeting, we sit in the principal's office – on one side, the two classroom teachers, the school's resource teacher, the school psychologist, the vice principal, the principal, and the school board's program specialist – on the other, my husband and I. In this meeting, for the first time, someone says the words 'attention deficit disorder' and asks us to consider Ritalin (methylphenidate). She has not yet been tested, but they know what the solution should be.

I think, 'Well, maybe this is the answer.'

So begins a long investigation into the services and procedures available for children suspected of having attention deficit disorder (ADD) in the Calgary area. The school gives me a list, and from that list I branch out. The options are endless, as are the numbers of specialists. A multimodal assessment is apparently the ideal procedure – at least according to the private, fee-for-service agencies that offer them. The fees are beyond our ability to pay. The Children's Hospital has a one-year waiting list for multimodal assessments covered by public health care insurance. Then there is the option of going to a pediatrician specializing in ADD, all of whom have at least six-month waiting lists.

Finally, we see a pediatrician. Twenty minutes later, we leave her office with one photocopied sheet of questions and a triplicate prescription for a double-blind Ritalin test. The pills are split between Ritalin and placebos. We and the teacher are each to complete a daily questionnaire, and then I will bring the completed forms back to the doctor for assessment. I read the questionnaire; it asks about the child's ability to sit still, take turns, stand in line, work in groups. There is nothing about her life outside the classroom – at home, on the playground, or with peers.

The first pill that I give her puts Hilary into a panic. Our placid, easygoing child hyperventilates during a shopping trip, and we have to take her home. There is no place on the form for me to provide this information.

The teacher fills out her forms assiduously: a neat row of Xs that are easily related to Hilary's classroom experiences. My forms look like examination crib notes – sentences are underlined, and the margins are filled with lists, comments, and clarifications . When I give both stacks to the pediatrician, she carefully removes those that were completed on the weekend. She tells me those days were not necessary, as it is school behaviour that is really of concern. She will call me in a few days, after she has been able to run the statistics on the forms against the coding for the blind Ritalin trial. To this day, I suspect the pediatrician never looked at my forms.

I begin to think, 'Someone should write a book about this.'

The answer comes. Yes. Hilary has ADD. So I begin, each morning, to place two small blue pills next to her plate. Despite her complaints of a stomach ache. Despite the continued complaints from the teacher about her organizational problems. Despite the ongoing grind of ever-increasing homework. Despite my own ambivalence. I can think of no other way.

I say, 'Whatever it takes.'

We watch and wait. Hilary continues to take Ritalin. She also continues to bring home homework that inexorably erodes our family's relationships. We work each night for two or three hours, my husband and I taking turns, as each of us reaches the point of no more to give. Hilary has no option for taking turns – she must endure this in its entirety. She regularly misses Girl Guides. She does not ever miss her regular private math tutoring. Still, the phone calls come from the teachers:

'Hilary is not doing well in Math class. Is there something wrong at home?'

'Hilary's homework has not been done. Is there something wrong at home?'

'Hilary's agenda has not been signed. Is there something wrong at home?'

'Hilary doesn't seem able to connect with her peers. Is there something wrong at home?'

Yes. There is.

We are worried sick for our lovely, struggling, quiet, uncomplaining, slowly fading-away daughter.

End of Grade 3. Hilary is going to go into a special classroom for children with learning disabilities (LD). The school says, 'It will be good for her. No, we take special care to ensure that children are integrated with the rest of the school. She will still be able to be with her friends. She will take some subjects in the regular class, and do English, math, science, and social studies in the LD class. It will be fine. It's what she needs. We've seen this before, and we know it will work. It's what she needs.'

There is no time for mourning. There is no room for doubt. We hope. We trust. We sign the report card and its placement suggestion. I think, 'Well, maybe this is the answer.'

We say, 'Whatever it takes.'

For the next two years, Hilary attends this special class. I volunteer – two and sometimes three times a week – helping children read, keeping peace in the library. I am not a teacher, but I sometimes wonder whether this class is such a good thing. Granted, there are only twelve children for the one teacher, but they range in age from six to twelve years old, and a great deal of time is spent coming and going, gathering up materials, or sitting and listening while the teacher tells one group or another what she expects. The teacher seems tired and impatient. My daughter never quite seems to understand what she is to do. Much later, I learn that this teacher has no training whatsoever in special education. She is just another weary teacher, ready to retire, who has been given a small class full of special children to teach.

We find that we are still doing the same amount of homework. I start to believe that anything that Hilary is learning, she is learning with us. But at such a cost. Now not only are there tears, but raised voices, and arguments – and sometimes, refusal.

There is something else. The little girl she used to play with after school and went to Guides with will no longer play with her. The other little girl who lives at the end of our road says, 'I will still be your friend, but only on the weekends. When we're at school, I cannot play with you. So don't try to be my friend at school, okay?'

Our daughter – our gentle, forgiving daughter – agrees.

The end of Grade 5. We receive a letter along with Hilary's last report card. Funding for the special LD class has been withdrawn, and Hilary will now attend Grade 6 in a regular classroom. I meet with the school, and they assure me that this is a good thing. The tell me that Hilary will be happier if she is integrated in the regular classroom. They tell me that a segregated setting, as we know, is a burden socially for these children. Again, they say, 'It will be fine. It's what she needs. We've seen this before, and we know it will work. It's what she needs.'

Hilary's LD classroom teacher makes up little certificates with a picture of an eagle on the front, and a note inside telling the children that, now that they are no longer in the special class, they are ready to fly like the eagle.

I taste the bile in my throat, and think, 'Someone should write a book about this.'

Grade 6, and surprisingly, the regular classroom is going fairly well. Hilary's teacher is very structured and stays with her every night after school to do her homework with her. I cannot believe how much time we all have in the evenings, or how pleasant life can be with Hilary when we are not fighting over school work.

Still, I begin to wonder how Hilary will manage next year in junior high school, when she has to move to eight different teachers a day in a school of 700 children, and when her social life is already filled with taunts, and slights, and incredible sorrow. Will she be one who falls through the cracks? Will she be one who, socially outcast, decides to do drugs or hang with the wrong crowd because she feels she has no choice?

I make an appointment to see the vice principal at the junior high school Hilary will attend the next year. I ask her what services the school will offer. She provides me with a very short list. She also suggests that, in preparation, we send our daughter to a two-week camp to teach children organizational skills, that we hire a tutor for math and English from a private school for kids 'like her,' that we sign Hilary up for a computer keyboarding class, that we send her to summer camp for children with learning disabilities to help her build up her self-esteem. All of this will be, of course, at our own expense.

It is October, and I start to make inquiries with private schools that offer specialized programs for children with attentional and learning difficulties. I am told we are probably too late to apply for next year; the waiting list is about eighteen months long. I apply anyway. I am desperate.

The application forms are long, and they ask difficult questions. There are questions about our lives as a family, about our pasts, about our own problems as parents. One of the questions asks, 'Has your child ever experienced any trauma?' I answer, 'Yes. She has been in the public school system for seven years.'

I apply to these schools despite my job in a university department that teaches about and advocates inclusive education for children with disabilities. I do this despite the fact that we cannot possibly afford the tuition. I do this despite my fears that having to pay for this school might mean giving up my own return to school to complete a PhD in the fall. I say, 'We'll worry about that later. Whatever it takes.'

In Grade 6, every student in Alberta must write province-wide examinations. These examinations are used to assess and rank the performance not only of the student, but also of the teacher and the school. Our daughter is provided extra tutoring, extra completion time, and a scribe who will write down the answers that our daughter tells her to. These are things that, in the assessment she received in Grade 3, were identified as services she requires to achieve to her potential. She has never received them until now, but with these services, Hilary receives the highest marks in the school on the provincial examinations.

At the year-end awards ceremony, a great deal is made of our daughter's exam marks. She receives a golden pencil and a laminated certificate. I am pleased for her, and she is rightly proud. But I am also furious. I believe that she could do this kind of work all the time, if she had the proper kind of support. And I am convinced she only received it at this time because it would improve the school's scores.

I receive her year-end report card. For the first time in all of her schooling, the report card includes a comparison between Hilary's scores in reading, spelling, and arithmetic with those of 'grade level expectations.' The scores tell me that, in Grade 6, she is spelling at a Grade 2 level, doing math at a Grade 3 level, and reading at a Grade 8 level.

It is June 1996. I receive a phone call from one of the private schools. A place has come available. Are we still interested?

My husband and I have talked about this. He's not so sure. Perhaps she'll be embarrassed to go to a school for kids with learning disabilities. Perhaps it won't make any difference anyway. Certainly, we cannot afford it.

My daughter and I have talked about this. She's pretty sure, then she's not so sure. Maybe it won't work. Maybe it will be like the LD class. Maybe it would be better to go to school with her friends – well, with the kids she knows.

I swallow hard, and say, 'Yes. Yes. We are still interested.'

As I hang up the phone, I stand in the quiet summer morning, feeling more hope than I have dared to feel since that winter morning at the bus stop so many years before.

I think to myself, 'I am going to write a book about this.'

1   Why Attention Deficit (Hyperactivity) Disorder, Why Mothers?

I saw your notice in the Education Tower seeking volunteers for ADD interviews. While I can't meet your need, I do have two questions about ADD, which you might be able to answer for me.

Is there any relationship between ADD and Fetal Alcohol Syndrome?

Of the three ADD-diagnosed children I know, all come from single-mother families. Is this just a coincidence?

Teacher education student (male)

E-mail correspondence

20 January 2000

The above e-mail came in response to a public call for research participants that I posted in the faculty of education at the University of Calgary. I believe it eloquently expresses some of the unfounded assumptions that circulate about mothers, about difference, and about attention deficit order (ADD). This brief letter reflects assertions in popular and professional discourse about ADD that tie it to both neonatal and postnatal maternal failings. In these discursive claims, mothers of children who are different are suspected of poor prenatal practices, including alcohol and drug use during pregnancy. They are also criticized for providing inadequate nutrition, relying on fast foods, working too much outside the home, and of laying inadequate moral, psychological, and emotional foundations for their children because of single motherhood (Malacrida, 2001, 2002).

When I received this letter I felt horrified and, in a grim way, satisfied. My horror came from learning that the young man who wrote it was at the time a Sunday school teacher at his church and a student teacher with the Calgary Board of Education; he planned to graduate as a teacher within three months of his letter. In short, he was someone who ought to know better, and someone who was in a position to do considerable harm through his misguided insights. My grim satisfaction came from seeing that my suspicions about maternal blame, my scepticism about the ability or intentions of at least some helping professionals to be compassionate and non-judgmental, and my hunches about the moral imperatives attached to mothers' and children's 'normality' were well founded.

I originally thought to study how mothers deal with their child's diagnosis of ADD and/or attention deficit hyperactivity disorder (ADHD)[1] because of my own experiences of parenting a child with that diagnosis. As a result of our daughter's label, I have struggled with the ambiguity of my own guilt, my desire for some way (any way) to help our child, my cynicism about the 'nature' of her problems, my hope for a solution to them regardless of their etiology, and my despair at finding none that fully satisfies. I have struggled to obtain appropriate services for her, to avoid her and my stigmatization, to retain her and our dignity and quality of life, to attain an education for her that is adequate in terms of fulfilling her social and educational potential. At times, I have complied with the label, at others I have resisted the psychiatric and educational strategies that were ostensibly designed to help her. Throughout, I have been guided by a desire to protect her while acknowledging that what I do has the potential to do her harm. Throughout, I have also understood that her attributes, somehow, cast a shadowy light on mine – because she has encountered troubles, I have been seen as troubled. I would be lying if I said it has been easy.

In this research project, I undertook to speak with two groups of mothers, one in Canada and one in England, whose children were diagnosed with AD(H)D. My focus in this comparative research was *not* to examine macro-level medical, educational, and psychiatric practices related to AD(H)D in Canada or England, nor was I hoping to determine which country's practices are more 'accurate' in terms of locating and responding to the 'real' nature of AD(H)D. Further, I was not interested in providing evidence one way or another to add to debates over the legitimacy of AD(H)D, where some argue that it is a

1 In this book, reflecting common language used in both research sites, and also the diagnostic practices of these countries, I will use ADD when speaking of Canadian data, and ADHD in referring specially to British material; when speaking generally, I will use AD(H)D.

legitimate neurobiological condition and others just as virulently claim that AD(H)D is little more than a symptom of poor educational and medical practices, aggressive pharmaceutical marketing, or the demise of 'the family.' Instead, I sought to understand what it is like within two different cultural contexts to be a mother confronting multiple 'helping' professionals while dealing with this highly controversial diagnosis.

I suspected that mothers of children who are identified as troubled would be both objects of surveillance and bearers of blame and that their narratives would provide insight into the workings of power in the handling of children and families that are deemed problematic. Hence, I asked these women about the ways that lay and professional controversies and professional practice intersected with their mothering of a child who is 'different.' In doing so, I sought to understand the problems they faced in understanding their children's difficulties, and the factors that helped or burdened them in the process of finding solutions.

My experiences of the dilemmas of care attached to parenting our daughter inform this study not only in terms of its focus on mothering and the choices that other mothers confront. The mixed messages I have encountered in my search for information that might help our daughter, the often-ambiguous 'helping' practices I have experienced, and the ways that AD(H)D has acted as a site of public surveillance and intervention into the private lives of the members of my family also inform my analytic and theoretical approach in this study. These experiences led me to believe that AD(H)D was an important topic because of its contested nature, because of its intersection between personal lives and normative public discourse, and because of its operation as a site of surveillance and intervention.

The intersections between public discourse and private experience that relate to AD(H)D include norms of good motherhood, of childhood as both innocent and dangerous, of psychiatric normalization in which increasingly narrow categories of difference are attached to increasingly broad ranges of attributes, of shifts in educational discourse from the production of good citizens to the production of docile workers, and of competition within schools and between schools. I will discuss each of these intersections more fully later in this chapter. Professional discourse and public media, over the past fifteen years in Canada and the past three or four years in England, have combined to create a confusing 'truth' about AD(H)D. Psychiatrists, psychologists, physicians, nutritionists, and educators have contributed to the debate, with members of each professional group presenting both support and dissent over the legitimacy, etiology, and treatment of AD(H)D.

In addition to debates over the legitimacy of AD(H)D and methyl-phenidate (Ritalin), lay and professional discourse has constructed a parallel, and in many cases, demonizing view of mothers and their children with AD(H)D. Those who see AD(H)D as a legitimate diagno-sis have claimed that mothers are to blame because of poor pre- and postnatal nutrition, resistance to breastfeeding, reliance on fast foods, and as a result of the stresses of modern, dual-income family life (Adams, 1998; Adduci, 1991; Baker and McCall, 1995; Maté, 2000a; 2000b; Stordy, no date; Ullman and Ullmann, 1996). Conversely, detractors of AD(H)D's legitimacy describe AD(H)D-like behaviour as a product of mot-hers who are irresponsible, undisciplined or self-absorbed, or who are overachievers who simply are not satisfied with their 'normal,' if rambunctious, children (Breggin, 1991; Foss, 1999; Schatsky and Yaro-shevsky, 1997). Regardless, then, of whether experts accept or reject the legitimacy of AD(H)D, there seems to be some agreement that mothers of children who are diagnosed with AD(H)D contribute to their chil-dren's problems. Some additional charges levelled against mothers are the following: these mothers are poor disciplinarians, preoccupied with their own problems, overwhelmed with the stresses of modern life, working outside the home to the detriment of their children's mental health, and are in bad marriages, or worse, are not married at all (Atkins, 2000; Browne, 2000a; 2000b; Foss, 1999; Maté, 2000b; Rees, 1998a; Schatsky and Yaroshevsky, 1997).

Children with AD(H)D have been portrayed as children 'at risk' for social isolation, low self-esteem, potential school failure, depression, and suicide (Brooks, 1994; CHADD, 1995; Choate, no date; Johnston, 1997; Kewley, 1998; Minde, 1987; Murphy and LeVert, 1995; Schuckit et al., 1987). Conversely, these children are portrayed as potentially dan-gerous to society because, it is claimed, they tend to be antisocial, lacking in judgment, risk-takers, and have high rates of alcoholism, unemployment, and criminality in adulthood (Choate, no date; Farrington, 1989; Forehand et al., 1991; Franklin, 1994; Halikas et al., 1990; Johnston, 1997; Minde, 1987; Schuckit et al., 1987). As we can see from this very brief overview of the discourses of blame, risk, and danger relating to mothers and to children diagnosed with AD(H)D, the choices women must make over AD(H)D are accomplished not only within the frame of considerable ambiguity about AD(H)D itself, but women's choices about care also carry some very high moral stakes.

The sites of surveillance involved in the management of AD(H)D include the home, the community, the day care or preschool setting, the psychologist's office, the hospital, the physician's office, and most especially, the school. In both Canada and England, mothers' practices, feelings, and understandings about their children are brought into question by nurses, teachers, school administrators, psychiatric and psychological professionals, and medical practitioners. Thus, although in this study my goal was not to determine 'best practice' relating to AD(H)D, or simply to compare macro-level structures relating to the handling of AD(H)D in both sites, I did attempt to understand the intersections between these professionals, their institutions, and maternal practice.

I also hoped to examine how mothers' responses unfold within each context. What influences did professional or lay discourse have on maternal knowledge and experience in each instance? What relation did discursive practice have to maternal experiences? How do mothers come to terms with each 'choice'? What are the possibilities and limits for women as they negotiate with or struggle against teachers, physicians, psychologists, psychiatrists, special educators, educational administrators, and social workers in hopes of getting their children's needs met? What are the specific dilemmas, risks, and benefits attached to an AD(H)D diagnosis for one's child in southern England? in southern Alberta? In both places, how did mothers struggle to provide care, protection, and assistance to their children? What factors, be they textual or interactional, contributed to maternal decisions? These, and other subsidiary questions, were the foci of this research.

The purpose of this research was to understand what is it like, as a mother, to confront and come to terms with the diagnosis and treatment of one's child with AD(H)D in two differing cultures of AD(H)D. In addition, a major interest in conducting this research was to undertake an examination across cultures and contexts of discursive practices relating to the medicalization, psychiatrization, and normalization of school-aged children as a way to examine maternal compliance and resistance. A third focus has been to attempt a method that uses Foucauldian discourse analysis along with feminist standpoint theory to construct a *feminist discursive ethnography*. My hope has been to create a bridge between the discursive professional practices relating to AD(H)D and the lived experiences of women as they attempt to mother within the highly contested discursive fields of AD(H)D. Finally, in comparing the experiences of mothers and the discursive practices of professionals within the divergent contexts of Britain and Canada, I hoped to provide insight into maternal dilemmas of care for a 'different' child, regardless of the culture's acceptance or rejection of the AD(H)D label. My suspicion was that, regardless of the particularities of the diagnostic procedure or the national setting, mothers would face similar difficulties and dilemmas in dealing with their children's problems.

To understand the complexity and ambiguity of mothers' coming to terms with an AD(H)D diagnosis, it is important to understand the historical, cultural, and discursive background against which these women's experiences are played. Thus, in the following sections, I will provide some historical and cultural background on AD(H)D, and some insight into the controversies over the AD(H)D diagnosis. First, however, I consider the implications of poststructural theories of knowledge production, medicalization, and normalization as the backdrop against which AD(H)D, like many psychiatric categories, came into being.

Medicalization, Psychiatrization, and the History of AD(H)D

Roy Porter has pointed out that a great deal of psychiatric practice has developed not as a response to conditions that are or have been necessarily problematic, but as a result of new ways of thinking about difference. As western society has become less tolerant of difference, and as medical and psychiatric professional infrastructures have developed, the range of behaviours identified or perceived of as pathological has grown (Porter, 1987). This decreased tolerance of and increased psychiatric surveillance over a broad range of behaviours and signs that once were accepted as part of the continuum of human possibility, but that now have become problems to be resolved through expert practice, has been termed the 'psychiatrization of difference' (Castel et al., 1982). Others have noted that the psychiatrization of difference is part of a broader trend in modern western society towards the medicalization of difference (Conrad and Schneider, 1980; Conrad, 1992). Medicalization refers to the process whereby previously non-medical situations come to be defined as medical and are conceptualized as only being treatable through medical means. Irving Zola has referred to medicalization as the 'process whereby more and more of everyday life has come under medical dominion, influence and supervision' (1983: 295).

Poststructuralist David Armstrong (1983) has described the development of pediatrics and child psychology in the first half of this century as part of a more general trend in medicine and psychiatry towards normalization – or a policing of the normal. Armstrong notes that new technologies of the dispensary, of the school clinic, of pediatric medicine and psychology, and particularly of developments in medical surveys and knowledge exchanges between hospitals, infirmaries, schools, and clinics, led to an increased knowledge about child populations and about what constitutes 'normal variability' (1983: 43.) Hence, a systematically derived range of the more-or-less normal (rather than an absolute normal) came to govern judgments about children so that 'every child was normal' and, at the same time, 'all normal children have behaviour problems [so that] ... diagnosis and the medical problem [became] a constant normalizing gaze exercised by a new medical discipline over the growth and development of *all* children' (1983: 63, emphasis mine). Armstrong notes the rise of a number of not-normal categories in the mid-1920s that were not typified by extreme difference, but that actually encompassed most children in one way or another. These include the difficult child, the neurotic child, the eneuretic child, the maladjusted child, the unstable child, the delicate child, and the solitary child: in each case, these children were 'construed as precariously normal, as liable to slip into inappropriate or problem behaviour without constant vigilance' (1983: 27). Armstrong also notes that, unlike earlier conceptions of madness that had acted as rituals of exclusion, these milder forms of neuroses 'celebrated the ideal of a disciplined society in which all were analysed and distributed' and in which all members were retained (in a disciplined form) in community life (1983: 22).

Nikolas Rose has described how childhood, as 'the most intensively governed sector of personal existence' has in modernity become the focus of economic, moral, and developmental regulation (1990: 121). Here, the child is seen as requiring protection from physical, sexual, and moral danger, and as a site where professionals 'actively promote certain capacities of attributes such as intelligence, educability, and emotional stability' (ibid.). Drawing on both poststructural theory and feminist analysis, Rose notes that during the nineteenth and twentieth centuries, a number of 'large and little projects,' such as philanthropy, mental hygiene, and the child-saving movements came into play to elaborate a 'set of doctrines for rearing healthy children, and to pose many issues of moral conduct in medical terms' (1990: 128). In particular, Rose notes, these doctrines, and the profession of psychology, gave rise to new notions of the normal child. These included normality as a state of naturalness and health, as a set of standards against which 'the actual is judged and found unhealthy' and 'as that which is to be produced by rationalized social programmes' (1990: 130–1). Hence, through technologies such as demographics, statistics, and particularly through objective and repeatable testing measures, the study of large numbers of children was used to create a mythical 'normal' against which *all* children could be measured. This process, of constructing a large body of ever-expanding attributes that categorize the normal and the abnormal, occurs in a process Rose names 'normalization.'

As a poststructuralist, Rose also notes that correction for those attributes that testing deemed abnormal was located in a set of professional discursive practices that operated through public health clinics, social work offices, schools, and physicians' and psychologists' offices. He also notes that the norms of childhood, parenting, and motherhood that built up around normalization opened up the psyches of children, and their mothers, to a new kind of regulation. In Rose's view, mothers and children were not only regulated from without through the discursive practices of professionals, but 'it has become the will of the mother to govern her own children according to psychological norms and in partnership with psychological experts' (1990: 131).

Rose's explanations provide us with a way of understanding how mothers might be both 'victims' and 'users' of these psychological norms. The knowledge production and dissemination of the helping professions, and the language of professional–maternal teamwork, does more than just position mothers as objects of surveillance. Rather, through knowledge consumption and through technologies of the self, modern mothers have come to 'partner' with teachers, health workers, and mental health professionals in the moral, spiritual, and psychological regulation of themselves and their families.

AD(H)D: Some Historical Background

The 'discovery' of AD(H)D can be seen as part of the psychiatrization, medicalization, and normalization process, in that it appears to have developed from clinical trials that serendipitously both defined the problem and discovered its solution. In short, the discovery of AD(H)D did not result from the search for a treatment to a long-identified medical, social, or psychiatric concern.

ADD is a relatively recent term, but its history can be traced back to the 1930s and the work of Kurt Goldstein, a neurologist who studied a number of brain-injured veterans of the First World War. Goldstein found that these individuals exhibited high distractibility and a forced response to any stimulus (i.e., a high inability to concentrate and an inability to distinguish the essential from the trivial). Building on this early work, in the early 1940s, Heinz Werner and Alfred Strauss set out to generalize Goldstein's findings through a comparative study between children who were developmentally delayed and children who had a dual diagnosis of developmental delay and brain injury. They found that the brain-injured children exhibited more signs of distractibility than did the non–brain-injured children. Despite some controversy (particularly about the accuracy of their post hoc identification of these children as brain injured), their findings and the teaching and assessment procedures they developed proved influential; for a number of years, the syndrome they helped to discover, define, and test for was commonly known as 'Strauss's syndrome' (Hallahan et al., 1996).[2]

In 1937 Charles Bradley observed that recently discovered amphetamine drugs, when administered to a small group of school-aged children with reported high levels of distractibility, were effective in reducing distractibility and in subduing the children's behaviour (Conrad and Schneider, 1980). Despite the success of Strauss and Werner's assessment tool, and Bradley's almost parallel discovery of a seemingly appropriate medical treatment, however, Strauss's syndrome remained a fairly rare diagnosis (Hallahan et al., 1996). It was only in the mid-1950s that the syndrome and the medication came together in a way that promised a generalized and relatively safe applicability. Ritalin, a drug with the effectiveness of other amphetamines but few (tested) undesirable side effects, was discovered in the mid-1950s, making the use of amphetamines appear less threatening; Ritalin was approved in 1961 by the Food and Drug Administration for use in the United States. As well, in 1957, Maurice Laufer first described a constellation of attentional and behavioural symptoms that had 'no clear-cut history of organicity' and labelled it 'hyperkinetic impulse disorder' (Conrad and Schneider, 1980). Laufer's new diagnosis was able to accommodate an entirely new population: hyperkinetic impulse disorder was implicated neither specifically for developmentally delayed nor brain-injured children as

2 Subsequent names of this syndrome included minimal brain damage, minimal brain dysfunction, hyperkinesis, and hyperactivity, reflecting a gradual shift away from making the label depend upon a history of brain trauma.

earlier syndromes had been, but simply attributed pathology to a set of specific behaviours that could be located in any child.

Following the development of a broadened, behaviourally based diagnostic category that could be applicable to all children, and the development of a reputedly benign medical treatment (Ritalin), the disease as a medically accepted diagnosis developed fairly quickly. Peter Conrad and Joseph Schneider traced the growth of this disorder through the number of publications in scientific and academic journals that were related to the disorder. They note that 'there has been a virtual flood of papers and research published since the early 1960s' on the etiology, diagnosis, and treatment(s) of AD(H)D (1980: 57). My own survey of educational, psychological, sociological, and anthropological literature related to AD(H)D confirms that literally dozens of articles related to AD(H)D are now published each year in academic journals. Similarly, popular parenting and family magazines and newspapers frequently offer coverage on various aspects of AD(H)D. The 'parenting' section in any local bookstore will readily provide several advice and resource books directly related to AD(H)D, and no parenting how-to book today could be considered adequate without some reference to it. In short, AD(H)D has become normalized in popular discourse: it has grown from an obscure medical anomaly found in a specific subset of the population to a disorder that is commonly encountered in popular and professional discourse, and it is represented as a disorder that will likely affect many children and their families.

Although Conrad and Schneider simply report the increase in academic and popular representations of AD(H)D as evidence of the success of this diagnostic category, a Foucauldian reading would implicate the discipline-based production of knowledge about AD(H)D as a contributor to the disorder's growth. The burgeoning literature about AD(H)D not only reflects professional and disciplinary concerns about the care and management of AD(H)D, it also represents an increasingly public education about AD(H)D by these disciplines. These texts explicate the ever-finer categories of assessment appropriate to AD(H)D, the ever-broader criteria of inclusion for an AD(H)D diagnosis, the ever-growing professional and academic understanding of the problems, and they convey an increased knowledge of current challenges, risks, and solutions in managing the AD(H)D-diagnosed child in the physician's clinic, the psychologist's office, the teacher's classroom, and the family's home. Through this explication, a historically situated 'reality' is conveyed to parents, teachers, physicians, counsellors, advocates, psychiatrists, and researchers about the complexity, seriousness, and pervasiveness of AD(H)D.

ADD vs ADHD – Some Cultural Background

The diagnosis and treatment of children with AD(H)D is culturally as well as historically situated, as can be noted in the differences between the current handling of the label in Great Britain and Canada. According to British pediatrician and ADHD activist Geoffrey Kewley, diagnoses in Great Britain are typically based on the International Classification of Diseases, tenth edition (ICD-10) criteria (see Appendix 1) issued by the World Health Organization (1993), which restrict identification to '*severe, persistent hyperactivity*' (Kewley, 1998: 1595, emphasis mine). In Canada, criteria set out in the American Psychiatric Association's *Diagnostic and Statistical Manual of Mental Disorders* (1994) (DSM IV) are typically used in diagnosing children with ADD (CHADD, 1995). In the DSM IV (see Appendix 2), the diagnostic criteria are broader, including attention deficit disorder of the 'predominantly inattentive type' or the 'predominantly hyperactive type' or 'predominantly impulsive type.' In the DSM, a diagnosis of ADD is 'indicated when children display inappropriate inattention, impulsivity, *and sometimes hyperactivity* for their mental and chronological age' (Scott, 1987, emphasis mine). Thus, in the United Kingdom, one is more likely to see the narrow diagnosis of ADHD, rather than the more inclusive label of ADD that is typical in North America.

This difference is more than a matter of semantics: it results in differing rates of diagnosis and treatment between the United Kingdom and Canada. Although it is difficult to know how many children in any country are actually diagnosed as having ADD or ADHD, Kewley notes that Parliamentary Office of Science and Technology figures for 1995 indicate that 6,000 (or 0.03%) U.K. schoolchildren were being treated with psychostimulants (e.g., Ritalin, Dexedrine, Talwin, or Cylert), presumably for ADHD (1998: 1596).[3] Following the more inclusive DSM IV criteria used in North America, it has been speculated that 'approximately 20% of the population will be diagnosed as having ADD' (Scott, 1987). Despite Dr Scott's enthusiastic predictions, however, it appears that in 1995, some 3 per cent (100 times the U.K. rate) of U.S. schoolchildren were being treated with psychostimulants

3 Kewley does not provide background information on how this percentage is derived.

(American Academy of Child and Adolescent Psychiatry, cited in Hough, 1997). In 1995 in Alberta, approximately 2.5 per cent of school-aged children received Ritalin prescriptions, representing a four-fold increase since records began to be collected in 1987 (Alberta College of Physicians and Surgeons, 1999).[4]   Clearly, the ways that AD(H)D is understood, recognized, and managed vary across time, countries, and cultures.

The labelling of one's child with any psychiatric disorder is an extremely complex issue, and this particular psychiatric category is further complicated by its ambiguous history and the very public controversies that surround it. This labelling also intersects with a number of institutions and norms that span broad areas of any culture: it is the nexus at which the normative and disciplining institutions of the family, education, psychiatry, medicine, motherhood, and childhood meet. In the following sections, I will explore the ways that a number of institutions and discursive practices intersect with AD(H)D. Here, I am particularly concerned with discourses and practices that relate to knowledge production within the disciplines of psychology, psychiatry, and social work, which Robert Castel (1991) terms the psy sector, as well as educational practices, medicalization, and discourses of motherhood, risk, and the family.

Disciplines, Knowledge Production, and AD(H)D

Part of the phenomenal rise of AD(H)D has come as a result of a 'sustained interest over the past several years in better understanding, managing and treating attention, behavior and conduct disorders in children' by professionals (Cotugno, 1993). In turn, this interest has 'resulted in significant progress in the definition [and] diagnosis' of these disorders (1993: 118).

The development of an arsenal of assessment tools that can in a relatively straightforward way categorize a child with AD(H)D can be understood within the context of broader social developments related to health and normality. During the early part of the twentieth century

4 These figures are based on prescription rates for Ritalin provided by the Alberta College of Physicians and Surgeons (ACPS) and numbers of school-aged children in the public system, provided by Alberta Education. This rate does not include children not attending the public system. In addition, it excludes information concerning Dexedrine, Talwin, Cylert, Prozac, or other drugs that are also prescribed for ADD, but that are not recorded by ACPS.

and the later part of the nineteenth century, the development of numerous scales, measures, and instruments of categorization and differentiation proliferated. As Rose has noted, 'These tests were, indeed, the gateway to the psychological kingdom ... [they were] ... undoubtedly the basis of psychology's social vocation' (1985: 141). According to Rose (1990), eugenicists, philanthropic reformers, and governments all argued for an increasingly effective array of screening devices that would enable professionals to identify and manage the 'feeble-minded.' Rose notes that the psychological test represented a new, and more invasive, level of scrutiny. Because the stigmata of the moral or intellectual deviant could not be easily read on the body, these new tests became ways to identify the invisible and to assess the hidden marks of the mind and the soul (1990: 138).

It is also important to note that the project of identifying and labelling an increasingly broad range of mental and psychological traits as pathological has continued to the present. First published in 1953, the *Diagnostic and Statistical Manual of Mental Disorders* (DSM) listed sixty types and subtypes of mental illness; in 1969 the DSM II had expanded to include 120 disorders, while the DSM III of 1987 listed over 200 (Armstrong, 1993: 14). The currently used DSM IV comprises no less than 353 disorders (American Psychiatric Association, Personal Communication, 1999).

The success of AD(H)D as a disciplining category can be seen as a part of the growth of what Jacques Donzelot has termed the 'tutelary complex ... the constellation of social workers, special educators, family court workers, psychologists, psychiatrists and medical experts who form concentric circles around the child: the family circle, the circle of technicians, and the circle of social guardians' (1997: 103). The late nineteenth and early twentieth century development of psychology as a profession was concomitant with the advent of compulsory public schooling, a development that resulted in an increased number of children being available for screening and a broader arsenal of instruments being used to assess an increasingly sophisticated range of pathological classifications. The hoped-for outcome of such screening was to identify, treat, and contain individuals who were 'hereditarily unfit,' a financial burden on society, and a drain on national resources (including public education institutions), and who were at risk for exploitation by corrupt and criminal elements. The expectation was that, unless properly identified and treated, these individuals would become involved in the 'crime, poverty, destitution, physical ill-health, and immoral habits that philanthropists and social investigators had revealed at the heart of our great cities' (Rose, 1990: 135–7).[5]

Conrad and Schneider offer an alternate explanation for the success of AD(H)D as a diagnostic category, basing their analysis in a 'social problems' approach, in which various interest groups (or 'moral entre-preneurs') act in formal and informal ways to legitimate an aspect of social life that is problematic. Conrad and Schneider identify a number of interest groups in their analysis including pharmaceutical compa-nies, the medical complex, government, and parental lobby groups. They note that, in addition to the 'burgeoning interest in child mental health and psychiatry' of the mid-twentieth century (1980: 157), the pharmaceutical revolution that dates from the 1930s forward has had a tremendous impact on the medicalization of a broad range of deviant behaviours that were previously seen as the purvey of the church, the family, and the state (1980: 17–19). They observe that only after 1960 did it become common practice for pharmaceutical companies to advertise in medical journals, through direct mail to physicians, and through sales representatives who visited physicians' offices to promote their products. They content that this intensive marketing effort resulted in a general use of pharmaceuticals to remedy psychological problems and in a specific use of Ritalin to remedy children's behavioural problems (Conrad and Schneider, 1980: 157–9).

In addition, they note the impact of patient (in this case, parents of patients) advocacy in fostering an increased understanding of AD(H)D as a medical rather than a behavioural problem. In particular, Conrad and Schneider note that the Association for Children with Learning Disabilities (AACLD) in the United States, through conferences, social support groups, and lobbying efforts to legislate educational reform that would ensure programs and services for children with learning disabilities, did a great deal to legitimate AD(H)D as a medical diagnosis and Ritalin as the preferred treatment for it.[6] According to Conrad and Schneider, AACLD endorses a biological rather than social or psychological model of AD(H)D. To these parents, the advantage of a medical rather than a behavioural or familial label is that children

5 As will be seen later in this book, notions of the child 'at risk' persist in present-day psychological, medical, and professional discourses concerning AD(H)D.
6 'Attention deficit (hyperactivity) disorder' is often regarded as a learning disability; in other views, it is considered to be a separate diagnosis, but one that is often co-morbid with learning disabilities.

become labelled as 'sick' rather than 'bad' and are more likely to receive services than punishment from educational, psychological, and social work personnel. Further, parents of children whose problems are deemed to be medical rather than social or psychological in origin are themselves less likely to be stigmatized in terms of perceptions by professionals about their parenting abilities.

A third factor cited by Conrad and Schneider in the medicalization of AD(H)D reflects Foucauldian notions of the interdisciplinary nature of power. U.S. government support of a medical definition of AD(H)D developed as a result of a congressional subcommittee that examined the claims of psychiatric lobbyists who were concerned that children were being overmedicated by general practitioners who simply relied on 'teachers' and parents' reports that the child was doing poorly in school' (1980: 158). The U.S. Congress, on the recommendations of a special Department of Health, Education, and Welfare committee comprised primarily of physicians, in 1973 passed legislation that 'only physicians make the diagnosis and prescribe treatment, [and] that pharmaceutical companies promote the treatment of the disorder only through medical channels' (1980: 158). Thus, according to Conrad and Schneider, government, psychiatry, medicine, and pharmaceutical manufacturers came together to determine a route of identifying and appropriately treating AD(H)D that (despite the behavioural markers used to identify the existence of the disorder) privileged a medical rather than behavioural or social interpretation of its cause and treatment.

It must be mentioned, however, that medical hegemony over the handling of AD(H)D has not gone uncontested: it is interesting to note one of the more populist indictments of the diagnosis and medication of AD(H)D has been launched by a psychiatrist, Peter Breggin. Breggin's book (1991) is one that sits in multiple copies on the shelves of popular bookstores; he is also quoted in newspaper and magazine articles regularly, and he has appeared on national television (including the *Oprah Winfrey Show*) as an advocate against the improper diagnosing and overmedication of children imputed to suffer from AD(H)D. Breggin's contention is that *psychiatrists*, rather than pediatricians or other doctors, should be the professionals who decide on the AD(H)D diagnosis: his claim is that typical childhood behaviours such as restlessness, frustration, and anger are quickly diagnosed as biochemical in origin, when in many cases the problems are more psychosocial than neurobiological.

Education and AD(H)D

In North American practice, more often than not, neither the pediatrician nor the psychiatrist manages children's diagnosis and treatment. Rather, the schoolteacher acts as the shepherd of the child and its family throughout the assessment and treatment process. Typically children are first identified as AD(H)D in the early primary grades, and the assessment tool used to gauge the effectiveness of AD(H)D treatment privileges behavioural norms that are more relevant to the classroom than the home or playground. Indeed, the American Psychiatric Association has supported the ascendancy of teachers' over parents' perceptions and foci in relation to assessing and treating children with AD(H)D. They have formally stated that in the case of discrepancies between parent and professional assessments relating to AD(H)D, 'primary consideration should be given to the teacher reports because of greater familiarity with age-appropriate norms' (Kiger, 1985: 79).

Researchers who shift their focus away from understanding AD(H)D to be the result of medical or psychiatric claims-making activities have noted the role of the schools in the growth of AD(H)D. Gary Kiger (1985) argues against Conrad and Schneider's social problems approach to the history of AD(H)D. Agreeing that the many influences Conrad and Schneider detail in the growth of AD(H)D are legitimate, he also claims that their model fails to account for material and economic interests attached to the various stakeholders who have lobbied for a medicalization of childhood behaviours related to AD(H)D. Instead, Kiger believes that economic factors have contributed to the rise of AD(H)D, noting that transformations in the labour market during the late 1950s (from an industrial towards a technological revolution) demanded an increasing maths- and science-based curriculum that required higher levels of attention and concentration from children. As well, the new economic context required a longer training period to bring children to employability, creating a need for a more docile, compliant student body. Further, while the U.S. student-to-teacher ratio did not change during the 1960s, the number of classroom aides was reduced, and the ways that education was delivered became increasingly democratized. Specifically, the *Gault* decision of the U.S. Supreme Court in 1967 made it difficult for schools to expel, suspend, or punish unruly students in ways that had been previously unchallenged, making drug-based therapeutic control much more attractive. Finally, legislation at the federal level (these are U.S. data) resulted in benefits to schools for having children with medical rather than behavioural labels; the transfer of additional funds to schools with identified AD(H)D children was part of the All Handicapped Children Act passed in 1975. To Kiger, then, these economic and governmental factors, including transfer funds for children with disabilities, the need to keep children in school longer, the demands inherent to training children in increasingly technical ways, and changes in disciplinary practices in the schools, all combined to make a medical response to unruly behaviour extremely attractive. Finally, the low cost of treatment (Ritalin is a relatively inexpensive medication), typically assumed by parents rather than schools, provided schools facing increasing retention and instructional challenges with an effective and fiscally attractive solution.

AD(H)D as a disciplinary category has specifically been linked to the development of the relatively new fields of special education and school psychology. Roger Slee has noted that the management and classification of children, through psychometric testing and increasingly defined expert-based classifications of pathology has resulted in 'the expansion of the behaviour management/special needs professional ranks' in school systems (1994: 156). Further, it has incidentally allowed school systems to be relieved of responsibility for student failure (1994: 156–7). Slee believes that a shift from punishment practices to disciplinary practices has been the ground upon which AD(H)D's growth has thrived. He notes that moving discipline policy 'from "punishment" to "treatment" has the capacity to disempower young people at an unprecedented rate in more profound ways' than earlier interventions did (1994: 149). Paralleling Slee, Leifer (1990) has speculated that the problem with a medical model of behaviour, such as the model currently attached to AD(H)D, is that the label itself becomes deterministic: the disorder's course is seen as inevitable, and the individual's freedom and responsibility become irrelevant.

Slee notes the risk of a medical and/or psychiatric label lies in its permanence: individuals become identified as pathologized rather than troubled, and their problems are presumed to be both permanent and remediable only through medication. Slee notes that this transformation from 'bad' to 'sick,' while reducing the tendency to blame the child for 'delinquency' or 'unmanageability' and the parents for bad or inadequate parenting, has two outcomes. First, reminiscent of Foucault's technologies of the self, individuals (parents and children) become co-opted by medical and educational personnel: 'formerly "hostile" parents and students, because of their newly respectable status as "special" become willing participants in the remedial processes outlined by medical and educational experts' (Slee, 1994: 159).

A second outcome related to a medical rather than behavioural label, Slee points out, is that teachers are less pressured to develop skills that can accommodate children who are different in their classrooms (1994: 159). Children labelled as having 'special needs' are either routinely segregated from main classes, or they are made responsible for obtaining counselling services, skills development workshops, and social remedial programs that will make them able to fit into the regular classroom rather than have the classroom find ways to accommodate difference. In short, teachers, because it is the child who is labelled as deviant and lacking, are not compelled to find ways to include or to reach children who fall outside normative behavioural and academic standards (1994: 158–60).

Barry Franklin (1994), taking a historical and less critical approach than the above writers, also notes that inconsistency and financial exigency has played a major role in policies and programs for children with disabilities and for those who have required special services from educators. Tracing the practices of two American school boards, Franklin provides evidence that although progressivist discourses claim additional funding and the development of special services *should* be attached to children identified with learning disabilities (in which he includes AD(H)D), the funding for these services has in actuality been woefully inadequate (1994). Echoing the claims of Conrad and Schneider (1980), Kiger (1985), and Slee (1994), Franklin notes the advantages to teachers, educators, and parents in a label that is medical, rather than behavioural. Nonetheless, he provides evidence that, despite the less-stigmatizing application of a medical rather than behavioural label, actual services and assistance for identified children have frequently shifted, and have been subject to the whims of individual school boards and individual principals and teachers.

One wonders why (outside of 'letting parents off the hook' for being labelled as inadequate), a medical label that offers so little in terms of real assistance continues to act as such an appealing alternative. Perhaps discourses related to children and risk can offer some insight; in the following section, I will offer an analysis of some current theories concerning the AD(H)D 'child at risk.'

The 'At-Risk' Child and AD(H)D

These youngsters may not have close friends because they are so bossy ... Later at school they may have the role of the class clown and look for friends among younger children whom they can dominate more easily.

During adolescence, they may seek excitement through illegal activities such as joy riding in the cars of others, cutting classes or even stealing. In adulthood, about 25% of these youngsters still show difficulties in concentration and in their relationships with others. As a consequence, they have more motor vehicle accidents, more job changes and fewer friends and confidants.

Klaus K. Minde, MD, FRCP (C)
Learning Disabilities Association of Alberta, 1987

The label of the child as 'at risk' rather than 'bad' or 'dangerous' does more than relieve parents and teachers of the suspicion that they are inadequate. It also establishes the 'truth' that children who are not treated appropriately are in danger of serious social, intellectual, and emotional deficits if they remain 'untreated.'

The notion of the child as at risk has broader implications than simply the prediction of a dire future for the individual child diagnosed with ADD. As Robert Castel and colleagues (1982) have noted, the psy sector (psychiatry, psychology, and social work) has been active throughout this century in devising ways to identify 'populations at risk.' Castel ties the psy sector's risk discourse to late nineteenth- and early twentieth-century eugenics and mental health movements. He notes the point was (and is) not so much that these 'at-risk' populations are dangerous to themselves, but that their containment will improve the general social good (1982). Further, in this discourse, risk is reduced not by responding to situations that are dangerous now, but through prophylaxis, through early interventions that will preclude the risks inherent to a given population. To Castel et al., this results in 'a new mode of surveillance: that of systematic *predetection*' (1991: 288).

Children identified as having AD(H)D seem to have become conceptualized as a population at risk, and it is anticipated that early intervention, in the form of medication that enables them to pay attention, particularly in school, will result in avoiding a number of negative outcomes before they are even vaguely evident in the individual. Professional discourse about AD(H)D includes claims that, not only will properly medicated children be capable of receiving an education in the immediate sense, but also they and society will be protected from a number of future ills. Appropriately treated children, it is claimed, will achieve higher personal and economic goals, and they will be able to avoid the following: low self-esteem; alcoholism; drug addiction; unemployment; poor family, marital, and working relationships; and even criminal careers. In short, society will have fewer dropouts and misfits to tend to in their adulthood (Adams, 1998; Brooks, 1994; CHADD, 1995; Choate, no date; Johnston, 1997).

In actuality, research indicates that AD(H)D is not necessarily a predictor of alcohol or drug abuse (Boyle and Offord, 1991; Boyle et al., 1992; Halikas et al., 1990; Schuckit et al., 1987). Some literature does seem to indicate the juvenile delinquency and aggression are tied to AD(H)D; however, these studies typically are retrospective studies conducted on incarcerated youths, and thus cannot claim a predictive relationship between AD(H)D and aggression or criminality. Even so, in these studies AD(H)D has only a secondary influence on delinquency and aggression, with 'conduct disorder' being the primary influencing factor (Farrington, 1989; Forehand et al., 1991).[7]

Frederick and Olmi, who performed a meta-analysis of literature that connects AD(H)D with social failure, note that research that characterizes AD(H)D-diagnosed children as at risk for social failure has been conducted with children who are already in trouble in one way or another (1994). They suggest that tracking *all* AD(H)D children, including those who do not come to the attention of social workers, courts, and prisons, would be more accurate in determining the actual risks for AD(H)D-diagnosed children (1994). Despite the research-based evidence to the contrary, however, the spectre of risk for children not properly treated for AD(H)D appears to hold particular sway for parents, teachers, physicians, and mental health workers who manage the medicalization of AD(H)D.

Conrad notes that medicalization need not be directly administered by medical practitioners or medical regulators (1992: 211). Instead, he argues that medical definitions and typologies can operate in ways that permit non-medical personnel to accomplish the routine, everyday work of applying the medical label and treatment. Pediatric and psychiatric medicine acts as the gatekeeper to the treatment of AD(H)D, because only physicians or psychiatrists can prescribe Ritalin. However, it is the teacher (and the school psychologist or special education teacher) and the parent who typically administer the routine acts of identifying possible candidates for medicalization, steering those candidates towards medical services, performing the actual assessment of the identified child, and then ensuring that compliance to medical treatment is enacted.

---

7 Conduct disorder is another, relatively new diagnostic category, with seemingly fluid boundaries and its own history of increasing inclusion per the DSM.

Therefore, it is important to understand the roles of educators and parents (mothers in particular) in relation to the production of children who are what Foucault has called 'docile bodies': regulated, scrutinized, productive, well-disciplined, trained, and socially integrated citizens (1995: 142–55). I will begin with a brief consideration of what educational theorists have called the 'hidden curriculum' and will then discuss the role of the family (and mothers) in the moral and social regulation of children.

The Hidden Curriculum

Henry Giroux (1981) points out that there have traditionally been three kinds of rationality in educational theory: traditional, interpretive, and reproductive. Traditional educational theorists have not acknowledged schools as necessarily being sites of oppression; rather, they have assumed that the negative effects of education can be eradicated with adequate tinkering and a will to reform on the part of legislators and administrators. Interpretive critiques argue that schooling should be fluidly tailored to student needs on a consensual basis: such educational theories presume a more or less willing partnership between teachers and students who share a common goal and who can negate power imbalances through consensus-making. Reproductive theories, the most critical of these three bodies, see schools as places where, through ideological means, class and other social relations are reproduced (Giroux, 1981).

The rhetorical ideal of equal educational opportunity for all children that is embedded within both traditional and interpretive educational theories holds within it the promise of emancipatory transcendence: in short, the educated child will be capable of moving beyond differences of class, race, gender, and ability. Reproductive theories of education offer a different way of understanding the latent functions of education, and its proponents have developed a theory of a hidden, yet extremely potent, curriculum. Reproductive critics of education note that a 'hidden curriculum,' conveyed through student–teacher interactions, classroom structure and bureaucratic organization, and deployed through both intentional and unintentional ways, actually replicates rather than supersedes 'values acquisition, socialization, [and] maintenance of class structure' (Vallance, 1983: 10). Hidden curriculum critiques have included the claim that schooling is more a site for learning about teachers' authority (Jackson, 1983), the transmission of (primarily middle-class) moral standards (Purpel, 1988), the replication of social class structure (Apple, 1995), and gender stereotypes (Gilligan, 1983; Grumet, 1988). In addition, schooling has been understood as the avenue by which a national character is formed, in which coercive detention of children occurs, and in which a trained and docile workforce is forged: in short, a place in which one finds children as objects of social control (Vallance, 1983). Although some argument remains about the deterministic nature of this hidden curriculum (cf. Giroux, 1981; Apple, 1995), there can remain little doubt that schools do not necessarily do what they manifestly claim to. Rather, they create latent effects that are well outside the bounds of providing equal educational opportunities unproblematically to all students.[8]

Poststructural educational critiques add to this criticism of educational practice, connecting educational power, knowledge production, and discursive practices to normalization. Poststructural critics see that education, like psychology, medicine, and psychiatry has had as its primary effect (rather than as an unintended consequence) 'the establishment of measurements, hierarchy and regulations around the idea of a distributionary statistical norm within a given population' (Ball, 1990: 2). Thus, the knowledge and practice of teachers and schools is seen in poststructural accounts to operate in much the same way as other discipline, like medicine and the psy sector function: to organize, categorize, differentiate, scrutinize, and discipline young people in ways that make them easier to manage and easier to know. An additional insight offered by poststructuralists is that of the intertwining relationship between institutional orders in the management of children: schools work together with other disciplines and institutions (including medicine, psychiatry, psychology, social work, health promotion, and perhaps most importantly, the family) in this production of docile young bodies (Donzelot, 1997). Thus, the disciplinary aspects of educational practices are interrelated with normatively defined familial roles in the medicalization and normalization of AD(H)D. I will now turn to a discussion of the family and some theoretical insights that may illuminate familial roles in the medicalization and normalization of AD(H)D.

The Role of the Family

Many theories of the family have situated it (and often 'it' is either overtly defined as, or simply assumed to be a 'modern' family – a

---

8 As noted earlier, children with 'special needs' are often even less accommodated as part of the ideological claim of public schooling (Franklin, 1994).

nuclear, heterosexual, two-parent, father-headed unit) as the most fundamental social institution in western society. This 'modern' type of family has been seen as a 'haven in a heartless world' (Lasch, 1977) or as a domestic unit in which members share a common emotional climate, one that members feel 'they must protect from outside intrusion, through privacy and isolation' (Shorter, 1975). These understandings of the family see its role as a protective one: the modern family acts as a private and enclosed bulwark against the pressures and strains of a modern, industrial society.

Feminist critiques of the 1970s and 1980s challenged this view of the family as a private arena in which the desires of individual members were met unproblematically. In terms of intrafamilial roles, feminists criticized a sexual division of labour that privileged male freedom and female dependency (Friedan, 1963) and provided insight into relationships of violence and the abuse of power wielded by men against women (MacLeod, 1987; Walker, 1979) and children (Butler, 1985). In a critique of theories of the family as a private unit that can provide protection against institutional and social penetration, feminists pointed out that women's bodies and women's roles as mothers are neither private nor uncontested. Feminists instead argued the private and personal is both public (in terms of penetration by economics, legislation, and the helping professions) and political (in terms of political and social implications in women's reproductive and mothering acts) (Diprose, 1994; Ehrenreich and English, 1978; Fraser, 1994; Lupton, 1995; Martin, 1992; Oakley, 1984; R. Rapp, 1999; Rowland, 1987; Thorne, 1992). This argument acknowledges implicitly the importance to the state and to society of women's roles in materially reproducing healthy children (as evidenced in state, medical, and public health education interventions in maternal and obstetrical care) and in the moral reproduction of well-socialized and well-adjusted children (as evidence in psychological theory and practice related to proper maternal attachment, and social work theory and practice related to maternal child abuse and neglect). Nonetheless, such theoretical work often seems to regard women as little more than targets of professional, political, and discursive interventions into their maternal practice.

Poststructural theory, which informs this study, moves beyond understanding women merely as targets of power and acknowledges the active roles of women themselves as purveyors of social and moral reproduction within the family (cf. Badinter, 1981; Donzelot, 1997). Taking up this notion of an active subject, I thus asked women to tell me about how they themselves complied, pushed for, or refused the labels and treatments their children ultimately obtained.

Discourses of Motherhood

Some theorists note that fathers have taken an increasingly active role in the intimate rearing of children (McKee and O'Brien, 1982). Others argue that, while men seem to be moving into new masculinity and parenting norms, social policies that deter active fathering (such as poor paternal leave policies and barriers to custody rights for gay fathers) continue to undermine long-term changes in fathers' roles in the family (Rotundo, 1987). Still others argue that the 'new father' remains something of a mythical construction and that fathers themselves are mixed in their ability or willingness to live up to the rhetoric of egalitarian parenting (Daly, 1995; Lupton and Barclay, 1997).

Despite the claims that the role of fathers is shifting in at least some families, there remains a tendency on the part of social, educational, and governmental agencies to consider the mother as the primary moral guardian in the modern family. Caroline Knowles's recent study of multiagency interventions of the family when violence occurs in the home indicates, for example, that not only are women themselves conceived of by policy-makers, social workers, teachers, and medical personnel as responsible for the care and safety of their children, they are also conceived of as being responsible for choosing safe partners and for regulating the behaviour of their (typically male) partners: ultimately, mothers are held culpable when *any* type of family 'breakdown' occurs (Knowles, 1996: 123).

Further, Knowles observes, the range of maternal behaviours and problems that are deemed 'high risk' (i.e., appropriate for regulation through social policy and professional intervention) are comprehensive and include psychological maladjustment, maladaptive behaviour, negligence, being devious, being deemed dangerous, as well as actually being involved in any behaviour that is harmful to the child (1996: 169). In other words, 'dangerous mothers' are evaluated as such not only on the basis of their actions, but also on their personal, emotional, and psychological traits; all aspects of women thus are scrutinized in terms of their potential to harm children. On the contrary, Knowles points out, fathers are typically subject to a much narrower range of interventions than are mothers, and these interventions are limited to fathers who are actually dangerous (sexually or physically), dysfunctional, or who are absent (as in interventions to enforce child support payments). In short, paternal intervention is limited to behaviours that are actually harmful, while maternal interventions include aspects of the mother's personality that are perceived of as *potentially* harmful, reflecting professional understandings of the role of motherhood as both more primary and more complex than fatherhood.

Professional perceptions that mothers are responsible for all aspects of their children's lives are evidenced in the extraordinary circumstances of professional interventions attached to family violence and child abuse. It is also evidenced in everyday interactions with professionals and quasi-professionals related to child-rearing: again, even when the mother is not necessarily present. As an example, my husband took our daughter to Brownies, Girl Guides, and Pathfinders for over seven years. He was the parent who typically picked her up, volunteered for the cookie sales, drove her and other children to special events, and made any necessary arrangements with group leaders at the meetings. Invariably, however, when one of these leaders called our home with any concern or information, even when my husband would answer the phone, she (and it does always seem to be a 'she') would insist on speaking with 'Hilary's mother' as the 'naturally' responsible parent.

Present-day practices and belief systems that hold mothers fully responsible for the good of the child and the safety of the family go back at least to the Enlightenment (Badinter, 1981). Since that time, mothers have been held responsible by experts not only for the preservation of their children physically, but they have been burdened with responsibility for the moral regulation of their children (Badinter, 1981; Donzelot, 1997; Ehrenreich and English,1978).

Rousseau's *Emile* ushered in a long tradition of expert advice on mothering, establishing a discourse of good mothering as a natural state, one in which 'the ideal woman would be the one who came closest to the animal' which naturally provided nutrients and care to its young (Badinter, 1981: 155–6). Women were made responsible not only for their child's health and physical well-being, but also for every aspect of familial 'success': the good woman attracted a responsible father and kept him around to help her raise a successful and integrated child: 'It was entirely on her that everything was to depend ... if the father was slow to assume his paternal functions, it was because the mother was bad ... the mothers would nurse and the fathers would then naturally do their part. The family would be united and society virtuous – which the police lieutenants and economists translated into political terms: 'The state will be rich and powerful' (Badinter, 1981: 166–7).

Mothers in eighteenth-century France were made primarily responsible for socializing their children, and according to Badinter, this shift occurred concomitantly with the development of new state agencies and academic disciplines, foremost among them medicine and education (1981: 222–36). A symbiotic relationship developed between physician, educator, and mother over time as child-raising manuals, home visits, maternal watchfulness, and the production of law-abiding and well-educated children came to be associated with proper mothering. Badinter claims that two benefits accrued to mothers in their new role as medical and educational handmaids; first, they were able to avoid the guilt and blame attendant with the label of 'bad mothering' by adhering to medical and social prescriptions and proscriptions. Second, mothers gained power and prestige through the new medical and educational discourse that promoted mothers as the primary and naturally expert caregiver and as the sole source of natural goodness necessary to the betterment of children and ultimately, the nation state. As Badinter says, 'By accepting responsibility for her children's upbringing, the middle-class woman improved her personal status. To the power of the purse ... she added power over human beings – her children ... the mother became the holy "domestic Monarch"' (1981: 189).[9] The irony of this new power for mothers was that the mother, according to Badinter, ended up becoming the enforcer of *other people's* rules (ibid.). With the replacement of the patriarchy of the family by the patriarchy of the state, a whole new range of accountabilities befell the maternal role: mothers became accountable to physicians, educators, truant officers, welfare and social workers, and family courts.

Donzelot, too, has noted the shared trajectory of the rise of the medical profession and the rise in the civil authority and social status of the mother during the eighteenth and nineteenth centuries (1997: 20–1).

---

9 Badinter points out that this shift to the 'good mother' was not uniformly embraced: poor women adopted it later and to a lesser extent, because of other demands on their time and labour, while wealthy women persisted in boarding out their children well into the nineteenth century (1981: 195–201). As we will see, class-based differences were also evidenced in the present study, both in terms of women's own attitudes about mothering, medicine, and education, and in terms of the treatment of women and their families by those institutions.

The alliance between mothers and medicine, which has continued to this day, was: 'profitable to both parties: with the mother's help, the doctor prevailed against the stubborn hegemony of that popular medicine of the old wives; and on the other hand, owing to the increased importance of the maternal functions, he conceded a new power to the bourgeois woman in the domestic sphere' (Donzelot, 1997: 20). The new role of mother as both consumer of and handmaid to disciplinary knowledge, including medical knowledge about raising a healthy child, social work knowledge about ideal socialization and emotional well-being of the child, and educational knowledge about rearing an intellectually developed and occupationally prepared child, shifted familial authority away from the father and resulted in new domestic power for women. On the other hand, Donzelot notes, when the woman became responsible for the health, well-being, and harmony of the home, she also became liable for any failing that might occur in the entire family: 'if the husband preferred the outside, the lights of the cabaret, and the children the street, with its spectacles and its promiscuity, this would be the fault of the wife and mother' (1997: 45).

According to Badinter (1981), the role of mothers as primary, expert caregivers is not a natural one. Her description of typical mothering practices in France prior to the ascendance of the 'good mother' discourse that began in the Enlightenment demonstrates that nurturance, selflessness, and expert mother knowledge are not only learned, but they are often resisted by women who would prefer not to take on these roles. In fact, Badinter's book presents a compelling argument that there is no instinct for mothering: nonetheless, the moral imperative inherent in a discourse of motherhood as nurturing and virtuous has resulted in a belief in the *natural* ability of all 'good' women to mother capably, wholeheartedly, and selflessly. Conversely, it has resulted in an understanding that women who fail or refuse these roles are not 'good' women; rather, they are seen as *unnatural*. Further, the 'maladjusted child' today continues to act as a symbol of the 'bad mother' who is, incidentally, an unnatural creature. This will become an important tradition to consider when discussing the reasons mothers of AD(H)D-identified children might wish to cooperate with medical, psy sector, and educational professionals in applying a medical rather than a familial or behavioural label on their children.

The belief that women naturally are responsible for the material and moral success of all members of their families persists in the present. Paula Caplan tells us that 'mothers are either idealized or blamed for everything that goes wrong' (1989: 2). She notes that mothers are not permitted to err and be human, because so much is at stake; her children's mental and physical health, and their future, is both the mother's purpose and her sole responsibility (1989: 68). Caplan has developed a typology of 'perfect mother myths' based on extensive research and counselling of mothers and daughters. Among these, the myth that 'the measure of a good mother is a perfect child' is perhaps most salient (1989: 74). If the child diagnosed with AD(H)D truly does run the risks of not having close friends, of being the class clown and depending on younger friends to dominate, of seeking excitement through illegal activities, cutting classes, or even stealing, and of continuing into adulthood with difficulties in concentration and in relationships with others (Minde, 1987), that child is certainly less than perfect. Further, if the child's imperfection is understood as a reflection of the mother's failings, those imperfections will be perceived as natural outcomes of poor mothering.

Because women are held responsible, because they are so often implicated as lacking or problematic when things go 'wrong,' and because they themselves may subscribe to these discourses of 'good mothering,' I believe that an examination of motherhood – rather than of parenthood – as it relates to the dilemmas attendant to an AD(H)D diagnosis has been an important strategy in accomplishing an understanding of the moral and social regulation attached to AD(H)D. Further, because it is mothers who, within the family, are generally the intersecting site between the public world of medicine, education, and psychiatry and the private world of child-rearing, a focus on women permits an examination of the nexus between public intervention and private care in an optimal way.

Motherhood and Medicalization

Feminists have created a substantial body of work critiquing women's medicalization, that is, the ways that many aspects of women's bodies come to be defined and treated as medical problems and how this medicalization operates as a way of controlling women's bodies and lives. This process occurs to young women upon whose anorexic and hungering bodies the brushstrokes of psychological pathology have been laid (Brown and Jasper, 1993; Chernin, 1981); women upon whose pregnant and lactating bodies the stamp of risk and responsibility has been pressed (Blum, 1993; Diprose, 1994; Martin, 1992; Oakley 1984;

Rowland, 1987); menopausal women upon whose bodies the label of madness and unruliness has been applied (Barbre, 1999); and ill and/or disabled women upon whose bodies the stigmata of pollution, inferiority, and deviance have been placed (Batt, 1994; Asch and Fine, 1997). Modern, western science and medicine have treated women's bodies throughout the lifespan, and across situations, as sites to control, improve, and blame.

A second stream of feminist analysis shifts its focus from women's bodies to an examination of how women experience medicalization in their roles as mothers. Here, mothers become targets of medical, educational, and social work professionals as maternal practice and knowledge is manipulated through discourse, policy, and actual intervention. As with women's maternal bodies, women's maternal experiences have been medicalized. In the place of earlier understandings of mothering as a natural and instinctual process, motherhood from the eighteenth century forward has come to be seen by medical professionals as a site requiring education and intervention through modern, enlightened, child-rearing regimens (Badinter, 1981). For mothers of 'normal,' healthy young children, modernist notions of good mothering were tied to the · new sciences of hygiene, illness prevention, and developmental psychology, deployed through public health visits, breastfeeding and immunization educational campaigns, and public health programs (Arnup, 1994; Burman, 1994; Ehrenreich and English, 1978).

Feminist analyses of medicalized motherhood have expanded from a consideration of the effects of medicalization on all mothers to more focused analyses of how medicalization intersects with marginalization. Feminists have examined the regulation of mothers who have used drugs during or following pregnancy (Boyd, 1999), are lesbians (Arnup, 1995; Nelson, 1996), are deemed to be too young (Flanagan, 1998), who are immigrants (Fraktman, 1998), or members of racial minorities (Collins Hill, 1994; Litt, 2000; Sparks, 1998), or who are disabled (Asch and Fine, 1997). Thus, feminists have exposed how 'good' mothers are situated in traditional medical and professional discourse as heterosexual, married, able-bodied, white, middle-class, stay-at-home caregivers, and how this is punitive to women, and serves gendered, classed, ableist, and racialized normative orders.

Although some consideration has been given to 'abnormal' mothers, most feminist analyses have been concerned with the medicalization of 'normal' pregnancy, infancy, and early childhood. A small number of writers have examined the experiences of mothers whose children are disabled, and argue that mothers of children with disabilities bear additional burdens of blame and guilt compared with mothers of non-disabled children. It has been noted, for example, that increased medical technology, particularly sonograms and amniocenteses, has placed pressure on mothers to produce perfection and to reject the 'abnormal,' making the 'choice' to continue an 'imperfect' pregnancy seem irresponsible at best, pathological at worst (Landsman, 1998; R. Rapp, 1999). Anne-Marie Ambert argues that mothers of disabled children must act as mediators and advocates with teachers, caregivers, and medical personnel for their children, that professionals often blame mothers for the child's difficulties, and that these negative outcomes are heightened when the child looks normal but acts in ways that are different (Ambert, 1992: 118–20). Thus, mothers' experiences of medicalization operate in unique ways when the child is a child with a disability, particularly an invisible disability such as AD(H)D.

Similar to other disabilities, the medicalization of children with AD(H)D acts as a mirrored surface upon which surveillance, normalization, and stigmatization is reflected: the AD(H)D child's problems become reflections of presumed problems in mothers. For mothers of children with AD(H)D, child and maternal medicalization occurs later in childhood, lengthening the arena of surveillance and intervention into mothers' lives. Further, because of its intersection with the *tutelary complex* (not only physicians, but educators, counsellors, psychiatrists, and juvenile authorities), the scale and complexity of intervention broadens beyond traditional conceptualizations of medicalization to include a wide spectrum of 'professionalizations.' Finally, the medicalization of AD(H)D extends maternal responsibility to an ever-widening range of children's (both immediate and threatened) qualities: from poor schooling and lack of social skills in childhood to threatened alcoholism, drug dependency, criminality, social isolation, and unemployment in adulthood.

Conclusion

In the preceding sections I have outlined the cultural and historical background against which the management of AD(H)D is played out. In particular, I have described AD(H)D as a disorder that is treated quite differently between Canada and Great Britain, and that is not universally accepted as legitimate by lay people or by professionals in either national context. Further, I have shown that AD(H)D is an ambiguous diagnosis: neither its cause, nor its effects are undeniably established. Additionally, I have shown that mothers, even when not directly implicated in the causes of their children's difficulties, are subject to speculations about their character and intentions when their children encounter troubles. Finally, I have indicated that studying mothers as they attempt to understand the application of an AD(H)D diagnosis to their children will provide insight into the discursive practices and workings of power in a number of important social institutions, including childhood, motherhood, the family, medicine, psychiatry, and education. In the next chapter, I outline methodological considerations in conducting this study of mothers and AD(H)D in both Canada and the United Kingdom, with particular attention to my concern of bridging feminist standpoint theory with poststructural discourse theory.

2 Methodology

Poststructural theories of knowledge and human subjectivity have had a tremendous influence on recent research and theory related to psychiatry, medicine, health, and the body (Turner, 1997). Poststructuralism, informed by an understanding of the body and illness as both historically situated and discursively constituted, eschews debates about whether a particular illness has some prediscursive basis in nature. Instead, poststructural approaches seek to uncover how discourse, knowledge, and language circulate in ways that produce the effect of an illness that operates *as though* it is real and natural. The focus thus becomes a 'critical epistemology of disease categories as elements of the moral control of individuals and populations' (Turner, 1997: ix). This is the approach that I am taking in studying mothers and AD(H)D. Thus, I am not particularly concerned in this research with the question of whether the children in this study were indeed 'properly' diagnosed with AD(H)D, nor whether AD(H)D itself is a 'true' disorder. Rather, my central interest lies in understanding the ways that knowledge and language relating to AD(H)D are deployed in professional discursive practice and in lay discourse, and how women themselves respond to these discursive and disciplining practices. In short, I am interested in the *effects* of the discursive practices that surround AD(H)D and that permit AD(H)D to operate as a disciplinary category.[1]

---

1 It must be confessed, however, that the women with whom I spoke do not necessarily share my interest. Many of the mothers in this study have asked me 'what I've found out about AD(H)D.' *Their* interest, because of their precarious positions as mothers of vulnerable children, *is* in finding out the 'truth' about AD(H)D so that they can then respond accordingly.

Poststructural discourse analyses do not necessarily presume that material and economic interests are at the root of legitimation strategies, nor do they assume that underneath the machinations of interested parties some fixed 'truth' about the problem in question endures. While the poststructural focus might superficially be on institutions, theories, or ideologies, it is their *discursive practices* – 'what is said and what is done, rules imposed and reasons given, the planned and taken for granted' in handling social difficulties that are the central focus of analysis (Foucault, 1991: 75). In essence, poststructural analyses focus on *games of truth* (Foucault, 1987: 2). Truth games, to Foucault, are those discursive and knowledge-based activities that produce the *effect* of making one's claims act as though true, natural, and real, despite their constructed nature. Thus, in poststructural analyses, profit or material control is not necessarily understood to be the sole root of knowledge claims; rather, professional hegemony and control of knowledge are the 'interests' that inhere in truth games. Additionally, poststructural analysis is relatively unconcerned about the 'true' nature of the problems that underlie these truth games: rather, the focus remains on the effects of those truth games, and on how truth games work to effect social and moral regulation. Further, poststructuralists understand power as circulating and available to all human actors, rather than as operating in central and unitary ways. This permits a shift in focus from the study of lobby groups and professional bodies to the ways that all human actors (including patients and parents) engage in truth games.

Foucault's concept of governmentality is central to a contemporary poststructural analysis. In governmentality, top-down mechanisms for regulating, knowing, and disciplining individuals and populations through increased knowledge and surveillance intersect with the self-care and self-surveillance (technologies of the self) of individuals. This concept has permitted researchers to 'think about the medicalization of society within a new framework, where the exercise of medical power was seen in terms of local diffuse practices,' rather than something that operated from a central, state-organized position, as occurred in traditional medical sociology (Turner, 1997: xiii), or even from the powerful base of lobby groups and corporations.

Finally, in poststructural analyses, these truth games involve not only laying claims to the truth of one or the other way of handling and understanding AD(H)D, but they also involve technologies of the self that make responding in one way or another 'true.' Foucault's concept of technologies of the self provides a theoretical framework with which to understand how individuals come to desire and participate in discursive effects that make certain illnesses and their accompanying disciplinary practices operate as though real. Technologies of the self, 'permit individuals to effect by their own means or with the help of others a certain number of operations on their own bodies and souls, thoughts, conduct, and way of being so as to transform themselves in order to attain a certain state of happiness, purity, wisdom, perfection, or immortality' (Foucault, 1988: 18). Thus, for example, mothers who wish to count themselves as good mothers of cared for and deserving children may feel compelled to 'partner' with others in disciplining their children or in accepting an AD(H)D label for them. The 'others' who may assist parents in facing an AD(H)D label for their children include the family physician and/or pediatrician, the teacher, the school special education teacher, a school psychologist, a psychologist or a psychiatrist, family members, and other parents.

By employing a Foucauldian understanding of the human subject as constituted through discursive knowledge and as self-constituting through technologies of the self, I believe I have been able to examine not only the compliance of individuals to the AD(H)D label, but to explore examples of resistance and the use of power by mothers as they construct their own games of truth. Thus, my analysis includes not only how mothers come to respond to the label of AD(H)D in one way or another, but also explores how they constitute themselves as *good mothers* either in complying with or resisting professional practices relating to their troubled children. Finally, by taking up a poststructural understanding of power, I hoped to accomplish two things. First, by exploring maternal–professional interactions, I hoped to understand the complex workings of power and its multiple intersections in the lives of the women and children in the study. Second, by asking women how they understand and respond to these intersections, I hoped to understand how women themselves take up discursive power and use it to their own ends. Because AD(H)D is a contested category, I believed it might leave openings for mothers to respond and resist in ways that a less ambiguous diagnosis (for example, diabetes or cancer) might not permit.

Foucauldian Archaeology

In this study I have made a comparative examination of texts and interviews taken from one discrete moment in time and two distinct cultures as they relate to AD(H)D. In this sense, I have taken up a Foucauldian archaeology to examine the ways that language imposes itself on given systems of thought and gives rise to discursive practice and social effects. In archaeology, the researcher analyses *énoncés*, or discursive pronouncements, that give rise to certain ways of thinking and acting that operate as natural, but that are indeed connected to linguistic practice specific to time and place. Archaeology uses these *énoncés* as data, and takes as its focus an examination of 'the forms of regularity ... the discursive conditions, which order the structure' of certain ways of being and thinking (Olssen, 1999: 10).

I chose to use archaeology as a 'box of tools' (Foucault, 1977: 205) with which to analyse both official and informal or lay discourses and practices relating to the handling of AD(H)D. The *énoncés* that I examined include policies and funding provisions in educational discourse relating to the handling of students with special needs and statements by various medical, educational, and psy sector professionals about the 'proper' way to understand AD(H)D. As well, I examined pronouncements in the popular media and in professional discourse about the 'true' reasons that AD(H)D exists, about who is responsible for it, who understands it best, and what is the best and/or worst way to respond to it. By examining these texts, I aimed to undertake an investigation of the various 'games of truth' deployed by a wide range of knowledge producers, including educators, administrators, governments, physicians, psychiatrists, and special educators, that are engaged in handling 'different' children in two modern, western cultures. In addition, this examination of the truth claims circulating over AD(H)D illuminated the professional practices that form the backdrop against which mothers' stories unfold and help us to understand the dilemmas mothers face in attempting to find 'the right answer' for their children.

Standpoint Theory and Interpretive Methods

Research that is focused on discursive practice and knowledge production is important in exposing the constructed 'nature' of the social and the ways that knowledge circulates to constrain human experience. However, there have been criticisms of a research approach to the social that does not include the perspectives of human actors. Nancy Hartsock, for example, has criticized Foucault's usefulness to feminist studies, stating: 'Foucault's is a world in which things move, rather than people, a world in which subjects become obliterated or, rather, recreated as passive objects, a world in which passivity or refusal represent the only possible choices' (1990: 167). Hartsock goes on to state that, despite Foucault's theoretical and substantive focus on power, his methodological adherence to a structural rather than subjective position ironically results in work in which 'systematic power relations ultimately vanish' (1990: 168). Hartsock instead calls for a theory of power and a research approach that recognizes the way that human actors are able to understand their world. She argues for a feminist standpoint epistemology, claiming that people whose lives are subjugated in terms of race, gender, or class positions are better situated to expose the workings of power than are those who enjoy positions of privilege, a category in which, because of his gendered, raced, and classed position, she includes Michel Foucault (1990: 171–2).

Expressing a central tenet of feminist standpoint epistemology, Donna Haraway notes that daily practices and material life are experienced differentially according to gender, class, and race (1991). Further, she argues that the position of women, as subordinated subjects, offers a perspective on social situations that exposes social relations, power operations, and the effects of institutional practice with particular clarity (1991). Thus, we can see that feminist standpoint theorists argue against macro-level, historical research that adopts a falsely neutral, view-from-nowhere stance, because such approaches efface marginalized human subjectivities and leave little room for social change and resistance. Instead, they call for social research that is engaged from the standpoint of the oppressed, that includes the possibility of creating transformative knowledge, and that understands humans as not only objects of history, but as capable of constituting themselves through knowledge creation and consumption (Hartsock, 1990, 1996).

Conversely, a number of feminist philosophers have argued for the usefulness of Foucauldian theory in feminist analyses, and they find Foucauldian theories of knowledge and power to be productive tools in enhancing feminist standpoint epistemologies. Weedon, for example, has noted: 'Although the subject in post-structuralism is socially constructed in discursive practices, she none the less exists as a thinking, feeling, subject and social agent capable of resistance and innovations produced out of the clash between contradictory subject positions and practices. She is also a subject able to reflect upon the discursive relations, which constitute her, and the society in which she lives and is able to choose from the options available' (Weedon, 1987: 125).

Thus, Weedon argues for the usefulness of Foucauldian concepts not only as an important way to gain an understanding of what women themselves are thinking, feeling, and doing, but also as a way to understand the perspectives of women about the forces and structures that that shape their experiences and their identities. This argument is echoed by Amy Allen, who writes that Foucault's understanding of power as operating locally, circulating in the capillaries of the social body, and emanating from every point in the social field offers feminist scholars a position from which to understand the workings of power that is intimately tied up with women's bodies and daily practices. Further, she notes that Foucault's concepts of discourse permit researchers to make connections between the intimate workings of power, subjectivity, knowledge, and cultural meanings that operate at the micro-level of the subject and at the meso-level of discourse (Allen, 1990). In this research, I have attempted to undertake just such a combination of methods by playing interpretive, micro-level analysis against an examination of meso-level discursive practice.

Mixed Methods

Taking together Weedon's claim of a knowing Foucauldian subject and Allen's support of the usefulness of Foucault to understanding the connections between local practices and meso-level discursive practice, I believe it is appropriate to use Foucauldian analyses of power, subjectivity, risk, and knowledge with methods other than the historical, macro-level genealogy or the purely discourse-based archaeology described earlier. I am not alone. Sue Middleton, for example, has used life-history interview data to 'provide a view from the bottom up.' She interviewed students in her study to examine from a Foucauldian perspective the disciplining of adolescent sexuality in public secondary schools in New Zealand during the twentieth century (1997: 3). She also uses her student interview material as a counterpoint to interviews conducted with professionals, teachers, legislators, policy-makers, theorists, and researchers as a way to understand the ways that discourse constrains and produces certain types of understanding and behaviour around adolescent sexuality in students and officials alike.

Like Middleton, I used multiple methods of data collection, but instead I have combined interview data with discourse analysis of lay, professional, and policy texts as a way to understand women's experiences within the framework of professional discursive practice. My use of interviews played against professional and academic discursive materials is a methodological attempt to construct an account that connects subjectivity to structure. A purely interpretive account would consider the voice of articulate subjects as the central focus of analysis, while purely structural accounts would privilege textual and institutional structures as the appropriate focus of inquiry. My approach reflects the Foucauldian notion of a subject who is constituted through practices of normalization and inscription and who at the same time engages in her or his own truth games (Lacombe, 1994: 12–13).

Interviews and Methodology

Foucauldian notions of knowledge, power, and resistance informed my interview approach. I understood these mothers to be knowing subjects who are active participants in a discursive field of circulating, local, and practice-based power relations and whose perspective is able to provide us a rich penetration into the micropolitics of AD(H)D (Weedon, 1987). Mothers, as objects of medical, psychiatric, educational, and social work discourse, and as subjects who interpret, interface, advocate, and care for their children in conjunction with professionals, can offer a critical understanding of professional discourse and practice attached to AD(H)D. In addition, they have much to say about how women in relatively subordinate positions offer resistance and appropriate power in an attempt to be heard, respected, and served.

Thus, while Canadian mothers often struggle to avoid a label and British mothers typically struggle to obtain a diagnosis, my focus was on how maternal experiences in both sites are mediated by normative discourses of motherhood, knowledge, and risk. In this focus, mothers in both sites are subject to the 'truth games' about AD(H)D, as deployed by multiple professionals, in which claims are made to legitimacy through the use of language and reliance on common understandings of what is 'true' (Foucault, 1984). As a way of understanding how these truth games operate in both contexts, I asked mothers to tell me about the ways that medical, educational, and psychiatric professionals used language, knowledge, and common understandings about good motherhood, dangerous childhood, and pathology in understanding and treating children with AD(H)D. In turn, I asked mothers to tell me about the operations of professional truth claims in their lives, and to tell me about their own strategic truth games in dealing with professionals.

What I sought was insight into the subjugated knowledge mothers have about the ways that 'regularities, logic, strategy, self-evidence and "reason"' are used to codify the truth related to AD(H)D (Foucault, 1991: 75). Mothers are conspicuously silent in discourse, research, and theory relating to AD(H)D. I wanted to hear from women precisely because their 'naïve and disqualified' ways of knowing about AD(H)D would provide a counternarrative 'capable of opposition and of struggle against the coercions of a theoretical, unitary, formal and scientific [and psychiatric, medical, and educational] discourse' relating to AD(H)D (Foucault, 1980a: 74). I asked mothers to tell me not only about how they felt their lives to be scrutinized and constrained by professional discursive practice, but also to tell me of the ways they struggled to be heard, to effect change, and to resist stigmatization. By exploiting current feminist standpoint theory, and taking my understanding of AD(H)D from the perspective of mothers as they care for their children, I have exposed the operations of power in the AD(H)D medical–educational–psychiatric complex in a way that only mothers could illuminate.

Interviews typically began with the simple question, 'Please tell me the story of how you first came to think of your child as different.' The posing of such a question offered interviewees the opportunity to bear witness, name their injuries, and connect with others by breaking silence in a way that was not constrained by my own understanding of the situation (Riessman, 1993; Malacrida, 1998). I followed up this invitation to narrative with more structured, research-specific questions to ensure the data were comprehensive. The interview guide can be found in Appendix 4.

Interviews and Sampling Considerations

Ultimately, I conducted interviews with seventeen mothers of AD(H)D-identified children in southern Alberta and another seventeen in southeast England. I attempted to sample interview participants in ways that reflect some of the themes that arose from my review of the literature. For example, the literature on discourses of motherhood indicated that mothers who are single parents, lesbians, poorly educated, non-white, and living in poverty are more likely to be objects of scrutiny and intervention than are married, educated, white, middle-class women. Although these women may have fewer resources to bring to bear in resisting labels, I also felt that Badinter's insight (1981) about middle-class women's ready acceptance of 'natural motherhood' would be an important consideration. I wondered whether, despite meagre resources and higher levels of scrutiny, poor or marginalized women may be less prepared to buy into medicalization and psychiatrization because they perceive fewer 'partnership' advantages in doing so. Thus, I sought women in both cultural contexts who spanned a range of raced and classed positions.

In terms of racial heterogeneity, I was less than successful; both the Canadian and British participants were predominantly white. In the Canadian group, one mother is a First Nations person, another is Latina, and a third is of Chinese descent. In the British group, one woman is black and another is Latina. I was more successful in gaining a fairly broad range of women from different classed positions. Both British and Canadian women in the study ranged from single mothers with several children, to women who mother a single child within an intact and 'supportive' partnership and extended family. Mothers' educational and occupational status ranged from less than high school completion and receiving social assistance to possessing more than one graduate degree and maintaining professional (if not full-time) occupational status. We can only speculate about mothers' class positions; however, as most of the interviews occurred in women's homes, I saw evidence that participants' socioeconomic statuses ranged from very poor to wealthy. Despite efforts to 'capture' a wide range of women's classed, racialized, and sexual subject positions, this sample cannot be seen as 'representative,' and the stories of these women should not be understood to stand for the stories of all women who mother a child with AD(H)D. It would have been interesting, for example, to speak with women who are openly lesbian or bisexual in order to understand the ways that marginalized sexuality plays out in this situation or to speak with mothers whose experiences of AD(H)D were absolutely positive; however, I was unable to locate such mothers for this study.

Of the thirty-four women interviewed for this project, only two were employed full-time outside the home. All but six were employed on varying part-time bases; of those six, three women lived on social assistance, and the remaining three depended on their partner's income. All of these women stated that their need to be at home and to engage in more or less full-time advocacy or service delivery for their children had played a central role in their work-related opportunities and choices. They stated that the demands of tutoring, school meetings, doctor and therapist appointments, and ubiquitous child-related crises had led to decisions (often accompanied by regrets and/or resentments) within partnerships, or on the part of lone mothers to curtail paid maternal employment, at least during the child's school years. Although there are undoubtedly many mothers of AD(H)D children who do manage to work full-time, relatively few responded to my calls for interview participants. This might mean that the children discussed here have more difficult and demanding lives with schools and helping professionals than do other AD(H)D children, so that these mothers felt motivated to share their stories through participating in this research. Conversely, it may mean that working mothers of AD(H)D children have little time to sit down and tell their stories and that participating in this research would have added to what was already an overburdened life.

From the literature on poststructural theories of knowledge production and its effects on subjectivity, I understood that it would be important to attempt to speak with women who are members of support groups and to women who eschew support group services. I suspected that support groups have a role of educating and guiding parents towards a certain interpretation of AD(H)D – by speaking to mothers both from within and outside of the support group framework, I hoped to encounter different understandings of the legitimacy of AD(H)D. Thus, the women in both sites came to this study through a variety of channels. Participants in Canada were recruited in the following ways: through an article in a local parenting magazine (two mothers); a mail-out newsletter of the Alberta Learning Disabilities Association (two); a government-funded parent support group (four); flyers posted in the local university (four); a private school for children with ADD (three); and through snowball sampling (two). British participants were contacted through a national conference addressing AD(H)D issues (four mothers); Canadian personal connections (three); on-line grass-roots support groups (five); 2 local clinics in small towns (two); and snowball sampling (three). Again, although every attempt was made to recruit participants from a variety of sources, the final participants were self-selected, and thus they may have shared experiences that are quite different from those of mothers of AD(H)D-identified children in general. In particular, the stories told by this group of women may be more negative than those of other mothers; it can be surmised that perhaps women whose experiences of labelling and medicalization were pleasant would find little motivation to tell their story. Still, the women whose narratives are presented here shared remarkable similarities in the experiences they encountered.

The majority of the interviews were conducted in the women's homes. As has been noted by other feminist interviewers, this often meant dealing with the chaos of young children in the home and with the interruptions of children's questions and curiosity. In practice, however, I felt it was a benefit to meet the children who were being discussed, to watch them interact with their mothers, and typically, to note that there was considerable warmth in most of the relationships between mothers and their children.

Discourse Analysis – Theoretical Framework

In addition to interviewing mothers, I examined discursive materials related to parenting an AD(H)D-identified child in the belief that these texts offered me ways to organize my basic understanding of some of the themes and norms that women encounter and respond to (either consciously or unconsciously) while dealing with the diagnostic process. In my use of Foucauldian discourse analysis I employ the strategy of playing data from interviews with subjugated persons (mothers) against discursive materials directed towards mothers but generated by those in relative positions of power (psychiatrists, psychologists, teachers, physicians, and advocacy groups). I intended through examining this interplay – 'sometimes in harmony, sometimes as a cacophony [to] weave a coherent score' that would provide insight into the circulating power practices and truth games related to AD(H)D diagnoses (Middleton, 1997: 3).

Following Foucault, I was not interested in determining the absolute truthfulness of the claims that support AD(H)D as a legitimate medical and psychiatric category, nor in testing theories that see AD(H)D as a purely social problem for which mothers, teachers, and overzealous med/psy professionals should be held culpable. Rather, I sought to understand how the discursive practices of professionals and lay media in relation to AD(H)D act to constrain the choices and experiences of mothers. Rather than assume that AD(H)D 'is' in a natural and prediscursive sense, I assumed that AD(H)D, as it operates in the present in two western cultures, is an 'effect' of the discursive practices related to its medicalization and psychiatrization. Thus, through analysing textual materials related to AD(H)D in both Calgary and London, I hoped to outline discursive practices in each culture as a way of understanding the different and similar ways that AD(H)D has come to operate in each culture. In examining these AD(H)D-related texts, I explore the ways that claims are made to seem legitimate through the use of language and through reliance on common understandings of what is 'true' (Foucault, 1984: 74), particularly as those 'truth' claims relate to educational, medical, psychiatric, and governmental practice.

Foucault understood that a relationship exists between texts, economics, and politics. He stated that claims are made to seem legitimate through the 'ensemble of rules according to which the true and the false are separated and specific effects of power attached to the true ... it being understood [that it is a matter of] a battle about the status of truth and the economic and political role it plays' (Foucault, 1984: 74). However, for Foucault, the relationship between texts, politics, and economics is not determinative. He states: 'To put it very simply, psychiatric internment, the mental normalization of individuals, and penal institutions have no doubt a fairly limited importance if one is *only* looking for their economic significance' (1980b: 116, emphasis mine). Thus, while Foucauldian analyses of textual materials might include considerations of material practice, they also move beyond the 'relations of ruling' of neo-Marxist feminists (Smith, 1990) to examine the ways that truth is claimed in the handling of social problems.

I have used Foucauldian concepts in my analysis of discourse in both of these ways: through speculating on the economic and political interests at play in the claims that are deployed in the texts I examined and by considering the hegemonic knowledge interests that are at stake in handling the social problem of AD(H)D. In other words, I have examined these discursive materials not only to understand who can profit by their construction as 'true' but as a way to understand the nonmaterial benefits that accrue to educational, medical, and psychiatric professionals from the legitimation of the diagnosis and treatment of AD(H)D as 'true.'

The main 'tool' used within a Foucauldian archaeology is 'one of reversal. This entails examining official discourses which point to a particular conclusion, usually positive, and considering the implications of an opposite outcome' (Allan, 1996: 225). I have used this strategy of reversal in my analysis of texts relating to AD(H)D as a way to expose the things that are not said and the interests that are served by what is explicitly pronounced. In my analysis, I have identified several subterranean discursive themes embedded in texts relating to AD(H)D. These are the following: issues of gender specific to motherhood; professional discourses of childhood and the family as a place of lack and risk; discourse of expert knowledge that privileges medical, educational, and psychological interpretations and management; and notions of science as the truly legitimate purveyor of knowledge about health, illness, and treatment. Issues of social class are also embedded in these texts: in regard to one's ability to seek and purchase alternative therapies to mainstream medical, educational, and psychological treatments; in the ways that family and gender issues are constructed; and in the ways that medicalization and professionalization are traditionally upper-middle class projects. Finally, nationally located issues of professional hegemony are located in these texts, particularly in relation to the struggles over which professional groups in each site have ownership and responsibility for handling AD(H)D.

Sara Mills (1997) notes that employing an analysis of absence is also an important tool for feminist researchers undertaking Foucauldian discourse analysis. In this approach, discourse analyses should include a consideration of who is not included in the text and why that might be. Additionally, feminist Foucauldian researchers should consider that texts that direct women to behave in certain ways, or that construct women as certain kinds of subjects, are in fact responding to unspoken alternatives. In other words, the subject to whom such texts are addressed can be read as a resisting woman or unruly subject, one who is unlike the ideal type represented in the text (1997: 88–92). Thus, for example, texts generated by professionals that speak to partnerships between professionals and mothers should be read as a response to mothers who refuse or complicate such relationships.

I found Mills's strategies to be fruitful in my analysis of texts relating to AD(H)D. However, in addition to directly applying feminist concerns about women and texts, I extended my consideration of absences and of unspoken alternatives to include intraprofessional conflicts as well as profession–maternal difficulties. I felt this was important, as it illuminates the conflicted and ambiguous terrain upon which mothers' experiences, choices, and actions are played out and, often, made difficult.

In addition to taking a Foucauldian approach to discourse analysis, I have also used feminist research into the medical and professional surveillance and regulation of women who mother to inform my analysis. By extending feminist theories of medicalized motherhood to my analysis of texts produced by the lay media, and educational, psychological, and medical treatment providers, I hope to make several contributions to theories of medicalized motherhood.

First, I hope to convey that, in the case of disability, and particularly a disability with as much ambiguity as AD(H)D, the scope of professionals' maternal regulation moves beyond women's own bodies and personal qualities or the needs of the very young child. Rather, the disciplinary practices brought to bear on mothers of children with AD(H)D concern children who are school-aged or older, extending maternal regulation almost to the child's adulthood. Further, I propose that although the qualities these children exhibit have themselves been medicalized, with AD(H)D, the medicalized child becomes a mirrored surface on which the medical and professional gaze is reflected, creating maternal guilt by association and making mothers objects of medicalization and pathologization as a result of their children's difficulties.

Textual Sources – Sampling Considerations

Speaking for a textually based feminist standpoint epistemology, Dorothy Smith posits that the best way to understand the workings of power is to begin from our everyday lives, and to work up through the texts we encounter to uncover the institutional organizations of power that the texts represent (Smith, 1987: 175–6). The texts I examined intersect with the intimate everyday lives at a number of levels: from the direct, micro-interactional level of texts exchanged between physicians, psychologists, educators, and mothers, to meso-level discourse between professionals and between professional regulatory bodies, and finally at a macro-level of governmental policy documents and public media relating to AD(H)D.

Texts that intersect directly with maternal practice were culled from London and Calgary parenting magazines, materials distributed through parent support groups, and through local schools, pediatricians', psychologists', and psychiatrists' offices. This portion of the discursive data analysed in this study intersects institutional orders of motherhood, education, medicine, and psychiatry with the everyday lives of parents, and particularly mothers, as they struggle to find solutions for their children whose behaviours are noted as problematic. Often mothers themselves provided me with these texts during our interviews. I came across other texts through the British on-line support groups I used for participant contact; these groups disseminate considerable grass-roots information about AD(H)D from a remarkable array of perspectives to their membership. Thus, this selection of texts comprises materials that many of the mothers in this study have actually read and, in fact, have passed on to me.

Much of these data are in the form of pamphlets about various services provided by a number of different public, private, medical, psychological, and educational agencies. These texts include assessment tools, informational materials, brief articles and information about Ritalin. Some come from centres such as the Calgary Learning Centre and Renfrew Educational Services in Calgary that offer family counselling, tutoring, remedial mathematics, and reading workshops to children and their families. As well, I examined texts that come from private educational institutes that offer full-time education for learning-disabled[2] and difficult-to-educate children in both Calgary and the United Kingdom. Still other materials are of a psychoeducational nature: provided by parent support groups and agencies, they include descriptions of AD(H)D, of the diagnostic process, about typical treatments for AD(H)D, and about the risks of non-treatment.

The therapeutic and intervention-related texts I have collected also include materials from Mannatech, a U.S. producer and distributor of phytochemicals; Efamol, a British manufacturer and researcher of essential fatty acid supplements;[3] and Enrich, a U.S. organization that manufactures and distributes nutritional products. These are included as exemplars of alternative health responses to AD(H)D: their legitimacy rests on the claim that AD(H)D is the result of dietary deficiencies.

Also included are texts from a number of counselling and psychotherapeutic service providers offering family counselling; support services such as respite care; several self-esteem and life-skills-building camps; and out-of-school social skills programs for children. In addition, materials come from Myosymmetries International, a private biofeedback-training provider, and Calgary Academy, a private school that provides neurofeedback training to its students and to out-of-

---

2 There is considerable overlap between ADD and learning disabilities, both in professional literature and research and in lay understandings and responses to each syndrome. Thus, for example, the Association for Learning Disabilities in Calgary offers summer and weekend camps for children with ADD, while the Calgary Learning Centre, whose primary goal is 'improving services for people with learning difficulties' (CLC, 1997b), also offers workshops on parenting children and adolescents with ADD and on handling an ADD spouse (CLC, 1997a).

3 The British firm, Efamol, is a highly successful marketer of essential fatty acids in Canada. If the claims about the underrecognition of ADHD in Great Britain are legitimate, the notion of a British firm exporting ADD expertise to Canada is quite ironic.

school applicants in conjunction with a research program being conducted by academic staff at the University of Calgary.

The second group of texts collected for analysis comes from the meso-level discourse between professionals and between professional regulatory bodies about the proper handling of AD(H)D in both countries. These include a number of reports generated by professional bodies, as well as articles written by professionals that relate to issues of the 'proper' handling of children who are different and to the 'proper' kinds of professionals who should be involved in that handling. These articles were selected not only from professional or academic journals, but also from newspaper articles, magazine articles, and interviews in the popular press that were either written by or that extensively quote professionals who manage the handling of 'different' children. In addition, I have drawn some materials from an on-line discussion and information forum for special educational needs coordinators (SENCO's) in the U.K.,[4] and a North American on-line discussion group for parents, teachers, and resource specialists relating to inclusion issues for children with special needs.[5]

Finally, the third group of texts collected and analysed in this study came from macro-level discourse taken from television, magazines, and newspapers and from policy-level documents relating to education, medicine, psychiatry, and funding. In most cases, these texts are also directed specifically towards parents, but in some instances their intersection with parents is less direct. These texts include policies relating to special needs coding, to special needs funding, and to special needs accommodation at the school level. Thus, although mothers might not necessarily read them (although in many cases they had read some, if not all, of these materials), the practices these policies

4 In England, special education needs coordinators are specially trained educators who are attached to a school (sometimes on a part-time basis, or shared between more than one school). Their role is to offer guidance to classroom teachers and to coordinate assessment and service delivery for children in British schools who are identified as having special educational needs.
5 In Canada, resource specialists are also specially trained educators who are attached to a school, or shared between small schools. Their role is to work directly with children who are 'pulled-out' of their regular class for these services. They provide less coordinating services, although they may refer a child to board of education services such as a school psychologist, or they may suggest parents seek outside services such as speech or occupational therapy.

direct intersect intimately with the daily lives of mothers and their 'different' children.

An author-date list of the discursive materials analysed in this study is provided in Appendix 5. By collecting these materials through a wide range of avenues, and at a number of different levels, I hope to have achieved a sample of textual materials related to AD(H)D that is as representative of the intersections of public discourse and private experience as possible. Also, by collecting as many of these materials as possible through mothers themselves, I aimed to obtain materials that not only theoretically intersect with women's lived experiences, but that actually have been read by these mothers as they negotiate the terrain of AD(H)D.

Audiencing

My efforts to obtain and analyse textual materials that, in fact, have intersected with at least some of the lives of the women in this study reflects an attempt to illuminate the relationship between discursive practice and human subjectivity and subjection. My concern was to avoid an analysis that presumes that discourse (like ideology) necessarily produces subjugated readers. Rather, I wanted to explore the Foucauldian notion that discourse not only produces subjective identities, but that subjects are able to take up discourse in ways that are productive, resistive, and counterdiscursive.

This examination of the intersection between discourse and subjectivity was done through an attenuated version of what John Fiske (1998) has termed 'audiencing.' Fiske used observation of and discussion with people watching television shows to examine the ways that discourses interact with human perception and subjectivity. Fiske reads both the television program and his audience as texts, and he finds ways to connect the audience's responses to institutional practices, global consumerism, and gendered and sexual normativity (1998). In the same ways as Fiske, my use of audiencing reflects my understanding of participants as aware and instrumental human actors. Rather than presume that mothers dealing with children who are 'different' simply receive textual material as 'given,' I hoped to explore at least in a small way, the reactions of mothers to texts that are directed towards them and that speak indirectly about them. Most mothers who are going through the process of AD(H)D evaluation and treatment receive a number of professional texts that are either of a general nature related to ADD or that are specific to their own child. Thus, when setting up interviews with mothers, I asked them to bring along any textual materials they might have relating to AD(H)D. These materials included the kinds of materials listed above (information pamphlets, articles from magazines, etc.) and also included their children's assessment records, report cards, and medical and psychological reports. During the interviews, I asked mothers to discuss the various textual materials in their possession, in hopes of getting at the ways that women themselves perceive and respond to discursive practice. I asked them to speak not only to actual texts that they might possess, but also to tell me of the things they had read, or heard, or seen, and of the ways that they had come to know about AD(H)D, its assessment, and its treatment. I believe that this approach gave me some insight not only into the ways that women 'read' these texts, but also into the ways that they respond to them with their own complicit or resistant narratives.

In this way, I used a broadened application of Fiske's audiencing to obtain empirical data from which to counter the feminist critique that poststructural analyses fail to take into account an active human subjectivity. I hope by doing so to provide empirical insight into the ways that women subjects not only receive texts, but also how they interpret, refuse, resist, and comply with textual materials (Lather, 1991; Mills, 1997; Weedon, 1987, 1999).

An additional problem that I wished to address through my inclusion of women who can speak for themselves relates to the goal of critical social research as a vehicle for creating emancipatory knowledge. In modernist critical and feminist methodologies, the exposure of structural and fixed inequalities as a way to create a new, emancipatory way of understanding the social is a necessary research goal. In Marxist, class-based analyses, the financially exploited and culturally oppressed are the focus: knowledge is sought that will expose the conditions of oppression and that will raise human understanding to such extent that social change will be inevitable. Likewise, feminist, gender-based analyses have a goal of exposing systematic inequalities as a way to raise women's consciousness about the operation of power in their own lives as first step towards social change.

Poststructuralism has been criticized for lacking such an emancipatory centre: typically in poststructural research no one identifiable group of individuals has necessarily been the focus of an emancipatory knowledge production. In short, the feminist critique of poststructural (and particularly Foucauldian) approaches is that they run the risk of being relativist at best, and normatively bankrupt at worst. The concern here is that with poststructuralism, because of its focus on a decentred subject who is only constituted through discourse and who can take up power in her or his own right, structural inequities and oppression based on categories such as gender, class, and race become difficult to locate and account for (Benhabib, 1995; Hartsock, 1990). However, not all critical theorists and feminists agree with the notion that a decentred subject necessarily precludes an emancipatory knowledge production. Judith Butler, for example, has argued that a culturally constructed subject can also be a critical subject (1995). Further, Nancy Fraser, a pre-eminent feminist philosopher, has argued that by taking up post-structural notions of a subject constituted through discourse, we are offered new ways of critically understanding oppression, and that politically emancipatory research can indeed be an outcome of such a synthesis (1995).

My inclusion of women as knowledgeable and critical subjects who can and do speak about their experiences with oppression is, as noted, an attempt to accomplish a synthesis between poststructuralism and critical feminism. In undertaking this approach, my concern has been precisely to address the question of who would be best served by, and emancipated through, the knowledge that this study produces. It has been my hope that, by taking the perspectives of women as important and combining their stories with a discourse analysis of knowledge and discipline relating to AD(H)D, I will ultimately produce knowledge that will help mothers to understand power in ways that are indeed emancipatory.

Feminist Discursive Ethnography

In the end, what I have attempted to accomplish is a comparative *feminist discursive ethnography* of two cultures of AD(H)D. Through an examination of the discursive practices of mothers, teachers, special educators (SENCO's, resource specialists, and school psychologists), school administrators, governments, psychologists, psychiatrists, pediatricians, and physicians, as they relate to the identification and treatment of AD(H)D, I have hoped to provide a comprehensive representation of the ways that language and professional discursive practice are used to claim certain truths about children who are different. In so doing, I hope to describe the discursive aspects of a 'culture of special needs' that encompass the experiences of these mothers as they attempt to understand and care for their children

By employing a critical approach, I take up the premise that 'the structure and content of culture make life unnecessarily more nasty, brutish, and short for some people' (Thomas, 1993: 33). In this study, I argue that the discursive culture of AD(H)D makes life difficult in the first instance for mothers who must interface with 'helping' professionals whose practices are not only less than helpful, but are often exclusionary, blaming, and punitive. In the second instance, I believe that the discursive culture of AD(H)D makes life unnecessarily harsh for the children who are under the umbrella of care in a culture of professional fragmentation and uncertainty. There may be (and almost certainly is) a third level of hardship in the discursive culture of AD(H)D that is experienced by professionals themselves as they attempt to 'do the right thing' within constraining circumstances. Nonetheless, my focus in this study is on women and their children, because the potential harms to women and children move beyond the uncertainties in professional status or occupational practice that teachers, doctors, or psy sector workers face. Rather, for the mothers and their children who must navigate the murky waters of the culture of AD(H)D, the risks are huge: they include alienation, guilt, confusion, worry, and stress for the mothers, and stigma, loneliness, lost self-worth, and lost hopes for the children.

In any critical social research project, the notion of an emancipatory goal includes the question of service: the question 'For whom is this research being done?' is crucial. In this critical social research project, my hope and my goal has been that the research and my findings will provide some benefit for mothers and for children who suffer.

Conclusion

In the preceding sections, I have described the methods, as well as the methodological and epistemological considerations of my research approach. Again, my ambition has been not only with taking up Foucauldian theory and methods, but I have also attempted to incorporate feminist methodologies and epistemologies in my approach to the research problem. In reporting the results of this study, I will provide an analysis of the data that will hopefully support my claims to bridging poststructural and feminist approaches. However, before engaging in a discussion of the experiences of mothers as they encounter professional discursive practice relating to AD(H)D, I feel it is important to understand the macro-level contexts in which these interactions occur. Thus, in the following chapter, I will provide some information about knowledge production, discursive practice, and educational, psychiatric, and medical policy relating to AD(H)D in both Canada and the United Kingdom.

3   British and Canadian Con(text)ual Spaces

About a quarter million people in Canada are believed to be taking Ritalin, the majority of them children. Some health professionals believe Ritalin should never be used, calling it a prescription for a disorder that is a myth in itself. Dr Peter Breggin agrees ... he calls it the 'sit down and shut up drug.'

> David Palmer and Agnes Bongers
> 'Ritalin use in Canada up 36% – and climbing'
> *Calgary Herald*, 30 June 1997

Attention deficit hyperactivity disorder is a condition of brain dysfunction that is misunderstood and underrecognised in Britain ... Widespread ignorance exists about attention deficit hyperactivity disorder and the need for drugs as a component of treatment. Trite and simplistic explanations for the symptoms of the disorder are perpetuated which encourage the view that merely naughty children are being diagnosed to absolve parental responsibility.

> Dr Geoffrey D. Kewley
> 'Attention deficit (hyperactivity) disorder
> is underdiagnosed and undertreated in Britain'
> *British Medical Journal*, 23 May 1998

The above quotations exemplify central aspects of the general debate over AD(H)D and Ritalin as legitimate diagnoses and treatments. As well, the quotations reflect the relative positions of the debates within Canadian and British discourse during the time of this research. On the

Canadian side of the Atlantic, parents worry that ADD[1] has become an 'epidemic' and that Ritalin has been used irresponsibly as a way to compensate for educational, environmental, and social problems. In the United Kingdom parents struggle to an extent with these same issues. In addition, however, British mothers struggle to locate professionals who consider ADHD as legitimate, who are willing to provide a diagnosis and a treatment, and who do not assume that the child's problems result solely from family pathology.[2]

My first intimation of the differences in the culture of ADD between Canada and the United Kingdom came, as so often happens, through chance. In 1998 a colleague, knowing I was interviewing Canadian mothers about their ADD children, shared her British cousin Evelyn's annual Christmas letter with me. Evelyn is forty-four years old and has a Master of Laws degree from Cambridge University, although at present she works part-time as a college administrator; her husband is a lawyer, and the family is well-to-do.[3] In her letter, Evelyn described how, while listening to a BBC Radio program about children with ADHD, she felt she had finally understood her son and his difficulties. She went on to say that she had subsequently appeared on a television program for the BBC about children with ADHD, and how happy she had been to be able to do this as a way to 'spread knowledge here about ADHD and its proper treatment' (Evelyn, 1998). As a mother situated within the Canadian context of a very public debate about ADD and overmedication, I found the notion of 'spreading knowledge' not only novel, but perhaps a bit alarming. Nevertheless, as a researcher interested in the ways that professional practice impinges on private experience, the opportunity to compare maternal experiences within two quite different cultures of

---

1 Again, I use the term ADD when speaking of Canada, ADHD when discussing Britain, and AD(H)D when speaking generally. Mothers and professionals in the United Kingdom consistently use the label ADHD, reflecting British acceptance of World Health Organization criteria that limit the diagnosis to hyperactivity. Canadian parents and professionals more commonly use ADD, which includes the broader symptoms and assessment categories set out in the DSM IV, which is typically used in Canada.

2 As will become evident, despite a readiness to medicate, the actions of Canadian professionals also pointed out a presumption of familial problems as at least partially causal to the child's difficulty; thus, Canadian professionals effectively took up both a medical and a psychiatric framework to explain these children's problems.

3 For further biographical details of Evelyn and the other British and Canadian mothers who took part in this study, see Appendix 3, p. 264.

medicalization was not to be missed. Hence, I made contact with Evelyn and began to correspond with a number of professionals, support group leaders, and mothers in Britain as a means of laying the groundwork for research in England.

In early 1999, when I began these communications and joined a number of on-line support groups, there was reportedly very little in the way of public discourse (either positive or negative) relating to ADHD in Britain. By the time I conducted my field research in February and March of the following year, however, a number of television and radio programs and numerous newspaper and magazine articles about ADHD (both supportive and critical) had begun to appear. In the time since my field research, I have maintained contact with the on-line support groups, and it seems that the United Kingdom is now well on its way to a climate of controversy that is similar to the Canadian context. Thus, the picture I paint of the British situation must be taken as something of a historical artefact: for better or worse, the British context of ADHD I describe may indeed no longer exist. Today, there may be greater public consciousness and professional understanding of ADHD as a diagnosis, but this heightened consciousness has been accompanied by an increasingly negative media representation of ADHD.

British Border Crossings

In part, the shift in the British context is an example of the globalization of knowledge and truth claims made possible through the Internet. The British mothers I spoke with had, for the most part, Internet connectivity, and received much of their information through web-based discourse that was international in origin. While situated in the United Kingdom, the British support groups provide members regularly with links, downloads, and digested information from sites across the world, but particularly from the United States. Often, when these notices are posted, it is suggested that members download information to give to teachers, pediatricians, psychologists, and family workers. As will be seen in the later discussion of maternal resistance strategies, it is not certain how effective this type of information dissemination is in changing professional attitudes and practice. Nonetheless, the lack of professional knowledge about ADHD that British mothers have previously encountered has been eroded at least in part in recent years through information that has been imported from the United States directly into the homes of British mothers.

In addition to electronic knowledge dissemination, the importation of knowledge about ADHD has come from foreign professionals themselves. In early 1999, when Evelyn first provided me with a list of 'who's who' in ADHD in the United Kingdom, it contained five names. These included Dr Geoffrey Kewley, an Australian pediatrician working in the United Kingdom for the past ten years, and Fintan O'Regan, the director of the Center Academy, a Florida-based school providing services in London for children with attentional and learning difficulties. When I began to correspond with the Association for Workers with Children with Emotional and Behavioral Difficulties (AWCEBD),[4] a national professional association of teachers, special education needs coordinators (SENCOs), psychologists, psychiatrists, and pediatricians, they provided me with a publication about ADHD that they distribute to their membership (Cooper and Ideus, 1998). It contains eleven articles written by twelve contributors. Of these, six were Americans, including one by Dr Russell Barkley, who sits on the advisory board of Children and Adults with Attention Deficit Disorder (CHADD) in the United States (Murphy, 1995) and Andrew Hicks, the Florida-based CEO of the Center Academy. Other contributors included Robert Detweiler, the former director of the London location of the Center Academy, and Dr Kewley, the Australian pediatrician who now operates a private assessment clinic in Britain.

The book published on ADHD by the AWCEBD includes as an appendix the World Health Organization's International Classification of Diseases, tenth edition (ICD-10) criteria for ADHD, which are limited to hyperactivity and used traditionally in Britain to diagnose ADHD.

---

4 The AWCEBD publishes a peer-reviewed journal, organizes educational and research conferences, and advises the government on policy relating to special needs children. When I first heard the name of this organization and understood its role in promoting understanding about AD(H)D, I was taken aback. In Canada, perhaps because ADD has been a more medicalized diagnosis, it is not typical to speak (at least officially) of attention deficit disorder as a behavioural or emotional problem. Rather, in Canada, ADD is typically understood as a biological disorder or a learning disability. Allan Rimmer, the national administrative officer for AWCEBD, informed me that the name of the organization has been somewhat contested over recent years because some members feel that the title implies a certain 'wilfulness' on the part of those children served by the group, effacing the medical aspects of children's differences.

The book also provides the American Psychological Association's DSM IV criteria for ADD, which are not limited to hyperactivity, but include inattention and impulsivity as legitimate markers for the ADD diagnosis. Thus, British-based researchers and advocates draw on international (and typically American) professional knowledge to develop local knowledge about and acceptance of ADHD.

The third means of professional knowledge importation came through support group activities. CHADD, the U.S.-based support group that was central to the struggle to establish ADD as a legitimate diagnosis in North America (Conrad and Schneider, 1980), does not yet appear to be operating in the United Kingdom. Rather, over eighty local ADHD support groups are more or less affiliated under the loose umbrella of one larger network, ADDNet. ADDNet appears to have close working relationships with a number of prominent players in the ADHD landscape; at a conference they put on in March 2000, Dr Barkley, Dr Kewley, and Fintan O'Regan (present director of the London Center Academy) were all listed as presenters. Thus, British grass-roots activities, while not directly affiliated with U.S. advocacy and support groups like CHADD, do draw on American information and models to further the local cause.

A final blurring of national boundaries related to knowledge and discursive practice about ADHD in the United Kingdom came through less formal means. Four of the British mothers related that their first insight about a psychiatric label for 'symptoms' that the mothers had previously identified as simply difficult behaviour or lack of focus came from overseas relatives and friends. Moira, one of these mothers, had experienced very little success in having her child's difficulties taken seriously by local British educators and helping professionals. She said: 'It was over a few months in late 1995, a lot of things came together. There were some features on the radio about ADHD, uhm, also we have some friends in the United States of America to whom I'd written over a number of years about Teddy. And just as a kind of "throw-away" remark they said in one of their letters that they had some friends who *also* have a child with ADHD – I mean – they'd diagnosed it, just from the letters that we'd sent!' With this bit of knowledge in hand, Moira began a hunt for local information about ADHD. She did manage to obtain a book on ADHD, ordered specially from her local library, written by Dr Christopher Green, another American. From reading it, she became convinced that the label of ADHD was appropriate for her son. As she says, 'I read it in one go. And I remember lying in bed that evening, reading, and I kept saying, "Listen to this, Roger [her husband]. Who does this sound like?" It was Teddy. I mean, they had him absolutely pegged!'

Even though she was convinced that ADHD was a relevant label, Moira's approach to obtaining a diagnosis was carefully constructed. First, she went on-line to locate information about ADHD services in Britain, and found a website that provided information about a fairly local consulting psychiatrist who specialized in ADHD. Her next step was to find a local physician who would make the referral for her to this specialist. She explained:

> So the way I went about it was, I went to one of the other GPs – because we have a group of four, and you can go to whichever one you want, and the one I chose to go to was one who is really user-friendly, I think. Also, I was pretty sure he would take my word for it, if I would show him the book and could tell him that I'd read it cover to cover, and that I was convinced that he had it.

In addition to bringing along the book, Moira had prior experiences that led her to believe she would be taken seriously: some years earlier she had successfully suggested to this same physician that her own health problems stemmed from endometriosis. This earlier self-diagnosis had indeed been confirmed through medical testing. Thus, the notion of self-diagnosing, and her credibility as a patient with this particular doctor gave Moira the confidence to seek his help in obtaining the ADHD referral. As well, Moira brings considerable cultural capital to her dealings with professionals: she holds two master's degrees, is married to an academic, leads a local Scout troop, is a stay-at home mother, and is a prominent member of her church. Thus, although Moira relied on imported personal and professional knowledge about ADHD, her ability to obtain the desired referral for assessment rested in great part on her personal qualities and her history with the local general practitioner.

The acceptance of imported theories and treatment strategies relating to ADHD is not necessarily easily taken up, either by British professionals or British mothers. Penelope is another of the British mothers in my study. She is a homemaker, and her husband is an officer in the merchant marine; they have two children. Her son Morris is a member of Moira's Scout troop. In one of many conversations about Morris's challenges in school and the community, Moira suggested that Penelope might consider ADHD. Penelope says that, in fact, she had heard of ADHD before and was aware that there was a different classification for hyperactivity in America but that 'because it was being portrayed as something new from America, I'm afraid I probably fobbed it off.' Penelope's comments are important from two perspectives. First, although she herself had heard of ADHD, she only became willing to take the label seriously when it was supported by the testimony of a woman she knew and respected. Second, as she went on to say, her scepticism over the diagnosis reflects the attitude of many physicians and teachers in the United Kingdom who, as Penelope says, consider that ADHD is little more than 'an American fad that's coming over here.' Indeed, this notion of 'an American fad' receives significant support in public discourse relating to ADHD. Almost inevitably, negative British coverage relating to ADHD includes some reference to the United States. In these accounts, the United States is portrayed as a 'pill-popping' culture with skyrocketing AD(H)D rates and a willingness to medicate babies 'as young as one year old' (Anonymous, 1998a; 1999a; 1999b; 2000; Atkins, 2000; Browne, 2000a; 2000b).

Canadian Border Permeability

In many ways, the borders between Canadian and American ways of thinking and dealing with ADD are non-existent. The diagnostic criteria most often used to diagnose ADD in Canada come from the American Psychiatric Association's DSM IV, most of the parenting magazines available on Canadian newsstands are American, many booksellers in Canada are part of U.S.-based chains, and Canadian bookstores sell parenting and family books published predominantly by U.S. publishing houses, American television programming dominates Canadian airwaves, and CHADD, with over 600 U.S. chapters, has over forty chapters in Canada. Thus, Canada is certainly influenced by American popular discourse and professional approaches to ADD.

The border slippage occurs in local ways as well. For example, CHADD Canada (Calgary) holds an annual ADD Fair in the city of Calgary. The CHADD fairs are three-day events that couple a number of workshop and speaker presentations with an exhibition. The exhibition hall is filled with the booths of over eighty local, national, and international service providers and product distributors that are often American in origin. Speakers at workshops are typically local service providers, but the keynote speakers are inevitably big-name Americans brought in to increase audience appeal. Thus, although the fair is local, the interests represented and the content of the event blur local and national boundaries.

During the course of this research, a series of national newspaper articles nicely framed the Canadian controversy over ADD, and indirectly pointed to U.S. influences in the Canadian debate. This series, taken from the *Calgary Herald*, was written by Vancouver journalists for the Southam chain of newspapers – English-language newspapers distributed daily in most major Canadian cities. The majority of the articles sounded an alarmist note, referring to a sharp rise in the rates of ADD diagnoses, the increasing number of Ritalin prescriptions being written, and speculations that the diagnosis and treatment are often inappropriate and driven by adults (parents and teachers particularly) who cannot cope with normal childhood behaviour (Rees, 1998a; 1998b; 1998c; Rees and Dawson, 1998). These articles are typical of the antipsychiatry discourse that prevails in Canadian popular media, and they all draw heavily on the work of U.S. antipsychiatry activist Peter Breggin to shore up their claims. Breggin, the author of the popular books *Toxic Psychiatry* (1991) and *Talking Back to Ritalin* (1998), has made a career of criticizing ADD as a diagnosis and Ritalin as a medication. A popular and polemical speaker, he conducted speaking tours of Canada and Britain during the time of this research, enjoying broad press coverage, particularly in Canada.

In brief, then, U.S. organizations and individuals, both supportive and critical of ADD, have tremendous influence on Canadian discourse and practice. On the other hand, the Canadian context remains unique. For example, CHADD is not the only support group available to mothers in the Calgary region; there are several local and provincial groups that offer support, education, and advocacy to parents and their children. In particular, a number of these organizations are offered as formal, government-funded supports, provided through schools, hospitals, and child welfare auspices, reflecting the socialized nature of Canadian health and welfare services.

This symbiosis between official organizations and support services perhaps reflects Canada's unique position in relation to the United States and the United Kingdom. While Canada and Britain share similar publicly funded health care systems, the British medical profession's antipathy to the ADHD diagnosis precludes the likelihood of hospitals and schools offering ancillary support services for parents of diagnosed children. Conversely, while Canada and the United States share similar levels of diagnosis and medication, the privately funded U.S. medical system precludes offering cost-free support group services through medical institutions. Thus, CHADD, funded in part by Ciba-Geigy, the U.S. manufacturer of Ritalin (Merrow, 1995) is a powerful lobby, advocacy, information, and support network in the United States, while in Calgary CHADD operates as only one of many organizations that provide information and services in a support group environment. Conversely, while British support and advocacy organizations are grass-roots and lack the support of traditional medical and psychiatric insti-tutions, many support services available to Calgary mothers are either formally or informally connected with institutions that administer the assessment, inscription, and treatment of ADD. As will become evident in later chapters, the symbiotic aspect of the Canadian landscape is not necessarily ideal: support and advocacy groups that are tied to institu-tions do not leave much room for dissent or for information that might undermine institutional orders.

In the preceding pages, I have outlined some of the ways that the Canadian and British cultural contexts of AD(H)D are neither perfectly distinct from one another nor distinct from more global contexts. In the following sections, I explore the ways that a number of organizations and professions that relate to AD(H)D play out in the construction of AD(H)D diagnosis and treatment in both the Canadian and the British contexts.

Education and Normalization

Peter Conrad notes that medicalization, a process whereby 'nonmedical problems become defined and treated as medical problems,' need not occur directly under the auspices of medical practitioners or medical regulators (Conrad, 1992: 209–11). Instead, he argues that medical defini-tions and typologies can operate in ways that permit non-medical personnel to accomplish the routine, everyday work of applying the medical label and treatment. In Canada and the United Kingdom, pediatric and psychiatric medicine acts as the gatekeeper to the treatment of ADD, because only physicians or psychiatrists can prescribe Ritalin. However, in both sites, to varying degrees, non-medical professionals play a pivotal role in the process of what some poststructuralists have termed *normalization*.

Rose (1990) explains normalization as the ways that the concept of the 'normal' child has been constructed over the past two centuries through an increasingly detailed and expanding definition of what is abnormal. Rose notes that the advent of child welfare and child psychology arose not from a desire to protect children, but from a perceived need to discipline, manage, and observe them. He traces the ways that intelligence quotient (IQ) tests and similar psychological and educational assessment tools were able to expand the categorization of children as 'abnormal' beyond those whose differences could be read only on the body, to include those whose differences, like AD(H)D, were 'located in the soul' (Rose, 1990: 137). David Armstrong (1983) argues that schools have played a central role in children's normalization, effected through collaboration between educators and medical and psychiatric professionals. He notes that 'at the same time as the body of every child was subjected to educational surveillance through the introduction of compulsory education, the child entered medical discourse as a discreet object with attendant pathologies' (1983: 13). Thus, the daily scrutiny of children through compulsory schooling, the development of an increasing arsenal of assessment tools, and the interprofessional collaborations of education, medicine, and psychiatry all converge in the construction of an increasingly broad range of 'abnormal' behaviours and attributes that require professional intervention and management. Conversely, normalization serves to construct an increasingly narrow range of children who might be considered 'normal' and for whom intervention of some kind would be unnecessary.

In the stories of children in both sites who came to be identified as having AD(H)D, teachers and educational professionals played a central role in identifying and suggesting assistance for children who fell outside the range of what psychology and medicine have framed as normal developmental and behavioural childhood expectations. In the following sections, I attempt to outline some of the educational aspects of the normalization and medicalization of AD(H)D children.

The Canadian Educational Landscape

In Canada, teachers were the primary source of a tentative ADD label. Of seventeen Canadian children in the study, only two children had already been identified and at least tentatively diagnosed prior to attending primary school. Mothers of the remaining fifteen reported that, although their child had always been in many ways 'different' during infancy and early childhood, it was really only once the child went to school that these differences came to be so problematic as to require formal intervention. As will be seen later, even though teachers identified children as strugglers, troublemakers, or poor learners, they were not necessarily able to offer fruitful labels or treatment solutions. Still, teachers almost inevitably got the intervention started, if only by telling mothers that they should consider ADD as a diagnosis and Ritalin as a treatment.

In Calgary, there are two public school systems, the Calgary Board of Education (CBE), with over 95,000 children, and the Calgary Catholic School District (CCSD), with over 43,000 children. Both these school systems fall under the umbrella of Alberta Learning, the provincial department of education. I think it important to note that only two mothers out of the seventeen Canadian participants had a child that had attended a CCSD school, even though I did advertise for participants in two local Catholic schools and through a wide range of generic locations. Perhaps the CCSD has found ways to provide relatively satisfactory services to its children (although the two mothers of CCSD children described experiences similar to CBE mothers' experiences). Indeed, two of the mothers with children in CBE schools were informally advised by CBE staff that 'if your child can get into the Catholic system, you should go there,' indicating that even some CBE staff believe that the Catholic system has more resources for special needs children. For whatever reasons, my sample is limited primarily to mothers whose children at least passed through the Calgary Board of Education system, and so my discussion of policies and procedures will be focused primarily on the CBE.

CBE policy is derived entirely from policy generated by the provincial department of education, Alberta Learning. ADD is not explicitly included as a mild-to-moderate disability in the Alberta Learning guidelines. However, its inclusion as a mild to moderate disability is implied under the rubric of learning disabilities, which includes many of the hallmarks of ADD such as 'difficulties in ... attention, memory, reasoning, coordination ... and social competence' (Alberta Learning, 1997: 24). Thus, at least by symptoms if not directly by name, ADD is recognized in Alberta governmental policy as a special need.

According to CBE policy, the school principal or designate must ensure that all students with special needs 'are identified, assessed and placed within the school system' (CBE, 1999a). Although Canadian teachers frequently speculated that their students should be assessed for ADD, and hence in a sense did identify these children as having special needs, in this study the children were not typically provided an assessment by their schools. In fact, of the fifteen children identified by their teachers, only four (one CCSD child and three CBE children) actually received psychological assessments through their schools. Typically, parents were told that their children were behaving inappropriately, or not learning to their potential, and that something must be done. In most situations, mothers were encouraged by the teacher, school administrator, or special needs educator to see their family physician and to obtain a referral to a pediatrician. Other mothers were informally told of the Alberta Children's Hospital, where a multidisciplinary pediatric group specializing in ADD and learning disabilities (LD) provides publicly funded services to parents. Still others were sent to the publicly funded behavioural clinic at another local hospital. Some were told of the Learning Centre, a private clinic specializing in ADD and LD assessment and remedial programs, and finally some found their way to private psychologists who offer services relating to ADD/LD.

In short, the assessment and even the referral services offered to children in the Calgary region bore little resemblance to the promise inherent in CBE policy. Rather, mothers were sent in a seemingly haphazard way to a variety of agencies and services, offered through publicly funded government programs, or through private, fee-for-service means.[5] Often, parents who could afford private counselling, assessment, and treatment did so, as waiting lists for funded psychological services could easily be as long as eighteen months. Medical services were much quicker, and many mothers described giving up on waiting for a psychological assessment because they experienced continuing pressure from teachers and school administrators to obtain a diagnosis and begin medical treatment. Often, these pressures were expressed quite directly. Amanda is one of the Canadian mothers in my study. She is twenty-seven years old, divorced, the mother of five children, and living on social assistance. Amanda described the situation this way: 'The school suggested that I put Michael on medication. They kept

---

5 In actuality, there is no prescribed route that CBE educators might suggest to parents in obtaining an assessment. The service provider teachers would instead depend on the knowledge of the individual teacher, the resources of the parents, and the severity of the child's problems. A child with severe difficulties might receive a high priority in accessing CBE resources, while other children would be referred to a family doctor, pediatrician, or outside service provider (S. Peters, CBE psychologist, personal communication, 2001).

asking. Whenever we'd have a meeting – because I went in to the school quite often. When I would suggest some strategy to them, they always asked me if I'd thought about putting Mike on medication.' In addition to these direct demands, Amanda came to see medication as her sole recourse because of indirect pressures.

Amanda's son Michael had been identified as troubled by his kindergarten teacher. His physician, however, did not feel that medication was necessarily the proper route because of Michael's youth and because the physician saw his problems as borderline. By Grade 2, however, it had reached the point that Michael's teacher would simply call Amanda and say, 'Come and get him. We can't get him to settle down. He's crawling under desks. He's doing this. He's doing that.' As time wore on, Amanda worried that her son was missing a lot of school because of these incidents. She also noted that:

> He ended up getting very diffident – so he stopped playing with kids, he stopped – he would choose not to go out for recess – in Grade 2! And I had a couple of times when I would go to school to pick him up, and he would be across the classroom and she – she wouldn't see me, but I'd be standing outside the door ... and she would yell at him across the room – real sharp. And because he's very distractible, he won't hear you ... So she walked over there and she took him by the arm, and dragged him across the room.

Ultimately, Michael began to 'play sick' and would often leave for school only to return home mid-morning, saying, 'I don't wanna go to school.' Worried about the impact of missed school time on Michael's learning, the impact on his social development from being ostracized, and the impact on his self-esteem from being yelled at and humiliated by his teacher, Amanda went back to her family physician, saying 'Okay, let's talk about the medication. Because I don't see any other way that I'm going to be able to deal with this without having the school on my case all the time.'

Several of the Canadian mothers described similar situations, and even if evidence of classroom abuse was not present, the constant pressure of phone calls, meetings, and questions about medication left mothers feeling they should at least give medication a trial. Thus, Canadian teachers, although not able to perform a diagnosis or prescribe treatment directly, are able to exercise considerable influence in having mothers push physicians for a label and comply with medicalization.

It is important to note the ambiguity created when a Canadian child who is diagnosed with ADD has not been assessed by a psychologist, either through the school or privately. When this happens, it is easy for schools and sometimes parents to conceptualize the child's problems as medical problems rather than educational challenges. In the CBE, children become *coded* when a child is deemed to be 'in need of a special education program because of their behavioural, communicational, intellectual, learning or physical characteristics' (CBE, 1999a). A medical workup and diagnosis of ADD will not result in documentation that would support coding, because the medical view of ADD restricts the disorder to signs and symptoms that can be medically managed, while a psychological workup would be more likely to include the child's learning style, capabilities, and challenges. Thus, in Calgary, where most children have little choice but to receive their diagnoses through medical channels, educators and administrators are able to categorize the child's problems as medical, and to avoid coding the child as having special needs. Of the seventeen Canadian children in the study, although all were diagnosed as having ADD, only eight CBE children and the one CCSD child had been officially coded as having special needs.

Further, even when a child was coded, the mothers were often not aware of the implications of that coding. There are two levels of severity for coding in the CBE; *mild-to-moderate disability* and *severe disability*. However, only two mothers in the Canadian sample were aware of the level of their children's coding, and neither had any firm idea what services and benefits ought to accrue with the designation. Other mothers knew even less about their child's assessment status; they might know that their child had been tested, but not whether she or he had been coded, or they might think their child had been coded, but not know the level of the coding. Not surprisingly, these women also knew practically nothing about their child's entitlement to services. In most cases, while mothers of children who did get coded knew that their children were being tested, they only really became informed that something administrative or programmatic was attached to the testing when their children were provided with an individual program plan (IPP).

The IPP is a 'concise plan of action designed to address the student's Special Needs, based on diagnostic information which provides the basis for intervention strategies' (CBE, 1999a). The CBE policy states that, once a child has been coded as having special needs:

The Individualized Program Plan of a student with Special Needs must be developed, in consultation with the parent, and must include:

1 Special education and related services to be provided
2 Long-term goals and short-term objectives
3 Assessment procedures and diagnostic information on which the plan is based
4 Review dates, results and recommendations ... (CBE, 1999a)

In fact, IPPs were rarely constructed with the participation of parents, and even more rarely were parents made part of the evaluation process or invited to determine what their children's goals, objectives, and program reviews would look like.[6] More typically, mothers were presented with the IPP as a fait accompli and told to sign and return the form without an invitation to provide input, and without a clear explanation of the resources and meanings that might be attached to coding a child. As will become apparent in later chapters, the IPP, regardless of its content or construction, rarely delivered on its promises, and often ended up being written in such a way that the goals, objectives, and services that were written into them were so ambiguous as to be virtually useless. The IPP is an excellent example of the disjunctures between professionally generated text and maternal experience, between the written record and what mothers themselves believed to be true. Unfortunately, such disjunctures are a leitmotif in the mothers' accounts, both in Canada and in the United Kingdom, and regardless of the affiliation of the professional involved.

As noted earlier, a number of mothers in the Canadian group had withdrawn their children from public schools and placed them in private, specialized schools. For some mothers this withdrawal came as a direct result of the gap between CBE policy and practice relating to assessment and IPPs. Clarissa is another of the Canadian mothers in this study. She is married to a successful businessman, has two children, and immigrated to Canada from Argentina when Julio was three years old. He was identified and assessed through a pediatrician rather than a CBE psychologist, and as Clarissa explained:

The last year the principal gave us the keys to leave. Because ... she never acknowledged that Julio had any problems. So he never got that extra help for ADD and never once was tested in the way that is appropriate for ADD students. So he never got any ... explanation of the meaning of the ques-

6 Some mothers did participate in the construction of their child's IPP. However, this only happened after considerable struggle on the part of mothers who, through independent investigation, became aware of their right to contribute. No parent was included in the IPP process from the outset.

tions or anything. I know that is more work. But it is supposed to be that the child who has ADD has some papers filled out and then sent to the board, and the school gets some extra money. But they did not do that. So that told me we needed to leave.

In Clarissa's case, the knowledge that her child deserved to be coded came not from the school, but because she signed Julio up for a local summer camp specifically designed for kids having trouble in school. When she answered the intake worker's questionnaire, she heard about coding for the first time. Even when asked directly, however, the school declined to provide Julio with an assessment or an IPP.

Thus, the picture that emerges in the Canadian educational context is one in which teachers are the driving force behind identifying children for assessment and pushing for diagnosis and medication of the child. Conversely, although teachers might initiate the child's identification and need for evaluation, they provide little assistance in obtaining assessments or services, either within the school system or outside of the schools. Finally, although there is considerable awareness by teachers about ADD, there is less than universal recognition that ADD constitutes an educational special need, with its attendant obligation of assessment, services, and classroom accommodation. Instead, teachers and school administrators evidence through their practice that ADD is often seen as something that is a medical problem, to be 'cured' through appropriate medication rather than through educational intervention.

The British Educational Landscape

The British mothers provided a slightly different picture of the ways that teachers and administrators responded to ADHD. The U.K. data reflect many different educational jurisdictions, ranging from small private schools in rural settings to large public schools in numerous London boroughs. Each of these schools is situated under the immediate jurisdiction of local education authorities (LEAs) that, as the CBE does for the provincial Alberta Learning, administer policies and procedures that are set by the state Department for Education and Employment (DFEE). Thus, rather than discuss special education policies from each individual school represented in the British sample, I limit my analysis to policy and procedures outlined by the DFEE. In particular, I focus on the DFEE's *Code of Practice on the Identification and Assessment of Special Educational Needs*, which operates more or less as the 'bible' of policy and process relating to special needs, regardless of the individual school. Most of the mothers I spoke with owned their own copy of the Code of Practice, and relied on its 134 pages of text to assist them in understanding the educational system and in demanding their rights from teachers and administrators.

The DFEE Code of Practice policies and procedures are related to identifying, assessing, and providing services to children who have special educational needs. The code also clearly outlines the wide array of difficulties and disabilities that will be considered as reasonably indicating the need for a statutory assessment or, in the vernacular, a 'statement.' The statement operates as a permanent record that the child has special needs and moves the assessment of and service provision for these children out of the hands of the individual school and into the hands of the LEA (DFEE, 1994a: 52). In effect, the statement is equivalent to an official application of a *label*: a permanent mark of difference that identifies the child as abnormal wherever the child and the file go.

From the British mothers' narratives, there appears to be a strong antipathy, particularly on the part of British professionals, towards labelling children with psychiatric diagnoses, such as dyslexia, dyspraxia, or ADHD. British professionals specializing in ADHD have noted this as well (Cosgrove, 1997; Kewley, 1998; Taylor, 1997). Again and again mothers told me how they worked through one avenue of treatment after another, never having a name for what their children were struggling with, because the name itself was problematic to educators and helping professionals. Mothers were told things like, 'Oh, you don't want that [the diagnosis] to go on his record,' or 'If we label him, it will follow him wherever he goes,' or quite simply 'ADHD is just a label to excuse bad behaviour.' Inherent in these comments are several themes.

First, these comments reflect an understanding of labels that is in keeping with the anti-labelling/antipsychiatry movement that developed in the 1960s, 1970s, and 1980s. In this movement, psychiatric labelling was seen at its worst to be inherently harmful (Szasz, 1974a, 1974b) and at its best, to be a process fraught with opportunities for errors and abuse (Pfohl, 1978). One of the common charges in anti-labelling theory is that the label is itself stigmatizing, permitting educators, insurers, and future employers to prejudge individuals, to limit their options, and to exclude them from a full human experience (Leifer, 1990). Thus, one might readily speculate that educators (who in British schools are charged with directing the labelling process) in practice resist labelling these children with a psychiatric diagnosis on the basis of humanistic concerns. On the other hand, it may not be compassion, but time, effort, and money that guide British educators to eschew the labelling process.

Becky is one of the British mothers in this study. She is Latin American, has a master's degree, and works as a freelance editor. She is separated from Anton's father. As Becky, whose son was refused a statement at the third stage of the process rather bluntly put it: 'Education don't want to label children, so they say! They say – follow the social model of disability. The social model's trying to say we shouldn't be using medical labels, and that the problem with disabilities are mainly due to people's attitudes ... I have no doubt Nottinghamshire education are simply using this as an excuse to save money.' Becky may have a point. The process of obtaining a label under the Code of Practice is extremely onerous, and as we will see, the pay-off to schools for initiating and pursuing the statementing process may make labelling seem counterproductive.

The Code of Practice outlines five stages of assessment that a child must go through in order to be 'statemented.' These are:

1 Class or subject teachers identify or register a child's special education needs [SEN] and, consulting the schools SEN Coordinator, take initial action.

2 The school's SEN Coordinator takes lead responsibility for gathering information and for coordinating the child's special educational provision, working with the child's teacher [Author's Note: At Stage 2 and sometimes at Stage 3 an individual education plan (IEP), similar to the Canadian IPP, is produced].

3 Teachers and the SEN Coordinator are supported by specialists from outside the school [in fine-tuning the evaluation process].

4 The LEA consider the need for a statutory assessment and, if appropriate, make a multidisciplinary assessment.

5 The LEA consider the need for a statement of special education needs and, if appropriate, make a statutory assessment/statement and arrange, monitor, and review provision. (DFEE, 1994a: 3)

Each of these five steps involves complex consultations with parents, school professionals, different levels of administration, or outside consultants. In short, the process of statementing, because it is complex, time consuming, expensive,[7] and involves the synthesis of multiple perspectives, seems to be designed to deter educators from applying a label.

A further irony in the statementing process, and one that may act as an additional deterrent to schools in pushing for a statement is that, when a statement is finally made, the responsibility for the child's Special Education needs will move from the local school to the LEA. In turn, this can mean that schools, after all their efforts, ultimately end up losing the student, and the student's basic allotment and special needs funding. Indeed, of the six children who had actually received a statement, four had been moved to 'maintained special schools,' which are LEA-funded segregated schools that provide services where local and community schools are deemed unable to provide adequate educational delivery to special needs students (DFEE, 1999).

Finally, even if British teachers and administrators at the school and LEA levels are prepared to consider going through all the steps of the statementing process, it is unlikely that the label applied through the statement would be ADHD. In over sixteen pages outlining the various 'criteria for deciding to make a statutory assessment,' which include physical disabilities, specific learning difficulties, emotional and behavioural difficulties, visual and hearing impairments, speech and language difficulties, and medical conditions, there is no mention either specifically of ADHD or more generally of attentional and organizational problems (DFEE, 1994a: 52–69). Thus, although in medical and psychiatric discourse ADHD is often considered a medical problem that falls under the rubric of learning problems or behavioural difficulties, there is little in the language of the code that would offer teachers an incentive to pursue statementing on the basis of ADHD symptoms.

It should come as no surprise then that, in contrast to the Canadian mothers' experiences, not one teacher identified any of the seventeen British children as a child who should be assessed for ADHD. Mothers in the British group invariably obtained information about ADHD outside of the school system and, as we will see in later chapters, often encountered resistance from teachers to the ADHD label or to the information about ADHD that mothers provided.

Not only were British children unlikely to be provided the ADHD label by teachers, but it took longer for them to obtain the diagnosis

7 The average cost for an initial specialist's assessment is estimated at approximately £480 per student (NICE, 2000: 10).

through whatever means mothers were able to locate. While the Canadian children's average age at diagnosis was 7.60 years, the seventeen British children's average age at diagnosis was at 9.06 years. Further, British children start school at four years of age, while in Canada the admission age is five (and in some cases, six, because kindergarten is not mandatory in Canada). Thus, the British children in this study spent a minimum average of 2.5 years (and more probably 3.5 years on average) longer in school prior to being labelled than did their Canadian counterparts.

This is not to say that these children had not encountered school-related difficulties prior to actually receiving a diagnosis. In fact, mothers of children in England described similar confrontations with teachers, continual meetings over classroom and school-yard problems, and the same kinds of adversarial relations that Canadian mothers described.

Many of the British children in the study had made it at least part of the way through the statementing process, although few had managed to make it to stage 5. While children whose special needs are seen to have been satisfied during the first stage of assessment are typically processed no further, after two periods of review, children at stage 1 will then move on to stage 2, and likewise from there on to stage 3. At stage 2 and stage 3, an individual education plan (IEP), similar to the Canadian IPP, will be established for the child. Thus, twelve of the seventeen British children had indeed received IEPs, although only six had actually been fully statemented.

Like the IPP, the IEP is theoretically a plan, to be drawn up in consultation with the parents, subject to periodic review that should outline clearly the services, goals, and strategies that will be provided by the school. As with the Canadian IPPs, the lived practice of the British IEP was quite different from the textual promise. IEPs were not prepared with the full participation of mothers, but were sent home for signatures after the fact. Mothers' suggestions for services and program adjustments of individual IEPs were not acknowledged or included, and the review process tended to be shared with families on a post hoc 'information-only' basis, rather than through collaborative parent–teacher analysis. Thus, in Canadian and British school settings alike, although teachers were readily able to identify children who struggled, the labels and interventions teachers were able to suggest were often less than beneficial, and the rhetorical promise of parent-educator partnership was not delivered in practice.

Unlike Canadian educators, who more or less immediately presumed a medical diagnosis for children's difficulties, British teachers tended to understand these children's problems as behavioural or emotional. As a result, children and their families were typically sent, as a first line of defence, to family therapy. Dolores is one of the British mothers in my study. She is married and has four children. The family is working class; Dolores works nights part-time as a nurse's aide, while her husband works days as a gardener. When Dolores's four-year-old son Adrian experienced tremendous classroom difficulties in kindergarten, his teacher suggested that Dolores take him to a pediatric clinic. When the pediatrician was unable to find anything physically wrong with the boy, the teacher then sent Dolores to the local child guidance centre. Dolores explained why she agreed to go: 'We said "fine." At least, we thought, if we're doing something wrong, at least we'll know about it. If we're doing something wrong for Adrian, and that's what's making him go like that – then, fine, at least we can know and get it sorted out ... and when we finally got down to the unit, all it was talking about me and my husband. Our past. Our families. Our situations.'

Dolores and her husband spent seven years – *seven* years – attending weekly sessions at the centre in hopes of obtaining help for their son. Meanwhile, things at the school and at home continued to deteriorate. The school was aware of her involvement in therapy, and seemed satisfied that the family was making this effort, but therapy was having no effect on Adrian's ability to be part of the classroom, to attend to his work, or to behave in ways that his teachers found appropriate. Despite this lack of effectiveness, Dolores herself was loath to quit the sessions because it was the only help being offered. Finally, one of the counsellors the family had been seeing over the years admitted she 'didn't feel she could offer much help any more,' and she called in a group of clinicians to observe the family's interactions through a one-way mirror. Among these professionals was a psychiatrist who agreed to assess Adrian individually and who ultimately provided the diagnosis. Dolores admitted, too, that the therapy 'almost killed our marriage' and that it was this pressure on their home life that led them to agree to give up the weekly sessions.[8]

Once a child, through whatever means, was given the ADHD label and prescribed medication, British teachers, like their Canadian counterparts, seemed reluctant to understand ADHD as something that they

8 Considerable literature on living with an AD(H)D child argues that living with these children is extremely burdensome and that the child and his or her problems cause marital stress and family breakdown. However, Dolores stated that the interventions related to her son's problems were as much, or more, burdensome than life with her son.

would need to address in their own classroom and educational practice. An additional layer in the British schools, however, occurred in relation to Ritalin as a medication and the unwillingness of school personnel to administer a 'class A' drug. Class A drugs are restricted medications that require a prescription to be filled out in triplicate. The triplicate prescription is used for tracking purposes: one copy stays with the physician who writes the script, one is retained by the pharmacist, and one is provided to the appropriate regulating body for restricted pharmaceuticals. In Canada, the process for prescribing Ritalin is exactly the same. Canadian teachers, however, seemed to have no problem in handling the distribution of the medication in their classrooms as prescribed on a routine basis. This perhaps indicates there are deeper levels of refusal on the part of British teachers – and of acceptance on the part of Canadians – than juridical or practical problems alone would support.

In the United Kingdom, slow-release Ritalin has until very recently been impossible to obtain, so that two or three tablets will be prescribed for children to be taken at various points through the school day, necessitating that some adult assist the child in taking the mid-day dose(s). Several mothers described the difficulties they experienced in trying to have a school staff member administer Ritalin to their children. Dolores said that when Adrian did begin taking Ritalin his teachers were delighted with the change in his behaviour. However, problems with rebound from the Ritalin began to surface when his teachers would not give him his lunch-hour medication.[9] Dolores described what happened with Adrian:

> Well, they didn't have anybody qualified in the school. No nurse or qualified nurse to actually administer the tablet ... So I said, 'Look, I can bring this stuff. I've got a certificate [to administer medications], and if you pay me, I will come in and give him, and the other kids who have this problem, their tablets. And they wouldn't allow it. They wouldn't do it. So we actually got onto the psychiatrist who wrote letters, and got onto the education council and board, and really tried to push it through. The headmaster was all for helping, because he knew that it was a big problem. And none of the staff would take it on ... . So we actually won in the end, and one of the teachers did actually start to administer the tablets.

9 Mothers typically described their children as being irritable and 'unmanageable' (oppositional, hyperactive) during the hour or so after Ritalin wore off.

Dolores's speculation is that, in part, teachers refused to administer the medication because they understand this as a medical rather than a pedagogical responsibility and that the refusal was related to concerns about liability in the schools. However, she also notes that administration felt that teachers should hand out medications where necessary, and indeed, even though no training was provided to teachers, ultimately the headmaster and the psychiatrist prevailed so that teachers did dispense Ritalin during school time. One can also speculate that teacher resistance to providing Ritalin had less to do with liability or training worries, and more to do with their perceptions of professional roles (they simply did not feel this was an appropriate task for them to take on) or suspicions (despite the evident improvement in Adrian's behaviour) about the diagnosis and the medication. In any case, a picture begins to emerge of British teachers who are unfamiliar with the label ADHD and distrustful of the treatment Ritalin.

In the United Kingdom, schools appear reluctant to acknowledge ADHD as a legitimate diagnosis and reluctant to accept the management of medication as part of the school's educational routine. Additionally, it seems that schools and educators conceive of ADHD symptoms as evidence of emotional problems in more overt ways than is the case in Canadian schools – although, as we will see in later chapters, blaming mothers and pathologizing families were common in both sites. Conversely, Calgary educators tended to force the medication issue as a first response and to restrict ADD to a medical rather than educational issue. In both sites, achieving a school-based assessment or set of services for children with problems that might be related to ADD or ADHD was virtually impossible. Additionally, in each site, as we will see below, shifts in educational funding played important roles in the ways AD(H)D was handled.

Informal Exclusion in Canada

Although the Calgary Board of Education is the primary school administrative board in the Canadian data, it operates under the umbrella of the provincial government department, Alberta Learning. Since the election of the fiscally and politically Conservative government of Ralph Klein in the early 1990s, there has been considerable upheaval in and public controversy over the Alberta public education system. Budgets have been cut, massive early retirements have been implemented, and a new emphasis on outcome measures (as evidenced by newspaper and Alberta Education website postings of school average scores on province-wide academic tests) means that decreased institutional support for educators has occurred within a context of increased public scrutiny of educational practice. In Calgary during this period, a number of new private schools have opened in the city. While in 1996–7 there were only three, in 1999–2000 there were eight private schools specifically designed for children with learning disabilities. Indeed, the CBE, the largest school board in Alberta and the third largest in Canada, acknowledges that it has experienced significant student attrition. Although the city's population is growing in leaps and bounds, and individual class sizes may be increasing, student enrolment is not. Rather, private and home schooling is proliferating (CBE, 1999b). Further, this attrition is particularly high in children with special education needs, including children with ADD (Croskery, 2000).

Thus, although the Canadian educational system has a long tradition of publicly funded, comprehensive community schooling, in which admission is non-selective and based on the child's home address more than the child's ability, in Alberta this inclusive model has been eroded by market shifts:

- First, at the board level, policy has shifted over the past decade so that although the local school is still theoretically obliged to take its local students, students can also enroll in schools of choice rather than location. This, coupled with the publication of city and province-wide test results in local newspapers and on the board's website, has created the possibility for parents who seek a 'better' school in terms of academic scores to move their children into different schools.
- At the individual school level, desirable schools are more able, at least informally, to select their students, and to indirectly discourage difficult students from enrolling in their schools. Indeed, several mothers described to me how local comprehensive school officials actively encouraged them to approach schools in alternative locations that might serve their children better, particularly at the junior or senior high school entry levels. In addition, two Canadian mothers described to me how, during the province-wide examinations, their children were asked *not* to write the tests, so that test scores for the school would not be affected. Another three mothers described

how, for the provincial examinations, their children were provided with support that had been suggested in their IPPs (such as a scribe to write down the child's responses), but that had not been provided to these children at *any* other time during their school careers.

- At the parental level, mothers in the study described how the decreased acceptance of children who are different by teachers and administrators, and by children's peers made community schooling less appealing. Conversely, the proliferation of specialized private schools has meant that parents of special needs children are, where possible, 'voting with their feet.'[10]

In Calgary, despite a rhetoric of commitment to the inclusion of children with special needs in community schools (CBE, 1997), a competitive and exclusionary (both formally and informally) educational system has developed, with particular implications for children who are different and/or vulnerable.

Superficially, the use of standardized testing and public competition, whether on individual 'performance' or in terms of academic achievement in the entire student body, operates to prove to a presumably increasingly critical public that educators are accountable, and that schools do what they set out to do – teach children. Although it may be tempting to merely understand the development of formal exclusionary practices in terms of economic pragmatism, these practices of selection and exclusion also illustrate how normalization works in educational practice. In Calgary (and, as we will see, in England as well) these standardized 'outcome measures' also create boundaries inside which 'normal' (read: successful learners) children may stand and outside of which 'not normal' (read: different learners) children must remain. The result? Not only an exodus of 'not normal' children from the public system, but an increasingly narrow range of abilities in the students who remain in the system, meaning the 'average' student comes to represent an increasingly finite set of possibilities.

---

10 Often, popular discourse about public education and private alternatives is phrased in the terms of public education as a system in decline that offers few positive educational experiences to children, while private schooling is framed as inherently superior [Kenway, 1990]. I do not wish to contribute to this binarism: in fact, not all the private school experiences mothers described were positive, even in schools that were specifically organized around children with special needs.

Canadian Funding Arrangements

Within the context of an increasingly competitive public educational market and the burgeoning privatization of special education, Calgary mothers whose children continued to attend public schooling described tremendous difficulties accessing public funding to support their special needs children. As noted earlier, children who are not coded by the board do not receive an IPP or additional funding that might be attached to receiving an assessment and a diagnostic label. Again, not all children who were diagnosed with ADD in this study had actually been coded by the CBE. However, even mothers whose children had been coded were surprisingly unaware of how much money was attached to the code or how those funds should be allocated according to CBE policy. I telephoned the CBE several times attempting to obtain this information, but was never provided with a response by board specialists. The CBE website (http://www.cbe.ab.ca/) does provide information on special needs programs and policies, but the information is difficult to locate within the website, and it does not include information about dollar values or actual service entitlements related to coding. In the end, I obtained information about actual dollar figures attached to special needs designations from the provincial Alberta Learning website. In short, information about the specific benefits of having a special needs label is neither readily nor locally obtainable.

In fact, the amount of money attached to a coded special needs child attending the CBE is quite low. In September 1999 the basic instruction rate per student in grades 1 through 12 in Alberta was $3,976, and the student subsidy for mild and moderate disabilities was $345 per coded child (Alberta Learning, 2000a). Further, special education funding subsidies are not designated for the direct use of the coded student. Rather, these funds are folded into the basic instructional budgets of schools and apportioned according to decisions made by the administration of each school (Alberta Learning, 2000a).

The relatively low amount and the bundled budget arrangements of Alberta's special needs funding might account at least in part for the difficulties mothers experienced in obtaining assessments through the CBE. While only $345 per year per child is attached to special needs coding, the costs of a psychological assessment, even by a CBE employee, will be well over that amount. Further, because these funds enter into program rather than individual student budgets, it will not necessarily follow that children with special needs will be the direct beneficiaries of the extra funds, or that the child's teacher will receive direct assistance in providing an enhanced program for the coded child. At the same time, Alberta Learning policy states that to be coded, a child must be assessed through 'a variety of strategies ... which are multi-dimensional' and which must then be interpreted to 'parents, teachers and others involved with the student's program,' and then in turn be used to 'develop individualized program plans' that will include a wide range of essential information.[11]

A typical IPP is produced by the classroom teacher four times yearly and comprises between fifteen and twenty pages of text. Thus, an official assessment, coding, and program plan represents considerable paperwork, meeting time, discussion, consultation, writing, and labour on the part of educators, and particularly the child's classroom teacher. The return on this labour, $345 in funding that may or may not make its way specifically into the child's classroom, is barely worth the teacher's while. Small wonder, then, that Canadian mothers described difficulties in obtaining coding for their ADD children.

Although children who are coded as mildly or moderately disabled (as would perhaps fit most children with ADD) only receive a small supplement to their basic student funding, children who ultimately are coded as 'severe physical/mental disabled' or 'severe behaviour disabled' bring considerably more money into a school's budget. Respectively, in 1999, these amounts were $11,948 and $9,177 per student. One might think, then, that teachers, specialists, and administrators would be motivated to provide assessments in light of these funds and perhaps to even encourage use of the more severe coding category. However, the process of coding a child with severe special needs is much more onerous and involves not only the school and the local board, but requires the presentation and defence of a child's file for review by the provincial authority (Alberta Learning, 2000b). Hence, the labour

11 The required elements of the IPP include the following: the assessed level of the child's educational performance; strengths and areas of need; long-term goals and short-term objectives; assessment procedures for short-term objectives; special education and related services to be provided; review dates, results, and recommendations; relevant medical information; required classroom accommodations (e.g., changes to instructional strategies, assessment procedures, materials, resources, facilities, or equipment); and transition plans (e.g., return to regular classroom programs or movement into a more severe disability category) (Alberta Learning, 1997).

involved in obtaining the identification is far more complex, time-consuming, and expensive than with mild-to-moderate disabilities and includes the gatekeeping step of convincing the funder that such coding is legitimate.

In addition, schools that assume the costs of an assessment for coding students with severe disabilities are not assured that they will necessarily benefit from any funding attached to the coding. As noted above, in Calgary there has been a shift from a primarily public sector school system to a blend of public schools and private schools, many of which serve children with special needs. One aspect of public school services relating to children with special needs (both mild to moderate and severe) is the use of designated special education private schools (DSEPS) to take up program delivery that the public school cannot provide. Of the eight private schools operating in Calgary that offer services specifically for children with learning disabilities, six are DSEPS (Alberta Learning, 2000c). DSEPS are schools that, if the school board has mutually agreed with parents that the child would be better served at the private school, will receive not only the special needs child but the full funding attached to that child's coding (Alberta Learning, 1997: 7).[12]

Thus, public schools that perform the assessment and obtain the coding, but nonetheless are unable to provide a program that fully satisfies the child's parents because of poor resources or lack of expertise, can find themselves losing the child's severe special needs funding after all. It is not clear to me (despite numerous inquiries to the CBE) how many children with severe special needs coding actually are directed by CBE schools to attend DSEPSs in Calgary. However, a multiagency review of special education in Alberta notes that these funding arrangements have operated as a disincentive for identifying students with special needs and that they may indeed have penalized the publicly funded system (Alberta Learning, 1997: 12, 70).

---

12 The notion that the decision to remove a child to a private school will be necessarily mutually agreed to is problematic. Mothers of children in private schools in Calgary often removed their children without direction from the public school. They told of terrible barriers to obtaining funding, and several had appealed funding decisions at the school board and Alberta Learning to no avail. Only one out of the eight Canadian mothers whose children attended private schools had obtained funding through the Designated Special Education Private Schools policy.

British Funding Arrangements

The British Code of Practice, compared with the information available to Canadian parents, is a marvel of clarity and openness. In over 130 pages, it clearly and in painstaking detail outlines the steps to obtain a statement, the various criteria for determining entitlement to services, and the process of review and appeals. Nonetheless, there is no indication in any of the three primary government-generated documents on special educational needs as to what concrete funds might be attached to obtaining a formal statement for one's child (DFEE, 1994a, 1994b, 1994c). Among the women I spoke with, there was wide variability in funding attached to 'statementing a child,' as evidenced in the following examples:

- Gloria is a working-class mother of three children who is on permanent disability; she voluntarily runs an on-line support group for ADHD parents. Gloria's daughter and son, both diagnosed with dyslexia and ADHD, received over £4,641 per child, per year, based on a rate of £59.50 per unit of special needs 'matrix allotments.' However, when Gloria's husband was transferred, and her children moved into a new LEA, the rate dropped to the new LEA's rate of £49.50, reducing not only her children's total funding, but also their access to services.
- Madeleine is a lone parent living on social assistance and raising four children; she runs a very active social support group on a voluntary basis. Madeleine found out from her local LEA that funding is allocated on the basis of services only, so that the statement would include the number of hours of assistance a child is entitled to, with no indication of what the value might amount to in total.
- Christine is a psychoanalyst and her husband is a professor. The family is blended and consists of a child from the husband's previous marriage and two from this one. Christine, whose eight-year-old son now receives four days of classroom assistance per week, noted, 'Our latest worry is although he has a large statement at present, he may end up "zero" when he moves to secondary education. I'm not sure how they work that out, but we know the next round with the LEA starts in January when we'll hear what school Drew will be going to.'

As these comments indicate, not only is it difficult for mothers to know exactly what entitlements are attached to their child's statement, but these entitlements can shift between LEAs, or from one level of schooling to the next within the same LEA jurisdiction. Nevertheless, on average, the British statementing process, once complete, was able to offer more substantial supports to children than the $345 attached to coding Calgary children. Further, unlike the Canadian situation, where special needs allotments are folded into a school's general budget, in the United Kingdom, the specialist hours and student funding are designed to be specifically for the child and are not to be shared with the entire class or school.

Finally, as noted above, once a child *was* statemented in the United Kingdom, it was quite likely that the child would ultimately receive fully funded special educational instruction through a maintained special school, in a mechanism similar to that outlined in the Alberta arrangements for designated special needs private school funding. Despite the structural similarities between public and private school funding *policies* in Canada and Britain, in *practice* the British situation differed immensely from the Canadian context. In the Canadian group, although eight of seventeen children had opted to attend separate, private schools for children with special educational needs, only one of these had received full tuition reimbursement from the CBE. The remaining seven children were paying their tuition themselves, despite lengthy appeals to the CBE for funding. Conversely, although the British statementing process was difficult to achieve, and although teachers did not readily support ADHD symptoms as 'statement-able,' when British children did finally receive a label (and typically this label fell under the rubric of 'specific learning disabilities'), they enjoyed a relatively high level of support for their special educational needs.

However, when British ADHD children were not able to obtain a statement, they encountered serious difficulties in receiving appropriate educational services. In addition to the issues of teachers perceiving ADHD as a non-legitimate diagnosis and Ritalin as an unacceptable treatment, there were also structural problems in the British educational landscape that made life difficult for ADHD children and their mothers. In particular, these relate to practices of inclusion and exclusion that operated in both formal and informal ways in the British school system.

Like the CBE special needs policy, the Code of Practice outlines a special needs philosophy that positions schools as responsible for meeting the educational needs of all students in a way that is inclusive and responsive. The code states that 'the needs of all pupils who may have special educational needs either throughout, or at any time during, their careers must be addressed' and that special needs children should, 'where appropriate and taking into account the wishes of their parents, be educated alongside their peers in mainstream schools' (DFEE, 1994a). Thus, educational policy calls for mainstreaming of special needs students in their chosen school unless, as in the case of the maintained special school children, the local school is unable to offer an adequate range of services. The structure, however, of the British educational system is quite complex, and this has created a more complicated situation than the code's inclusive educational policy might indicate.

The notion of comprehensive community schooling, in which children are admitted on the basis of home address rather than ability, is a relatively new one in Britain. Prior to educational reforms initiated in the 1960s, British children were assigned at the age of eleven to either a grammar, technical, or trade school, depending on their achievement levels.[13] By the mid-1980s, however, 90 per cent of students attended comprehensive schools, where student admission was based on community affiliation rather than academic selection (Booth et al., 1998). This shift at the secondary level created changes in the elementary schools as well: rather than focus on preparing children for a selective secondary examination system, primary schools became more integrated and inclusive (Booth et al., 1998).

With the election of Margaret Thatcher's Conservative government in 1979, however, a series of educational reforms were introduced and schools came to be run in more competitive ways. Universal national testing at ages seven, eleven, and fourteen was implemented, and 'league tables' that list school results began to be published nationally in the media and through the schools (a model that, as noted above, has been followed to a less formal extent in Alberta). Parents became able to apply to schools outside of their 'catchment' area (i.e., neighbourhood) on the basis of these league tables, and this in turn permitted successful schools to choose students on the basis of their grades and their pre-

13 Of course, there is a long-standing tradition of private schooling in the United Kingdom. However, the percentage of schools that are privately funded is not as high as one might expect. In 1996, approximately 6 per cent of British school-aged children attended private schools (DFEE, 1996).

sentability (Booth et al., 1998).[14] Recently, the erosion of comprehensive schooling access has been furthered, as Tony Blair's New Labour government introduced a five-year program that permits school-specific admission and program standards and the selection of up to 10 per cent of the student body on the basis of achievement. Blair is quoted as saying, 'Our best schools have moved decisively to a post-comprehensive argument. They take inclusion and equality of opportunity for granted but are highly flexible in the ways they meet them.' He goes on to say that the traditionally inclusive comprehensive system 'had too often held back individual students' (Blair, quoted in Woodward, 2001).

In Prime Minister Blair's comment, and in the exclusion policies of British and Canadian schools, we see some of the ironies attached to discourses of risk and danger. Although troubled children are often framed as being 'at risk' for negative outcomes, they are also represented as posing a danger of 'pollution' to other students and an undue drain on resource allocation by educators and policy-makers (Dehli, 1996). Thus, removing such children from the schools is justified in terms of making the schools safer or more conducive to learning for other, less problematic children. The self-fulfilling prophecy of refusing an education to children who struggle, resulting in subsequent decreased life chances is not acknowledged: rather, these children are made culpable for the outcomes of the system's failures to meet their needs.

Theoretically, local British schools are obliged to accept area children, and they are discouraged from selecting students. However, at least four mothers described trying to register their child in a local school and being discouraged from doing so 'because the school wouldn't be able to offer an appropriate program' (Cassandra) or 'because the focus in this school was on high academics and they felt that would be no good for my child' (Diane). These mothers speculated that in reality their children had been unable to obtain a place because their local schools, both of which enjoyed high league table standings, were filled with more desirable students.

The struggle to find an appropriate placement was particularly evi-

---

14 The practice of exclusion is both publicly acknowledged and highly contested in formal, political policy. While the Conservative government during 1980s and early 1990s encouraged student selection on the basis of ability, New Labour has recently reversed this policy, ordering schools to cut the numbers of pupils selected on ability (Anonymous, 1999c). Nevertheless, considerable ambiguity persists in public educational policy (and hence practice) relating to exclusion, student selection, and competitive reporting in school league tables.

dent at the transition between primary and secondary school. For example, Evelyn's nine-year-old son Harry was accepted into no less than three of London's top five league schools on the basis of his academic examinations. However, the admission process for these schools included not only an assessment of his academic record, but involved entrance interviews with Harry and both parents, as well as a set of screening examinations administered by each of the prospective schools. Evelyn is convinced that Harry was refused a place in the first two schools on the strength of his interview, and more importantly, his poor performance on the school's examinations, which were specifically geared to test memory and organizational skills. In her mind, Harry was excluded because of tests that were designed to screen out attributes that make student management difficult – and that are indeed specific to ADHD.

The Role of Exclusion in Britain

As we have seen, in Britain, as in Alberta, exclusion can operate in informal ways. Children are asked not to write examinations, to stay home when inspectors come (as will be seen in later discussion of British funding), to register at non-local schools because programs cannot or will not be made available to them, or they are kept from attending the 'right' school because these schools are able to screen out children who are different. In Britain, however, there are also more formal and regularized avenues for excluding schoolchildren.

According to the BBC News, there were approximately 137,000 temporary exclusions in 1998, with a 450 per cent rise in permanent exclusions or expulsions between 1990 and 1995 (Anonymous, 1998b, 1999c). The temporary exclusions are made on the basis of DFEE regulations, which allow the exclusion of children for up to forty-five days in a school year:

- In response to serious breaches of a school's discipline policy; and
- If allowing the pupil to remain in school would seriously harm the education or welfare of the pupil or others in the school. (DFEE, 1994d)

The implications of these criteria for ADHD children are enormous. Children whose inattention would make educating the child difficult, children whose hyperactivity would disrupt their own and other children's learning, and children whose problems are not seen as medical but as disciplinary problems are particularly vulnerable to exclusion under these regulations. Indeed, the DFEE itself acknowledges that 'the level of exclusions for pupils with a statement of SEN is extremely high; the most recent data show that the permanent exclusion rate for such pupils was seven times higher than for pupils without a Statement' (DFEE, 1994d: 3). Thus, if special needs children who have received a statement are unduly affected by these regulations, we can only suspect that children with ADHD, who typically will not receive the assessment and support of a Statement, but who exhibit problematic behaviours, will be particularly vulnerable to exclusion policies.

Indeed, of the seventeen British children whose mothers I interviewed, fully eleven had been excluded from school for varying lengths of time at one point or another. During the period of the interviews, five of these children were out of school on exclusions ranging from two to six weeks. For example, at the time of my interview with his mother Fran in late February, six-year-old Angus, although not officially excluded, had been out of school since school started in September. The school had decided, on the basis of Angus's transfer records from his previous school, that it could not handle Angus in the classroom. Still, the school acknowledged its obligation to offer some formal schooling to him, so he was provided with a home tutor for core curriculum ten hours a week. Technically, then, Angus was still being provided an education by the local school, but socially and emotionally, he most definitely was not part of the educational world shared by his peers.

As in Alberta, the effect of fiscally conservative educational policy on vulnerable British children can be seen in the problem of 'standards' in educational discourse. Throughout the 1980s and 1990s, under the government of Margaret Thatcher, there was an increasingly public debate about failure in schools and teachers and a concomitant emphasis on creating and imposing educational standards so that British children would be competitive in world labour markets (Booth et al., 1998). Thus, in addition to implementing the earlier-discussed annual school league tables, a four-yearly system of national inspections in state schools by the Office for Standards in Education (Ofsted) was established (Booth et al., 1998). The effects of these inspections for children with special needs were similar to the effect of province-wide examinations for Alberta special needs children: when the Ofsted inspections occurred, several of the mothers in the British group were asked to keep their children home. The implications for this are multiple:

- First, children who were asked to stay home missed school time, to which they were entitled, during the two to three-week–long inspection visits.
- Second, mothers were asked to accommodate school needs through keeping a child at home, which meant that they were charged with child care during school time; no mother was offered compensation for this, nor were they asked whether this request was a burden. Mothers were simply told to keep their kids at home.
- Third, because 'problem' children were literally made invisible through this practice, schools were able to provide inspectors with a picture of classrooms that were well run and competitive with other schools in ways that did not reflect their actual practice.
- Finally, and most importantly, because special needs children (and particularly special needs children who were experiencing difficulties in the classroom) were kept hidden during Ofsted visits, schools were able to show inspectors that they were *not* falling short of the 'fundamental principles' of the DFEE Code of Practice. These principles clearly state that pupils with special needs should be provided the *'greatest possible access* to a broad and balanced education ... *in the mainstream'* (DFEE, 1994a: 2–3, emphasis mine).

The overlap between practices of exclusion, competitive cultures of education as exemplified in the league tables, and children whose school performances may be problematic is highlighted not only in policy discussions, but has been part of a very public debate. In mid-1998, School Standards Minister Stephen Byers argued that 'cosmetic' expulsions were prevalent and that when schools expel students who are difficult to teach, they 'not only damage the future prospects of the individual excluded but also mislead parents and the public about the quality of education being provided at the school in question' (Anonymous, 1998b). As a result of concerns over the skewing of league tables, and the unfair exclusion of differently abled children, rules were implemented by the British government that required schools to continue to count the academic achievements of students excluded, in an attempt to provide a more accurate reflection of the practices of individual schools. This ruling has been strongly contested by teachers' unions in the United Kingdom. Recently, in response to lobbying by educators, these rulings have been softened, so that children who have been expelled are no longer required to be included in school ratings and examination results (Anonymous, 2001a). In arguing against the ruling,

John Dunford, the general secretary of the British Secondary Heads Association complained that the requirement to include students who had been excluded had affected 1,546 schools (almost half the total) by as much as 5 per cent on their league table scores (Anonymous, 2001a). Although Mr Dunford made his claim in light of the negative impact of the ruling on school scores, it must also be noted that his claim sheds light on the pervasive practice of exclusion and its impact on poor learners in the United Kingdom.

Thus, as we noted earlier about Alberta, in Britain as well the recent emphasis on standards and competitive educational models has created a need by schools to compete at all costs and has resulted in exclusion and dishonest reporting with particularly deleterious implications for children with special needs. Further, these forced moves by schools exist within a set of contradictory terms. In both sites, government reforms have fostered competitive and exclusionary educational practices through increased inspection, testing, and publications of results, while concomitantly issuing educational policies that at least rhetorically commit schools to provide inclusive, community-based educational opportunities for all children, including those with special needs.

It has been pointed out that educational 'reform' is often a site for 'intervention that can promote the modernization of nations, enhance the viability of economic systems within world markets, and link macro issues of regulation with micro patterns of socialization and child rearing' (Popkewitz, 2000: 3). Reflecting Popkewitz's analysis, in these recent changes to special needs services and policies, both Alberta and Britain have created situations where schools that seek to compete in creating marketable students find ways to abrogate their responsibilities to vulnerable special needs children and their families. Further, as I hope to evidence in later chapters, not only do educators in both sites abrogate their responsibilities, but they actively put the blame for 'problem' students on children who are 'flawed' rather than simply 'different' and on mothers who are 'overprotective,' 'in denial,' or simply 'uncooperative.' Thus, with AD(H)D, the link between global macro-level shifts in regulations and local micro-level administration of children's educational needs is nicely illustrated in both sites.

Conclusion

In the above sections, I outlined some of the complexities of AD(H)D in terms of how practice and policy in both sites reflect professional ambiguity over AD(H)D's diagnostic legitimacy and treatment. As well, I described some fiscal arrangements relating to AD(H)D children. Finally, I constructed the groundwork of a feminist discursive ethnography and provided examples of how women's stories stand in contradiction to promises, policies, and discursive practices of the cultures of AD(H)D in Canada and Britain. My point is that mothers encounter uneven structures and patchy understandings in each medical, psy sector, and educational funding context in both Canada and Britain when trying to find answers and services for their children.

Normalization as related to AD(H)D is complex. At the macro-medical and -psychiatric level, diagnostic categories and professional discourse operate to create increasingly broad categories of the not-normal child, in turn creating a selectively narrower band of attributes that can be considered to be normal. Again at the macro-level, educational and government funding policy creates contexts in which the handling of the normal/not-normal categories becomes tied up with political and economic trends in public education. At a meso-level, the application of these categories is again selectively taken up so that children who fall within 'not-normal' ranges are excluded. Further, diagnoses, treatments, and programs are provided to these children in ways that maintain institutional rather than familial or child-centred goals. Finally, at the micro-interpretive level, women are left to fend for themselves in terms of learning the 'truth' about policies and funding and in terms of accommodating the schools' requirements that their children find services outside of the promised routes.

In the following chapters, I offer a narrative of the ways that the children in this study came to be seen as different, the kinds of problems they and their mothers encountered, and their interactions with a wide array of helping professionals. These professionals include not only teachers and school administrators, but child care workers, psychologists, special educators, family physicians, pediatricians, and psychiatrists in the management of AD(H)D. I examine public and professional discourse as it relates to difference and play these data against mothers' stories about their children in a feminist ethnography of the discursive practices relating to AD(H)D. In offering up mothers' narratives, I highlight connections between the public context of lay and professional controversy and the private experiences that mothers and children encounter during diagnosis and treatment; the ways that professionals dismiss, confront, and delegitimate maternal knowledge about their children and about AD(H)D; and the ways that self-interested professional discursive practice is deployed in mothers' and children's personal lives. I also show how many of the incidents in these women's stories reflect or illuminate the lay and professional controversies over many aspects of AD(H)D. Finally, I demonstrate the ways that mothers strive to know about AD(H)D and to resist professional inscriptions of themselves as inadequate, unknowing, overprotective, or non-compliant and of their children as disruptive, poorly disciplined, lazy, or, quite simply, bad.

4 Mothers Talk about the Early Years

Dr Maté believes ADD starts when the bond between a parent and a new baby is fractured by one or many factors: stress, conflict between two parents, maternal depression, money worries, separation and divorce, alcoholism, even abuse ... For the child, there is ... an emotional injury ... The search for relief is constant. 'It's like you've been shot down. Rather than collapse, you tune out the pain so you can keep running,' Dr Maté says.

Krista Foss
'Helping mom and dad help Johnny'
Globe and Mail, Health Matters
20 April 1999

The above quotation, from a Canadian psychiatrist who has published a book, made a country-wide speaking tour, and given several interviews to the Canadian press on his theories of ADD,[1] provides some insight into the suspicions that professionals can bring to their assessments of children who are experiencing social, educational, and behavioural difficulties. Dr Gabor Maté is somewhat unique among critics of AD(H)D in that he agrees that AD(H)D is a biological problem. To him, however, this biological problem stems from poor early childhood bonding, resulting in defective brain development. For the vast majority of

---

1 In August 2002, I received an invitation to the 5th Annual ADDISS (the umbrella parent support group network in the United Kingdom) conference for parents and professionals on ADHD, to be held in London, England. Dr Maté was among the invited speakers, again reflecting the movement of North American knowledge producers to the British scene.

AD(H)D sceptics, however, the intermediate step of a brain dysfunction is not an issue. Instead, the causal equation between bad parent (mother) and troubled child is seen as a direct one. In this chapter, I would like to examine some of the ways that mothers whose children are different and troubled experienced some of these assumptions from the professionals they sought help from and from the communities they lived in.

From the preceding chapter, one might assume that the only struggles mothers face in negotiating for services and inclusion on behalf of a child who is different[2] come through dealings with teachers and schools. Second, one might presume that the differences between British and Canadian social and knowledge contexts might shape mothers' experiences in predictable ways: for example, we could assume that mothers in Britain might have more difficulty in obtaining clear information than mothers in Canada or that mothers in Canada might encounter more public acceptance of the diagnosis than mothers in Britain. Third, one might presume that in both sites, the ambiguity of mothers' struggles are acted out in an arena of professional discursive practice that has little to do with lay viewpoints and controversies over AD(H)D.

This chapter, however, explores the very early experiences of mothers and their children from women's perspectives, to show that often, even before these children became school-aged, family members, physicians, pediatricians, psychiatrists, and community members added to the burden of mothers and children who are perceived as difficult. It is evident that, although the British and Canadian educational and professional discursive contexts might differ considerably regarding AD(H)D, the dilemmas women face in obtaining meaningful assistance in both sites are not always very different. Finally, I show that mothers and children's difficulties in both sites were not only acted out in maternal–professional interaction, but that these interactions were

---

2 I am conscious that I am slipping here into language that presumes AD(H)D as both real and legitimate. It is difficult to write fluidly without doing so. While I presume that, for the most part, the ways that AD(H)D is handled are primarily social, I do not take on a purely social or antipsychiatry model of disability, wherein it is claimed that there is nothing inherent in certain sets of attributes that would make them disabling. Although I agree that schools, public places, homes, and communities are indeed social, the effects that AD(H)D children experience in these spaces *as a result of their difference* are, at least to them and those who love them, quite real. This is the perspective I hope to convey throughout.

embedded within controversies over AD(H)D that played out both within professional discourse and in highly polemical debates in the public media.

Although mothers' narratives in the previous chapter provided a counterpoint to the promises and claims of discursive practices relating to special needs, the focus in that chapter remained primarily on the policy, procedural, and professional truth games employed in managing children who are different. Here, I turn my attention towards the narratives of mothers' experiences of stigma, confusion, and isolation in their encounters in the community and with professional interventions related to their children's difference. I also make connections between public policies, professional knowledge claims, and maternal experiences.

Narratives of Difference – Ontological and Epistemological Considerations

A critical feminist perspective recognizes the importance of women's own interpretations of the problems in their lives. I began the interviews with mothers by asking them to tell me the story of how they first came to understand their children as different. Thus, although most mothers acknowledged that schools were the first places that their children's differences became so problematic as to require formal intervention or demand a label, the troubles often began at a much earlier point in the child's life. As Glenda (a British mother), reflecting the narratives of the others, said, 'Where it all began, and where he got diagnosed are two different things.' In this chapter, then, I would like to offer an overview of how it was that these women came to understand their children as different, of how those differences came to be problematic, and how that problematization was handled through various medical, educational, and helping professional interactions.

Every one of the British mothers and a little over half of the Canadian mothers described children who exhibited high levels of activity, even in infancy (from birth through to eighteen months). I suspect this difference in reporting may be related to the different cultures of AD(H)D diagnosis in Canada and the United Kingdom. We may recall that in Canada diagnosis is based on more flexible DSM IV criteria that include inattention, impulsivity, *or* hyperactivity, while in England the WHO ICD-10 criteria *must* include hyperactivity for the diagnosis. As a result of the different cultural handling described earlier, I suspect it is likely that most (if not all) of the British children discussed in this study have been diagnosed because of hyperactivity alone, while some of the Canadian children were diagnosed for other attentional concerns besides hyperactivity.

Perhaps the British children were a more active group than their Canadian counterparts, even in their early development. However, regardless of the level of activity mothers described, mothers in both sites reported that these children had somehow seemed special. Their stories began with phrases like, 'He was always a busy, busy boy – no naps during the day,' or 'Well, I first thought of him as different when he was in the womb, because he never stayed still – totally different to the other two,' or 'I tried to ignore it but from the time he was twelve months there was something different about him.'

In each of these beginning stories, there are three possibilities. First, there is the possibility that memories, filtered through mothers' histories of struggle and concern, have shifted over time to include a narrative beginning that frames the child's problems as both ontologically and medically legitimate. A second possibility is that mothers, because they are exquisitely aware of the discourses of blame and responsibility that are attached to ADD, offer these narratives up as proof of their innocence – in a sense, creating a counternarrative to professional and lay discursive claims that AD(H)D is the result of bad mothering. A third possibility is that these are the stories of children who always, in some ways, actually *were* different.

I mention these three possibilities because I am aware of how doubts and suspicions circulate in western culture around the legitimacy of AD(H)D and how western culture is imbued with discourses of motherhood and blame.[3] I also recognize that mothers themselves are aware of these discourses of uncertainty and blame and that this might compel them to tell their stories in a way that offers a counterargument. Most importantly, however, suspicions may be present in readers' minds as they encounter these women's accounts. Rather than ignore these suspicions, I wish instead to ask readers to remain open to the women's stories as they stand. As a feminist researcher, I take women's 'truths' about motherhood and AD(H)D as though they are *at least* as legitimate as those 'truths' that claim AD(H)D is nothing more than a cultural

3 By 'western culture' I mean, and for the purposes of this study only, Britain, Canada, the United States, Australia, and New Zealand, as these countries seem to contain the lion's share of lay and professional English-language discourse on AD(H)D.

artefact driven by inadequate mothers, poor schools, drug company profits, and medical ambitions. The following chapters provide my reporting of women's perspectives in their own words. I ask that the reader suspend judgment on why women tell their stories the ways they do and remain open to learning a different 'truth' about mothering an AD(H)D child in these two cultures.

Infancy – Exhaustion, Worry, and Self-Doubt

For whatever reasons, whether biological or social, mothers report that these children were quite often disquieting at early ages, describing their children as being cause for concern at worst, bemusement at best, even as infants. Samantha is one of the Canadian mothers in this study. She is twenty-five years old, divorced, remarried, and the mother of four children; she describes her family as 'working poor.' Samantha claimed that Justin was always different from his siblings. She explained:

> Justin was my first, so I didn't know any better. I just thought that was what babies did. From the beginning, he never really slept ... By the time he was about twelve months old, he *would* go to sleep, but it was like he was some kind of lunatic. You'd hear him in there, thrashing and crashing around before he actually passed out. We actually had to look for him once he'd fall asleep – he could be in the closet or under a pile of toys, wherever.

> Eventually, we stuck all his toys and furniture in the hallway – we even had to take everything off the walls – and we put his crib in the middle of the room. We'd stand outside and listen to him, then go in after he'd fallen asleep to make sure he hadn't hurt himself.

Samantha's experiences were not unique. Most of the mothers in the study spoke about infants who slept very little and who were difficult to feed and settle. Mothers described children who gave up on their daytime naps at very early ages, who demanded continual interaction and stimulus (or who refused it), and who left mothers feeling tired, burdened, and inadequate.

In addition, many mothers described children who, from the beginning, had been difficult to hold or to comfort. British mother Moira described her son's early demeanour: 'From the beginning, he was different to our daughter in that, whereas she had been easy to sit down and cuddle and talk to, or sit together with a book ... he would show no interest. Uhm, he was just desperate to get away all the time, and appeared to be avoiding eye contact, which was quite alarming, because it meant that he was very difficult to get to know. Those were the earliest days with Teddy. And I really was exhausted. Exhausted from the worry, really.' For Moira, then, as for a number of these mothers, the child she cared for was difficult to manage, to get close to, and to understand. This left mothers feeling vulnerable about their capabilities as caregivers, particularly if the child was a first child and the women had no other experiences to draw upon in framing their competency as mothers.

Not all mothers had experiences of children who were distant or aversive to interaction: indeed, many of the mothers spoke of the loving, cuddling nature of their children, and how, knowing that side of the child enabled them to know that their children were not bad, but struggling. Other mothers spoke, too, about infants who never stopped needing some kind of interaction. Teresa is a Canadian mother. She is middle class, married, and raising three children. Trained as a teacher, she recently re-entered the paid workforce after a hiatus of fourteen years. Teresa said, 'I felt, when Neil was little, like I was his own personal walking, talking television set! If I sat down, or stopped playing with him, he'd just howl! It was like he needed something from me *all the time* – we could never just sit together quietly – I always had to entertain him.' For mothers whose very early child-rearing experiences were shot through with worries about feeding and sleeping, difficulties in achieving physical or even eye contact with the child, or exhaustion from constantly entertaining or cajoling a child, the struggle of providing care caused not only worry, but self-doubt. While these mothers worried about the possible problems their children might be facing, they also worried that they themselves were doing something wrong.

Belinda is a Canadian mother in this study. She is forty-six years old, a professional, married, with three children. At present, she is a stay-at-home mom. Belinda described her son's early behaviour, and her concerns and feelings about the situation:

> When he was born, he wouldn't eat, things like that. And then when he was going to the babysitter with his older sister, she couldn't handle him. He didn't sleep an awful lot at night. If you picked him up and cuddled him it wouldn't calm him down – he'd still scream. Sometimes, if you put him down, he'd actually stop – which was pretty upsetting ...

In the back of my mind, I had guilt, and I was beginning to feel that maybe I was causing his problems, because I was feeling so tired – uh, impatient and crabby. I assumed he was feeling it from me.

In this last worry – that mothers themselves might be to blame for their children's problems – mothers received a tremendous amount of support from 'helping' professionals. Indeed, many women described very early interventions with professionals that left them clearly understanding that their mothering itself was under suspicion.

Daphne is a Canadian woman who moved to the United Kingdom when her daughter Melanie was just four weeks old. She is a part-time medical researcher with a graduate degree, married, with two children. Daphne encountered professional care in both sites that cast suspicion on her as a mother rather than specifically on her child's problems. A bright and articulate woman, Daphne has a master's degree in nursing and had worked some time in pediatrics prior to Melanie's birth. She described her early experiences with her child:

> It was a very stressful time for us – even from the very beginning. She cried a lot, and couldn't seem to latch on when I breastfed. Very difficult. And her developmental milestones were delayed. So there were all of those issues – what is wrong with this child? Yet, she was very affectionate, and had a tremendous sense of humour. So I knew that she was bright, and she loved to be around kids.
>
> But, every time the public health nurse would come it would be 'well, she's not sitting up yet – what are you gonna do?'

For Daphne, as for many of the mothers in the study, early interactions with helping professionals were fraught with a sense that mothers' competencies were being scrutinized and that the child's difficulties were presumed to stem from inadequate mothering.

The public health nurse's visits are a standard element in birthing and raising an infant in Canada and the United Kingdom. While ostensibly positioned as a way to aid 'normal' mothers in learning to be with their 'normal' babies, visits from public health nurse have been and continue to be an opportunity for nurses to scrutinize mothers and to identify mothers who are abusive or neglectful (Arnup, 1994; Lupton, 1995). Daphne, in part because of her professional training, but also reflecting the narratives of many other mothers in the study, understood quite clearly that she herself was a suspect in the problems her child was encountering. She said: 'They were all telling me that some-thing was wrong with her, but the doctor and the nurse were both saying "failure to thrive." Well, in Canada, "failure to thrive" is a euphemism for abuse. And the public health nurse would come – unannounced. To me, unannounced visits are, uhm – you know, in Canada if someone comes unannounced, they're suspecting something.' Daphne expressed clearly that she knew herself to be under surveil-lance, as part of the 'normal' regimen of assessing her child. In other words, she knew that to get help for her child, she would have to tolerate the unspoken assumptions that she was part of her daughter's problems.

Daphne's experience of seeking help and instead finding her ideas discredited and herself censured was neither unique, nor was it specific to the United Kingdom. Lydia is a Canadian mother in this study. She is married and has one daughter; she is a professional woman with a graduate degree who works part-time to accommodate the family's needs. Lydia described a visit from the public health nurse during which she asked the nurse if her infant daughter's crying and difficulty in settling was normal and in which she admitted that she was tired, worried, and wondering what to do. After the nurse's visit she received a telephone call from a help line for abusive parents, telling her that the nurse had referred her to them, and assuring her that she could always call that number whenever she felt she might be at risk for harming her child. Although this health worker's response undoubtedly stemmed from a concern to protect the child, Lydia experienced the response as shocking and as betrayal. She described feeling that her request for guidance had not been heard and said, 'After receiving that phone call, I really felt that it would be long time before I confided to *anyone* again, and in fact, it was.'

The interactions with public health workers described by mothers in both sites provide vivid examples of ways that helping professionals, intentionally or not, operate to scrutinize and control the private lives of women as they mother. Feminist historians and social researchers note that although the manifest function of public health nursing, health promotion, and social work has traditionally been to help 'trou-bled' families, these professional have always functioned in latent ways as well. These include the surveillance of families as a way of identify-ing and containing 'high risk mothers' and their 'endangered/at-risk' children (Abramowitz, 1996; Arnup, 1994; Boyd, 1999; Daikin and Naidoo, 1995; Fraktman, 1998; Knowles, 1996). Carolyn Knowles, in discussing professional family intervention practices in Britain, Canada, and the United States, provides an extract from a government handbook used as a 'guide for medical staff on maternity wards who are involved in the business of risk prediction' (1996: 131–3). This list's indicators for maternal abuse include mothers who express 'excessive' doubt about their ability to care for the infant, who are bothered by the infant's crying, who claim to feel helpless or hopeless, and who perceive that their child is 'different' or 'not-normal' despite negative findings (1996: 132). The warning indicators listed for children who might be at risk of being abused include children who are difficult feeders, unresponsive, irritable, or difficult to console, and hyperreflexive (1996: 133).

Thus, health workers in this study, who may have been taught to look for certain kinds of warning signs (worried mothers and difficult babies who have not been diagnosed with a specific problem) when assessing for maternal abuse were not *professionally* incorrect in making these assumptions about the mothers in this study. However, one could argue that they were *morally* incorrect in their assumptions. These mothers were not covert in their worries or actions: rather, they were. asking early on in their children's lives for information and assistance that might help them to provide their children with appropriate care. Further, women's concerns about their *children*, at this early stage, ended up being interpreted and responded to by professionals as worrisome attributes in the *mothers*. Thus, mothers who asked professionals to consider possible problems in their children were not only wrongly judged for doing so, but their children's needs were left unconsidered.

In Daphne's case, the belief that she was being scrutinized was borne out when, at the age of two-and-a-half, her daughter finally was referred to a sympathetic pediatrician. Having presumably judged Daphne and her husband as good parents, he left the child's medical record open on his desk while he excused himself, saying, 'Oh, I just remembered I have a phone call I have to make. I'll come back in about twenty minutes.' He left Melanie's full medical file on his desk for Daphne to view. Perceiving this as an open invitation, she says: 'I read everything they had written about it, and the *Canadian* mother, underlined, and not compliant, not feeding her child, not accepting the fact that her child has all these problems, and – uh – inappropriate affect. And, "Please assess for Cerebral Palsy." And I thought to myself, 'Nobody's listening here.' On a concrete level, this incident illustrates the ironies of some mothers' positions as 'experts' in the maternal–professional 'team.'

While, on the one hand, Daphne was encouraged by the physicians and nurses who were involved in her 'case' to be open and cooperative, the medical file showed Daphne that these same professionals were not interested in Daphne's insights into her child's problems. Daphne had refused the cerebral palsy label several times, offering alternative explanations, providing articles to her daughter's medical team that suggested other possibilities, and still the referral to this pediatrician indicated that cerebral palsy was to be investigated by the new medical team member.

An additional irony was that, although the professionals who had been involved in Daphne's case had asked her to trust them, from the contents of their file on her, it was clear that *they* did not trust *her*. Thus, while Daphne had attended meetings, met with the home visiting nurse, followed up on professional referrals, and generally cooperated with helping professionals, her cooperation did little to protect her from being judged as inadequate and perhaps even as culpable in her child's problems.

Although in this instance the pediatrician did not accept the file at face value, this incident provides a clear example of how intraprofessional texts can potentially stigmatize women and their children as unruly, uncooperative, or undeserving. Additionally, this kind of interprofessional missive can preclude the possibility of creating a truly productive alliance with the mother or of permitting professionals to understand the child's problems in ways that are not clouded.

In a rare and remarkably compassionate act of courage, this professional broke the code of silence shared by medical, psychiatric, and educational peers, opening Daphne's own file up to her. In doing so, he permitted her to actually see herself through the eyes of the professionals who were dealing with her child and to bear their assessment of her in mind when making choices about her daughter's care. In fact, although Daphne remains grateful to this professional for his honesty, she conveyed an understanding of professional scrutiny and blame that was shared by other mothers in this study when she said, 'It was good of him, but there was very little in that file I hadn't already suspected.'

In conclusion, then, even in infancy, many of the children exhibited signs that something about them was different or difficult, and often these attributes and interaction styles left mothers feeling worried about or alienated from their children. In addition, some mothers began to feel uncertain about their mothering skills and guilty that perhaps they may be contributing to their children's difference. As well, even in these early stages, maternal–professional interactions were characterized by suspicion, mother-blame, and interventions that were characterized by assumptions of maternal pathology rather than a consideration that mothers might actually have insight into their children's legitimate problems. Perhaps not surprisingly, these early professional–maternal contacts often laid the foundations for mothers' long-term distrust of professional knowledge and care when it came to their troubled children.

Toddlerhood – Worry, Censure, and Isolation

Unfortunately, as these children grew older and became more active participants in the social world, the difficulties they and their mothers encountered in their families, in their communities, and with professionals increased as well. Once the children reached toddlerhood (from eighteen months to four years) safety, manageability, and public behaviour became more pressing areas of concern for most of the mothers. In Britain, Moira's son Teddy, because of being born prematurely and having some subsequent developmental delays, only became mobile at sixteen months. She says, however, 'As soon as he became mobile, then something was obviously different, because he didn't stop. He knew no fear. And he would just take off.'

Deanna, a Canadian mother, echoed this. Deanna is an adoptive mother, married, and in a working-class family; she works part-time in the service sector. She said that, from the time her daughter could walk, 'for us it was just a struggle, and a struggle and a struggle. It drove me crazy with safety issues. This was climbing, going into drawers, running out in parking lots. Even now [at age nine] I never let her hand go when we're on the street.' In Britain, Diane had a similar experience. She is the lone parent of three children; she lives on social assistance and receives no support from their father. She described an incident when her son was three years old, and how this reflected on her: 'We actually went to where he was completely naked running down the street. I was in the house, thinking he was playing in the garden, and he made a hole in the fence and he just went. And there was an older lady brought him back. She gave me a look, I can tell you! I mean, what could I say?' Indeed, it is difficult for a mother to defend her caregiving in such a situation. Even though the older woman who brought young Andrew home did not chastise Diane, she felt herself judged and was at a loss for a plausible explanation.

The uncontrollability of their children often reflected badly on the ways these women were perceived as mothers very early on in their mothering and affected their own assessment of themselves as good mothers. It also affected mothers' freedom of movement and their social integration. Mothers, particularly in England, commonly described one of their worst nightmares to be shopping. Children would literally run amok, picking up things that had not been paid for, running away from mothers in the line-up, throwing tantrums at the checkout. These were profoundly humiliating experiences, and often mothers described responding in ways that were personally disturbing.[4]

When asked about the reactions of other people in the community to her son's behaviour, Diane said: 'It was annoying to me that this poor kid was being told off all the time. And that I'm responsible always. I got it all the time, from the age of three. "What's wrong with him? He's mad! Can't you sort him out?" And I'd say, "What can I do? I've done everything I can do." And you end up smacking them then. You don't want to, but you feel you've *got* to." Diane raised an important point. Not only did she feel herself to be judged for her child's behaviour, but she believed public censure stemmed from an assumption that Adrian behaved this way because she could not discipline him properly. In response, Diane consciously displayed herself as a firm mother despite her own feelings. Other mothers described similar situations: scolding or striking a child in public as a way to show disapproving strangers that they *did* care and that they *were* trying to exercise some control over their unruly children. Further, they did this even though privately they did not like or necessarily even believe in these kinds of discipline. As many of the women noted, discipline really seemed to make no difference to these children.

In the end, there were tremendous costs, not only for children, but for the mothers themselves. Lydia, in Canada, said, 'I really don't think Karla ever understood why she got in trouble, but I do think she always forgave me. It was like she forgot it right away. But *I* didn't, and it tore me up to think that I could do that to her – smack her, or yell at her, just to make sure everybody else could see I was on the case.' In these instances, the mothers' perceptions of what constitutes *good* mothering

---

4 In the British group, shopping was always mentioned as a problem. For Canadian women, although these incidents were mentioned, they were less foregrounded. This may relate to the structure of British shops (street-level, small, and community-based) as opposed to Calgary shops that are typically in large, impersonal malls.

was something of a Catch-22. On the one hand, they understood that aggression or anger did not work for them or for their children, while on the other, they felt compelled to display precisely these characteristics as a way to exhibit their parental control for others.

It must be acknowledged as well that some of the mothers felt themselves pushed into violence or into leaving their children unattended (so as to avoid violence) as a result of interactions with the children themselves. Lydia spoke of leaving her three-year-old daughter alone in the house one morning after a battle to get her teeth cleaned. She sat outside in the car and cried, while Karla stood in the window, smiling, waving, and clearly not understanding that anything untoward had happened.

In England, Evelyn recalled how, when she began feeding her son solid food, 'There would be this sort of battle, and he would clearly take pleasure in building up the tension.' She would eventually get to the point where she could no longer bear it and would leave him in the kitchen and shut the door on him. She says, 'I knew it was horrendous, but I also knew that it was either him or me.' Indeed, sometimes, it *was* him. She explains how she felt about this: 'At the time, I felt horribly guilty. I remember if I'd smack him during the day, or I'd pushed him away from me because I couldn't stand it any longer, when he was asleep at night, I'd go into his room. And I'd sit there crying, because I thought, *'How could I have allowed this to happen to us?'* Evelyn's comments are telling. Fraught with guilt, feeling out of control, and unable to understand how things have gone so wrong, she assumes that these problems are because of her inability to make things right.

It is difficult, as a reader, not to judge Lydia and Evelyn's responses to their children. A mother who cannot control her emotions when interacting with her recalcitrant child, and who leaves her child unattended so as to avoid further escalation, can be readily understood to be a mother who is inadequate or immature. Indeed, mothers themselves were ambiguous about their imperfect responses, describing not only guilt, but also a deep chasm between their personal ideals of motherhood and their actual mothering. Experiences where mothers felt themselves to be out of control, incapable of 'proper' discipline, and acting outside the bounds of their own definition of good mothering led mothers to believe themselves responsible, if not for causing them, then at least for not being able to fix their children's problems.

As mentioned earlier, mothers who felt this kind of self-doubt did not have to look far for confirmation from others about their shortcomings. In addition to the scrutiny of public health nurses, physicians, and members of the general public, mothers encountered censure from their family and peers. In Canada, Amanda's family blamed her for Michael's behaviour, even when their own efforts to discipline him met with failure. She said: 'My family more or less thought I was a bad Mom because Michael was just completely uncontrollable. And they figured if I were a lot more strict with him, then he would listen, [but] if they tried being strict with him and it didn't work, they just said, "Well, you shoulda started this way long before – coming down on him." And it was like, "I've tried!" Basically, I couldn't win.'

Fran is an English mother in this study. Fran has two children, is separated, living with a new partner, and at present unemployed. Her six-year-old son Angus, at the time of our interviews, was informally excluded from school because of behaviour difficulties. As a toddler, her son was 'very lively – he never sat still.' She described constantly running after him, calling after him, chasing after him, entreating him to settle down. She found his behaviour problematic not only in public sites like shops or streets, but also when visiting extended family. She described her family's reactions: 'I just felt constantly worn down. And I was – my partner and my in-laws at the time used to say, "Oh, it's only with you he's like that. He's only like that with you. Nobody else." And I thought ... I'm trying my best, and I seem to be the only one who's disciplining him, and everyone else is sort of smiling and thinking he's cute, and they're blaming me for the way he behaves!' Fran's comments are quite insightful. Not only did she feel that she was the one held responsible for her son's behaviour, regardless of what she tried to do, but she also understood that the work of parenting and disciplining, even when there were other responsible adults around, was hers alone. Further, the blame when that disciplining and parenting work 'fell short' remained hers, even when the child's father and grandparents actively undermined her efforts. Although Fran describes blaming and alienating interactions with her husband, for the most part, the women in this study spoke of husbands who, at least within the context of the home, shared in their frustration and worry; it is worth noting that Fran is now separated from her husband and living with a partner who is 'very supportive.'

Just as mothers earlier described feeling pushed to discipline their children as a way to deflect public censure, some of these mothers described how they tried to evidence for their families that they were good disciplinarians. For example, in Canada, Deanna said that both her parents and her in-laws believed her to be an inadequate parent. Although she provided them with a brochure about ADD and its symptoms, she says, 'When she [Ariel] acts up, they don't understand it. They still think I should just discipline her, and then in the next breath, they accuse me of being too hard on her ... When I'm with them, I just feel like I'm raggin' on her all the time.' Deanna was not alone; several mothers described feeling pressured to provide discipline and care in ways they disliked in order to maintain peace in the family.

Finally, for many women, these kinds of family interactions ultimately resulted in self-imposed social exclusion. Dolores, whose family visits inevitably ended up with teasing, fighting, broken toys, and tears, said, 'I got to the stage where I couldn't take him to my family's house, or to my sister-in-law's, because they were both arguing constantly with me, because of Adrian.' It can readily be speculated that this kind of exclusion took its toll on the relationships between mothers and their children.

The kinds of censure mothers described from family members and, in rare instances from partners, spread into other arenas during their children's early childhood. Women, particularly in England, spoke poignantly about their difficulties in being social with other women and their children, and the resulting exclusion they experienced as community members.[5]

Whether at a mother–tot play group, a Sunday school setting, or in the local shops, British women experienced profound barriers in their ability to interact, to share adult companionship with other mothers, or to see their children interact with their same-aged peers. For Evelyn, a well-to-do British mother who stayed at home for her son Harry's early years, social situations became difficult to truly take part in. She said:

> Children's playgroups, toddler groups, were a nightmare. Other mothers would sit there – even other mothers with boys – would sit there with a cup of tea. I was always the one who never, ever was involved in the

5 As noted in Chapter 2, 'Methods,' British women were more likely to have chosen to stay home with their children in very early childhood, and were more likely to have remained full-time in the home, reflecting more traditional gender values relating to family and maternal work outside the home. Canadian mothers were more likely to work at least part-time, particularly once their children were school-aged. Further, Canadian women tended to describe their part-time or quality of career choices as having been constrained because of their children's needs.

conversation. I mean, you do get isolated because you can never just sit and chat while your child plays happily.

Instead, I was dashing around, going in and coming out, stopping him doing things, taking things away, sorting out arguments, hauling him out of some scene where he'd pinched another child, trying to smooth things over, apologizing for things he'd broken before I'd been able to head him off.

Evelyn said that although the other mothers in the groups never openly criticized her, and even though she did continue to attend these community activities with Harry, she felt herself to be isolated because of the constant need for vigilance. Further, because Harry's behaviour with other women's children was 'appalling,' Evelyn also acknowledged that despite the polite acceptance of other mothers, she felt stigmatized because her son's behaviour (for which she held herself responsible) was shameful to her.

In contrast to Evelyn, most of the British mothers *did* describe overt experiences of being judged and excluded by other mothers during their children's early years. Rosalind is one of the British mothers. She is married, has four children, and is a stay-at-home mother; her husband is a professional, and the family is very well-to-do. Rosalind described how at infant and toddler playgroups, her son 'would just knock children about – left, right and centre, not because he was nasty [but because] he was totally unaware.' She went on to say: 'Mums used to sit there saying, "Look at that terrible Mum. Why doesn't she control that child?" Whisper, whisper, whisper. And I used to feel about *this* big. And I *desperately* needed to go to these places, because I was a full-time Mum at home, and I wanted to meet other people. We were very, very isolated. Nobody could cope with him.' Rosalind's comments describe her feelings of isolation and the overwhelming burden of caring for a child who requires constant vigilance and whose behaviour reflects poorly on mothers in the eyes of peers and community members.

Again in Britain, Diane, a single mother living on social assistance with three dependent children, found these negative incidents in shops, tot groups, and playgrounds so painful that she ultimately stopped going out at all, because 'it was just too embarrassing.' For Diane, this choice meant more than simply missing the company of other adults and of not being able to provide her child with opportunities for peer interaction. Rather, because she was without resources or the support of a partner, running errands, shopping for food, and providing the necessities of care for her family came to be near impossible. As Diane says, 'I felt like a prisoner – we *all* were, really – because of my own child.'

Thus, in toddlerhood, to varying degrees, many of the mothers began to see their children as unmanageable and to note that children's unruliness and poor social behaviour reflected badly on their capabilities in the public eye and within family and community networks. Further, as a result of these interactions, they began to experience doubts about their mothering abilities and would often tailor their public parenting practices in hopes of avoiding disasters with their children and deflecting censure from other adults.

Censure from family members seemed to be fairly universal regardless of the location of mothers. Mothers in both Canada and Britain described embarrassment in front of parents, siblings, and in-laws, and often reported comments from these family members that were misguided, hurtful, and blaming. Difficult social integration in more public social settings, such as community groups, church, and playgroups seemed more problematic for British women than for Canadian mothers. Perhaps this is because the British women engaged (or at least attempted to engage) in more traditional social patterns than their Canadian counterparts, so that problems and barriers associated with church attendance or mother–tot groups for stay-at-home women were a more pervasive focus of the British narratives. Ironically, although these kinds of semiformal community settings may offer social support benefits for individuals who 'fit in,' for the British mothers of ADHD children, these were often sites of quite painful informal exclusion and stigmatization.

Public arenas, such as shops, malls, and streets, although problematic to mothers in both sites, seemed again to cause more problems for mothers in Britain. This is perhaps because many of the British women I interviewed came from smaller towns in which shops and streets are small and crowded and in which mothers and their children were known members of the community. Again, ironically, the traditions of a small town setting offered cold comfort to British mothers of ADHD children. Rather, because British children's difficult behaviour unfolded in settings where they were neither anonymous nor readily ignored, British mothers described additional burdens of stigmatization compared with their Canadian counterparts.

Early Interventions – Mothers' Concerns and Professional Dismissal

When the children were toddlers and began to encounter increasing difficulties in their communities, preschool groups, and day care settings, slightly over a third of the Canadian mothers (six of seventeen) and slightly over half of the British mothers (nine of seventeen) entered into some kind of contact with helping professionals regarding their children. While typically it was day care workers, playschool teachers, physicians, and pediatricians who initiated these investigations, a number of the mothers (two in Canada and three in England) approached professionals themselves with concerns about their children. In both sites, when it was the mother who broached the subject, professionals often failed to acknowledge the legitimacy of mothers' concerns. Rather, these *initiating mothers* – mothers who brought their concerns to professionals – were assured their children were just fine, or they were told that their children were simply exhibiting gender-appropriate behaviour.

Initiating Mothers, Professional Dismissal, and Age

Amy is a British mother in this study. She is divorced and remarried to the owner of a pub; she is a stay-at-home mother. Amy's daughter Jana was asked to leave her second playgroup at age three because of 'discipline' issues, Amy expressed concerns to her family physician about her daughter. She was told to relax, that her child was just 'busy' and would undoubtedly grow out of it. In Canada, Lydia asked her daughter's child care worker whether she thought three-year-old Karla might not be hyperactive, and she received exactly the same response. In both cases, not only were the mothers' concerns dismissed, but the dismissal left these women feeling that their questions had been treated as evidence of excessive maternal vigilance. As Lydia said in discussing the child care worker's dismissal of her concerns: 'I think she thought I was just another neurotic mother. I mean, I think she meant well with it. But I went to her because I figured she should know what was typical – I mean, she was the expert, right? I didn't know, because Karla's my only child. But she *worked* with kids, and so I accepted her take on things, when probably I should have trusted my gut.' The belief that a professional should be better equipped than she was to assess her daughter's behaviour led Lydia to dismiss her own feelings and concerns. However, in retrospect, both mothers believed these early interactions had led to delays in assessment and treatment, and they expressed regrets over acquiescing to professional assurances.

Thus, in these early interactions, we begin to see how conflict between maternal and professional knowledge plays itself out; while a mother might 'know' something is wrong for her own child, professional understandings of what is normal for 'children' typically prevail. If the worker or the doctor does not see it, then it does not exist. Perhaps not surprisingly, this privileging of professional over maternal knowledge is upheld in professional discourse relating to AD(H)D. The American Psychiatric Association (APA), for example, has affirmed the ascendancy of professional 'knowledge' over maternal 'opinions' when psychologists and psychiatrists are evaluating children for ADD. The APA has indicated that 'when reports of teachers and parents conflict, primary consideration should be given to the teacher reports because of greater familiarity with age-appropriate norms' (Kiger, 1985: 79). In England, the Royal College of Psychiatrists (RCP) asserts psychiatry as the privileged knower of child normality, stating that 'although parents or teachers may *wonder* if a child with these problems has ADHD/hyperkinetic disorder, making the full *diagnosis* requires an experienced specialist assessment' (Anonymous, 1999d: 2, emphasis mine). Further, the 'experienced specialist' should be 'a child and adolescent psychiatrist [who] will be able to provide a thorough assessment and offer treatment' (ibid.). In the RCP scheme of things, both parents and teachers are given little cachet in evaluating children or in being part of the professional team. Rather, child and adolescent psychiatrists alone have the ability to know and determine the 'truth' about difficult children.

Initiating Mothers, Professional Dismissal, and Gender

The second response that initiating mothers received from professionals about their 'difficult' children related to gender; this occurred when male children were the focus of mothers' worries. When Canadian mother Belinda went to her son's pediatrician with worries about his inability to pay attention, his difficulties interacting with peers, and his behavioural problems in preschool, she was told, 'He's a boy. He'll grow out of it. You're overreacting.' In England, Diane and Moira were told virtually the same thing.

Indeed, when mothers brought concerns forward about their *sons'* socially inappropriate behaviours and activity levels, a gender-stereotyped response was extremely common from playschool teachers, physicians, and pediatricians during the early stages of dealing with the child's problems. It seems that for many professionals, the 'natural' gendered behaviours of boys – aggression, high levels of activity, and a 'need' for more stimulating and active kinds of play (which are also among the hallmarks of AD(H)D) – can act as a smokescreen against early intervention. 'Boys will be boys,' mothers are told, even when these boys are described (as occurred with Diane) by their mothers as different from their same-sex peers.

Mothers did not always accept at face value these professionals' interpretations of their children's troublesome behaviour as simply gender-appropriate. When Moira's son first came under medical care, his physician first ruled out deficient hearing as a problem and then fell back on gender as the explanation. She described her response: 'And I'm thinking, "No. It's not like that." I do know that boys can be different, and usually are different, than girls. I had a brother – grew up with him and his friends. Moreover, I decided to watch Teddy very closely with his peers, when he went to playgroup or something, and I was pretty convinced that he was different in some way.' Thus, while the professionals might have exhibited incredulity over her perceptions about the degree of Teddy's difference, Moira exercised her own incredulity over professional knowledge claims in judging her child's problems.

The relationship of gender to AD(H)D as evidenced in these early interactions is interesting and complicates the literature on gender and AD(H)D. Numerous researchers have speculated that boys, rather than girls, are more likely to be identified with AD(H)D (Greenblatt, 1994; Berry et al., 1985; McGee et al., 1987). This research posits that girls are more likely to be overlooked because their stereotypically feminine behaviours of passivity, shyness, and non-disruptiveness are less problematic to educators and caregivers; thus, girls will typically be identified as academic underachievers rather than having AD(H)D (Greenblatt, 1994: 90). Conversely, the claim goes that boys, because of their tendency to exhibit more demanding and irritating behaviours, may be identified and treated earlier, more frequently, and perhaps excessively in comparison with their female counterparts (Greenblatt, 1994: 90). In the children described by mothers in the present study, however, the very fact that early childhood educators and medical professionals expected boys to engage in 'naturally' disruptive behaviours meant that these boys' problems were minimized and that assessments and interventions were delayed because of their gender.

It must also be noted that, often, the kind of behaviour these concerned mothers began to point out to professionals in relation to their very young children was often not all that 'natural' in terms of gender or age appropriateness. For example, it might be possible to simply dismiss Diane's earlier description of having her three-year-old son returned naked to her by a stranger as little more than a tale of boyish pluck and innovation. However, it is harder to dismiss this incident as a 'natural' expression of masculinity when coupled with her story of how, while playing with a puppy, he became so excited that the puppy actually died or how he lit the hair of the little girl in front of him on fire during a church ceremony. Likewise, it might be possible to consider that a child who was very active and wearing her mother down at home might indeed be seen by professionals a 'just busy' for her age. However, one wonders why a 'busy' child like Amy's daughter Jana was not seen as needing some kind of evaluation after she was asked to leave two separate preschools because of her inability to fall in with social practices that apparently posed no difficulties for her peers.

As we have seen through these examples, whether mothers were told that their children were simply busy and that mothers should not worry or that young boys were just 'being boys' and mothers should relax, mothers' first questionings – 'Is there something wrong with my child?' – were met with dismissal. In fact, the professional dismissal that initiating mothers encountered in these very early stages foreshadows professional interactions throughout all the mothers' experiences. As will be seen, when mothers in this study drew on their own insights about their children and their difficulties, they repeatedly encountered professional refusal to take those insights seriously and were assured that their concerns were unnecessary. At this early point, professional dismissal of maternal knowledge meant only that investigations into the children's problems were delayed or that the mothers' trust in professional judgment began to erode. However, I will show that, as these children matured and their problems became more complex and more serious, the effects of professional dismissal became increasingly deleterious. Also, as initiating mothers continued to come up against professional dismissal, they ultimately found themselves to be judged as overanxious, overprotective, or overachieving mothers whose standards for their children's behaviours were simply 'too-high.'

Early Interventions – Professional Incertitude and Maternal Surveillance

In the above section, we heard from initiating mothers who attempted to get professionals to investigate their children's problems during the early years. Maternally initiated concerns resulted in inaction and in counterclaims that mothers' concerns were both unfounded and inappropriate and professional truth claims outweighed maternal ones when it came to the problems of very young children. However, of the six Canadian mothers and nine British mothers who encountered professional interventions over their 'different' children during toddlerhood, most came into such interactions as a result of initiations by professionals. When professionals rather than mothers first raised questions about these children, more often than not, investigative steps were taken, reflecting the ability of professionals to turn their concerns into action and to have their concerns taken seriously by mothers and other professionals alike.

Nevertheless, these professionally instigated early investigations often took false turns, creating smokescreens that delayed appropriate assistance for the children and that undermined mothers' confidence in the knowledge claims of helping professionals. The smokescreens fell into three categories: the young age of the child, physiological problems that were of little significance in obtaining appropriate assistance, and psychosocial smokescreens that focused on presumed family pathology rather than on the child's symptoms per se. The following sections tease out some examples of each kind of smokescreen and the implications of those professional interventions for mothers and their children.

Age-Related Smokescreens

In Canada, one smokescreen that mothers of very young children encountered in obtaining an assessment or an intervention for the child, even if the impetus came from another professional, was simply related to the child's age. In Canada, for example, Deanna described how four-year-old Ariel's playschool teacher had to physically segregate her from the other children in order to maintain classroom peace. In a parent–teacher meeting, the teacher asked Deanna whether she had ever considered that Ariel might have ADD. Although initially taken aback, Deanna began to consider the suggestion as worth pursuing.

The playschool teacher suggested a local pediatrician who specialized in ADD, and Deanna obtained a referral to see him through her family physician. Upon assessment, the pediatrician's response to her concerns was, 'Oh, well, yeah, she probably *does* have it, but the true test will come out in Grade 1. We'll wait til then.' Thus, Deanna and Ariel left the physician's consultation with no more assistance than to be told to come back in two years. As it turned out, once Ariel had been in Grade 1 for a few months, the new teacher initiated the investigation once more, and this time, through the same physician, Ariel did receive a diagnosis and began taking Ritalin. Deanna's experience was perhaps the most overt example of a Canadian professional providing a tentative diagnosis while refusing to confer an 'official' one until the child reached a certain age. However, several other Canadian women also reported less formal conversations with professionals (teachers and physicians) in which they were told essentially that ADD was a likely diagnosis, but that 'it was too early to tell just yet.' Perhaps not surprisingly, none of the British women described interactions of this kind at these early stages, in all probability reflecting the general scepticism of British professionals towards ADHD.[6]

Deanna's experiences can also be understood as an example of how mothers' personal problems intersect with and are influenced by contentious professional and public discourse over specific aspects of AD(H)D identification and treatment. Professional discourse relating to AD(H)D in young children is characterized by controversy. On the one hand, there are strong arguments by the professions against identifying children three years old or younger with AD(H)D (Campbell, 1990; Anastopoulos et al., 1997). These arguments are based on 'evidence now available that 3 year olds with significant symptoms of inattention and hyperactivity have a high likelihood of remission of these concerns within 12 months' (Anastopoulos et al., 1997). On the contrary, there are professionals who argue that preschoolers showing high levels of limited attention span and impulsivity are likely to continue to have difficulties in these areas. In other words, they argue that a child who displays AD(H)D symptoms at age three will most likely still display them at age thirteen (Szumowski et al., 1986). Thus, there is

6 The National Health Service has set out guidelines that ensure that 'methylphenidate (Ritalin) is not currently licensed for children under the age of six' in the United Kingdom (NICE, 2000); thus, it is not surprising that ADHD and Ritalin would not be suggested diagnoses or treatments for the young British children in this study.

no clear professional consensus on this issue of age and early identifica-tion. As was noted earlier, the symptoms of AD(H)D are also quite ambiguous and can be conceptualized as 'abnormal' levels of 'normal' childhood attributes. This ambiguity of AD(H)D symptoms (are they 'normal childhood traits' or are they evidence of 'pathology'?), when coupled with debates in the research literature over early identification, can create a level of uncertainty for early childhood practitioners. Under these conditions, even Canadian professionals (who work within a context where acceptance of ADD as a diagnostic category is high) may err on the side of caution in applying a label in very early childhood.

It can also be speculated that, at least in part, professional caution over early diagnosis and treatment operates in response to the lay controversies that circulate over AD(H)D diagnosis and Ritalin treat-ment at early ages. In the popular press, the notion that children are being medicated inappropriately and at increasingly early ages is argued with remarkable frequency and stridency. In England, for example, the *Guardian* recently ran a front-page article decrying the medicalization of children with ADHD in the United Kingdom, stating, 'Children with mild behaviour problems are being drugged with Ritalin – dubbed the "chemical cosh"[7] or "kiddie crack" – simply in order to control them' and that 'children as young as two are being given mood-altering drugs' (Browne, 2000a). These sentiments are echoed in other British media as well (Anonymous, 1999a, 1999b, 1998a). The Canadian media have offered articles that are similarly alarmist in tone, noting not only a rise in the number of Ritalin prescriptions written, but in the decreasing ages of some of the children being medicated (Bongers, 1997; Hough, 1997; Rees, 1998c).

My point in raising these controversies in both professional and popular discourse is not to take up one side or the other's argument as 'true.' Rather, I want to point out how mothers' private experiences can be mediated through these discourses. Physicians cannot help but be aware of the controversy over diagnosing a very young child with ADD, and some will inevitably choose more conservative approaches because of this climate. As well, mothers who encounter the contro-versy through popular media will perhaps be less willing to push for the diagnosis as a result of doubts raised through these texts. Thus, it is perhaps not surprising that in Deanna's case, both pediatrican and

7 For non-British readers, my informants describe 'cosh' as a slang term meaning 'strap,' referring to the use of Ritalin as a chemical form of discipline and punishment.

mother accepted that even though the ADD label was appropriate, treatment would have to wait, and that this prudent course of action (although perhaps regrettable) was for the best.

Physiological Smokescreens

A second set of smokescreens that mothers encountered in obtaining an appropriate assessment or intervention for the child was related to a broad range of presumed physical pathologies in the child. These included suspicions of hearing deficits, visual problems, large motor deficits, bowel immaturity, speech pathology, mental retardation, and cerebral palsy. In these situations, physicians typically took the lead, as they noticed unusual behaviour and attributes or delayed developmental milestones during routine doctor visits. In these kinds of medical interactions, where children were subject to regular medical scrutiny even before entering any formal or informal educational setting, mothers described experiences with professionals that were both worrisome and less than confidence inspiring.

In Britain, Melanie spent Daphne's first three years going to a pediatric clinic on a weekly basis. The litany of problems that were investigated, treated, or ruled out is lengthy and eclectic. By the age of three, Melanie had at varying points been diagnosed with 'failure to thrive,' strabismus, cerebral palsy, low muscle tone, and mental retardation. She had been seen by family physicians, pediatricians, occupational therapists, optometrists, and psychiatrists. Yet, as each diagnosis was put forward and treatment failed, Daphne began to doubt the competence of these professionals to make judgments about her child. One of the smokescreens that early medical investigations raised was that perhaps Melanie's vision was to blame. She says:

> So we weren't sure what her vision was. She was three, and I was being reprimanded because she couldn't read the alphabet. And because she couldn't read the alphabet, they couldn't test her eyes – Well, Duh! I now know that such small children have a different kind of eye chart, but they never used it.
>
> And we went to a reputable eye surgeon, so she ended up having eye surgery there, to correct the strabismus. It wasn't evident. Like you really couldn't see it – just a bit of an in-turn. In fact, we had gone there on a Monday and he said 'bring her back on Thursday and we'll do surgery.' Like, *immediately*.

The surgery came on the heels of six months of placing drops in Melanie's eyes and having her wear an eye patch – neither of which had proved effective. Further, as Daphne states, Melanie's vision was not tested properly by the surgeon, and her strabismus was barely evident to Daphne. Still, at the surgeon's insistence, Daphne agreed to the surgery.

The example of Melanie's surgery provides insight into the ways that professionals, on the basis of reputation and expert knowledge claims, are able to push forward procedures that can be quite invasive, despite little evidence for their necessity, and despite little material evidence that the professional insights are correct. In Daphne and Melanie's case, professional authority and insistence led to a surgery that Daphne subsequently, and with some bitterness, has come to believe was unnecessary. Certainly the surgery, and the eye treatments that preceded it, did nothing to address Melanie's original presenting problems: Melanie's inability to pay attention in the preschool and her failure to read at age-appropriate levels of achievement.

The notion of age-appropriate achievement norms is something of a leitmotif in Melanie's early childhood story. That she did not walk 'on time,' talk 'on time,' colour within the lines 'on time,' or achieve numerous other early childhood milestones 'on time' led to a conclusion on the part of the multidisciplinary team at the clinic that her problems were quite profound. Her mother, Daphne, explained:

> When she was three, the [British] pediatrician said, 'We want you to register her in a school for the mentally retarded. We think she's mentally retarded, and we think that if you're going to stay in this country, she cannot go in the regular system.' And yet my daughter was laughing, telling jokes, playing with the kids in the neighbourhood ... and because she had such affect and such humour, I didn't feel at that time that there was significant retardation.
>
> It was really terrifying ... knowing there was something wrong, but never really believing that what we were told was the right reason.

As Daphne intimated, she herself *knew* that, despite her daughter's shortfall in terms of development according to age-appropriate norms, that somehow the professional label was inappropriate. Despite her doubts, however, Daphne continued to work with the clinic and the specialists, primarily because she knew *something* was making Melanie's life difficult and also because there was nowhere else to go for guidance.

A final consideration I would like to make that stems from Daphne's example is that often the signs and symptoms these children exhibited were indeed ambiguous and difficult to understand in terms of concrete diagnoses and treatments. Despite her conviction that the surgery was probably unnecessary, Daphne also admitted that at the time Melanie's problems did seem to be visual, because 'the fact [was] that she wasn't very good at colouring in the lines, or watching TV for a long time, or doing anything for a long time. And those are all clues that I should have picked up on, retrospectively.' Daphne's retrospective doubts over these early interventions, and her hindsight conviction that she ought to have known better, reflect comments made by other mothers as well. Repeatedly, mothers regretted that their children had waited too long for the 'proper' answers to their problems, and they wondered if some of the measures they had taken on behalf of their children had not perhaps done as much harm as good. Finally, they regretted that they had failed to acknowledge those doubts earlier, because by trusting in professional competence and authority, they had done their children and themselves a disservice.

Not every mother who encountered these early physiological assessments and interventions was willing to overcome her doubts about professional knowledge and comply with what she perceived to be invasive procedures. Clarissa, an Argentine woman living in Canada, has trained as a holistic practitioner. When physicians suggested that Julio's problems stemmed from hearing deficits, they also pushed for corrective surgery. As she stated, 'We started instead to take care of that in a natural way, and that took around two years, so eventually we knew that he had no problems hearing people.' Clarissa's response to the medical intervention was to substitute a natural or alternative one involving numerous essential oils, massage, and a restricted diet. Whether we accept that her treatment was effective, or if we are sceptical and presume that Julio's hearing problem never really existed and Clarissa's treatment simply offered a placebo effect, is moot. The point is that, had Clarissa relented and Julio's physicians prevailed, he would have undergone an invasive surgery for problems that were either resolved in less invasive ways or that ultimately proved unnecessary. Either way, the situation did not leave Clarissa feeling confident about the medical team's ability to identify and treat Julio's problems. In fact, after Julio's hearing problems were ruled out, his speech, attention, social, and learning problems persisted: the hearing deficit was just a smokescreen that delayed identification of Julio as a child with ADD.

In Clarissa's story we see an early example of a mother's resistance against professional claims to the truth about the child's problems. Clarissa, perhaps because of her training as a naturopath, expressed cynicism over and resistance to medical interventions almost from the beginning. At these very early stages, however, maternal resistance was quite rare. As we will see, as other mothers engaged in continued interactions with teachers, doctors, psychologists, and other professionals, they too began to offer up various strategies of resistance against professional opinions and treatments that they believed were incompetent or judgmental. But for now, most women, because they simply trusted the experts, or because they worried that they themselves might inadvertently be contributing to their children's problems, or simply because they could see no other way to obtain help for their children, continued to 'play' on the professional–maternal 'team.'

Psychosocial Smokescreens – Canadian Mothers

Sometimes, symptoms that were initially investigated as physiological problems led to interventions that were psychosocial in nature. Pat is a Canadian mother in this study. She is married and the mother of two children; she has a master's degree, but does not engage in paid work. When Pat's daughter Chloe was three years old, day care staff had pointed the family towards a hospital-based pediatric clinic for assessment and treatment of the child's poor bowel control (encopresis).[8] Pat began taking Chloe to the local children's hospital and attending a gastrointestinal (GI) clinic, which started her on a 'regimen that they do for encopresis' – high-fibre diet, suppositories, and enemas for constipation, and positive reinforcement protocols to be followed in the home. It has been noted that encopresis can be divided into physiological or emotional causal categories: the former is the result of 'lack of conscious control of the child,' while the latter may be related to 'an emotional disturbance such as Oppositional Defiant Disorder or a Conduct Disorder' (Anonymous, 2001b). Although these latter 'emotional disturbance' labels were never applied to Chloe, the treatment ap-

8 A number of the children discussed in this study, on both sides of the Atlantic, experienced bowel incontinence (encopresis), which often was framed by medical practitioners as 'immature' bowels. From mothers' narratives, these problems were caused by poor motor control or by the child's inattention and inability to stay 'on task' long enough to fully empty the bowel. In none of these children's assessments, however, did professionals consider attentional or impulsivity issues as possible causes.

proach for her encopresis moved swiftly from a physiological to a psychosocial focus. Pat explained: 'At the GI clinic – it's very difficult for a young child to be examined. She really reacted. So the doctor at the clinic suggested we needed her to see a psychologist – so we began. By kindergarten [at age 5] we were now going weekly ... Reflecting on that, I realize how much intervention that was. And they must have thought this was serious.' Indeed, the weekly sessions with the psychologist were coupled with regular appointments with the gastrointestinal (GI) clinic, and ongoing meetings with the clinic's pediatrician. In short, going to meetings and following regimes became a consuming occupation for Pat and her daughter Chloe. The time, and emotional strain of these meetings led Pat to move from full-time to part-time work: there was simply no way to accommodate 'how much intervention that was' and maintain full-time employment. As an additional burden, the psychosocial interventions did not remain focused on Chloe, but quickly shifted to include Pat as well:

And so we went for quite a few sessions. Terrible, terrible, terrible sessions. The kind of sessions that make my skin crawl when I think about it. Sitting in a room, people looking through two-way mirrors, your child spinning out of control, very difficult questions being asked of you, you're being attacked as a parent.

   Because all through this – you have to remember – as much as people want to understand, they're still seeing a young child, and they're still saying, 'Behaviour. Parenting. Why is this child acting out so much? Is there something wrong in the home?'

Pat also noted that the burden of dealing with these multiple professionals stemmed not only from the time demands of so much intervention and the emotional tension involved in attending sessions, being observed, and being asked invasive and difficult questions about her home and family life. In addition to these things, the role of interlocutor between professionals became another source of oppression for her, as each professional inevitably referred her to yet another specialist. She said: 'They asked these things *all* the time. Every group of them. And I have dealt with ADD with twenty or so different types and groups of people. And I have to, with each of them, be very patient and allow them to get past their initial conclusion that "child is acting out equals problem at home." I have to wait until I can gain credibility because somehow *this information* – that this is a little more complicated than that, that we are a *good* family – never quite makes it onto the records we bring with us.'

Pat's point is well taken. The chart, the file, the letter of referral – all of these professional documents ended up accompanying or preceding these children as they made their rounds from one professional to another. Rarely did a mother have an opportunity to see the contents of those files, and even more rarely did mothers express the feeling that they had been equal contributors to those records. However, all of these women were aware, or at least suspicious of the ways those documents operated to provide professionals with assessments, judgments, and suspicions about the women, the families, and the children involved – often before that professional had seen the child or the family. Thus, the work of mothers as knowledge brokers did not begin *anew* with each professional, but it became necessary to counter professionals' *prior* knowledge of the family, transmitted through interprofessional referral letters and the files that preceded mothers and children to each new professional's office.

In Canada, Pat experienced very early psychosocial interventions because of her child's physical problems. Scrutiny of the family's 'dynamics' rather than a focus on the child's behavioural 'problems' was a common difficulty in the Canadian group. Samantha and Amanda were guided at very early stages in their children's lives towards psychosocial interventions – because of attributes in the mothers. Both women were at the time sole parents, and they were referred by family physicians to see a social worker to 'sort out' the role of family breakdown in their children's problems. Although each of them described these sessions as invasive, unpleasant, and 'useless,' they went along with the physicians' suggestions. When I asked Samantha why she agreed to see a social worker, she said: 'Well, what else could I do? I said yes, just to keep them happy. I saw the worker a few times, let her check me out – it was stupid, but in the end that showed them that Justin wasn't like this because of me – it was something else. So it was worth it.'

Although it might be possible to consider Samantha as a victim in this situation – that she first had to prove herself free of blame before her son could obtain services – it is also possible to understand Samantha's motives as a canny reading of the situation. While on the one hand, she acquiesced and visited the therapist, on the other hand, she only continued the meetings long enough to prove her point and satisfy the doctor that she was a cooperative and caring mother. As we will see, very often women like Samantha, who, because of her low socioeconomic status, we might easily believe would be readily oppressed in professional–maternal interactions, are surprisingly resourceful. Perhaps poorer women are sceptical as a result of being more openly scrutinized by professionals, or perhaps they clearly see themselves as positioned outside of any rhetoric of professional–maternal 'partnership.' For whatever reasons, as we will see, poor women in both sites of the study often showed less willingness to comply, to play along, or to accept professional pronouncements and interventions than did more privileged mothers.

Psychosocial Smokescreens – British Mothers

In the preceding section, we heard from a few Canadian women who, during the early stages of their children's assessments, were themselves placed under the microscope of psychosocial professional scrutiny. As we heard in the last chapter, however, in England, psychosocial surveillance and scrutiny was not only a *possible* course of intervention, but it was often one of the first *probable* interventions. Regardless of the socioeconomic status and cultural capital of the mother or of the severity of the child's symptoms, British mothers of children experiencing difficulties were almost inevitably sent by family physicians to psychotherapeutic professionals. These psychotherapeutic interventions ranged from family observations to talking-therapy sessions to instruction on behaviour modification. Regardless, however, of the therapeutic approach, although the child's problems were what brought the mother into the therapy room, it often ended up that the mother and her mothering skills became the focus of intervention.

Moira and Rosalind, living in different areas of Britain, shared uncannily similar experiences. Sent to their family physicians by concerned child care workers, each woman was in turn referred to a local clinic for psychological counselling. Each spent several sessions being observed as she interacted with her child behind a one-way mirror. Rosalind explained that her referral came when things got out of hand after the birth of her second child. Not only was the child care centre complaining about Robbie's behaviour, but Rosalind herself was feeling overwhelmed. She described the intervention:

> He was two years old and three months, and just after she was born, and he was terrible. He loved her to death, squeezed her, kissed her too much, would always be doing things with her. Had to watch where she was

continually. I had to have eyes in the back of my head. I was worried for her safety because he would try and climb in the pram, and tip it over. He'd want to give her a kiss. I was desperate. I needed someone to help. I could not cope with this child, and I did not know why.

So they referred me to a child psychologist, and we all went. Robbie, myself, my husband, and the baby. And we were viewed between a two-way mirror. At the end of it, the psychologist said there was sibling rivalry. And I should stop favouring the baby. They didn't even take into consideration that he was like this before the baby was born.

As we have seen with other mothers, Rosalind's cry for help was not answered with meaningful assistance. Her information about her child prior to the observation was not considered or accepted by the professionals, and in turn, their assessment seemed neither credible nor particularly useful to her. In the end, her request for help was met with a response that not only failed to offer a solution, but only provided a criticism of her ability to parent in a loving way.

Moira's involvement with family therapy produced similar outcomes. In her case, she explained: 'The conclusion that this psychiatrist came to was that there was nothing wrong with Teddy. That, for some reason, I favoured the older child – the daughter. And that, uh, the problems weren't really with the father. It was me. And that my problem was that I didn't encourage him enough, and the area in which I was encouraging him – we had a star chart – was totally inappropriate. I needed to mother him more appropriately.'

For Moira as well, then, an intervention that began as an exploration of her child's difficulties quickly shifted to an indictment of her mothering. Interestingly, the star chart, identified by the psychiatrist as a site of inappropriate maternal encouragement, was a behaviour modification tool suggested to Moira by a psychologist at a local well-child clinic, in hopes of improving Teddy's behaviour at home. The psychiatrist's damning of the instrument provides one of the first explicit examples of a problem that mothers faced on both sides of the Atlantic and at all ages of their children's lives: interprofessional dissonance. Despite professional rhetoric that calls for interdisciplinary teams to assess and treat children with AD(H)D, very often, interprofessional interactions are characterized by scepticism, cynicism, or even hostility. Psychiatrists scorn psychological interventions, pediatricians doubt psychiatric insights, teachers ignore psychological protocols, and mothers find themselves situated at the crossroads of these conflicts. As a result, mothers are often confused by conflicting information at best, and found to be allied with the 'wrong' profession or idea at worst.

Conclusion

This chapter drew primarily on interview data with mothers about their social interactions related to mothering an AD(H)D child and painted a picture of the difficulties and uncertainties of mothering a very young child who is psychologically and socially different. I outlined some of the subjective experiences of the women as they began to integrate their very young children into the community and how they began to encounter discursive fields relating to mothers of children who are different. Reflecting 'common knowledge' that 'problem mothers have problem children,' very early interactions with family, friends, and the local community led mothers to believe that their 'bad' children acted as evidence of their 'bad' mothering. They understood through interactions with family, with friends, and with other mothers in the community that their children's problems were seen as symptomatic of maternal inadequacy, and the mothers felt they were perceived by their peers as poor disciplinarians, overreacting, or simply incompetent. They also began to experience some problems in terms of social isolation and stigmatization of both themselves and their children. These interactions often contributed to maternal feelings of inadequacy and guilt, and sometimes even led mothers to treat their children badly in order that they could show themselves to be trying to meet social expectations of 'good mothering.' In short, many of the mothers in this study encountered discourses of 'good mothering' in multiple ways in the community. Further, in response to these discursive fields, mothers offered a counternarrative about themselves as mothers by overtly disciplining their children, by choosing to withdraw from the world rather than experience the censure that accompanied public life, or by coming to doubt their own judgment and good intentions as mothers. As unpleasant as these experiences were, however, the negative encounters really intensified when these mothers began to seek help from experts in child development, pediatrics, and mental health.

There are several important points related to the ambiguity of mothers' early interactions with professionals. In these early stages, mothers approached medical and other early childhood practitioners in good faith expecting several things. First, they raised questions about their children assuming that their worries would be understood as legitimate and would result in action. Second, they initiated interactions with professionals or went along with professionally initiated assessments expecting that professionals would be competent, insightful, and helpful to the children. Third, they cooperated with the interventions of medical and helping professionals expecting to have their insights about their children included and that they would be consulted with as partners in a team that shared the best interests of the child as its focus. However, they soon learned to tailor these expectations.

In contradiction to discursive 'truths' about professionals as expert, knowledgeable, compassionate, and level-headed, mothers saw professionals make mistakes, misjudge situations, go down false avenues of exploration, impose incorrect treatments, and insist on seeing maternal pathology where none existed. Mothers also learned that discourses about professional–maternal partnership were misleading. They learned instead that often professionals did not treat maternal concerns honourably, nor were mothers treated as co-investigators and important contributors in the helping process. Rather, professionals responded by dismissing maternal concerns and insights out of hand or by turning them around in such a way that women who raised such concerns became themselves the focus of intervention. They learned that professionals believe that professional knowledge about what normal and abnormal childhood should look like is taken as superior to what a mother's knowledge about her own child might be. Further, they often learned through hard experience that these professional evaluations of the superiority of professional knowledge were simply not reliable. In other words, they came to believe that doctors, nurses, social workers, and early childhood specialists were fallible. Thus, mothers encountered discrediting and dismissal of their insights and concerns, while being expected to concede to professional insights and concerns, despite interventions that were ambiguous at best. Further, they engaged in these unsatisfying maternal–professional interactions within the framework of conflicting evidence in the medical discourse and the popular media.

A second issue that has been raised in this chapter is how professional–maternal interactions are heavily imbued with presumptions of maternal fault. When the children in this study came under the scrutiny of medical and psychiatric and psychological practitioners, inevitably, the mothers' parenting styles, marital status, disciplinary abilities, or insight into their own children were considered to be pathological. These themes recurred constantly in the maternal narratives: mothers' limitless culpability, sole responsibility, and working at odds with others who profess to know best. Whether with parents, teachers, friends, doctors, or psy sector workers, mothers struggled with other people who passed judgment while at the same time refusing responsibility. In this sense, non-mothers hold all the cards: they are in a position to offer advice, pass judgment, and they do so with relative impunity because mothers – and mothers alone – are seen as bearing the burden both of cause and cure.[9]

In the story of Samantha, the woman who was sent to a social worker because she was young and divorced, we gain our first insight into a third theme – the intersections of class, cultural capital, and women's resistance among these mothers of children with AD(H)D. Because of professional assumptions about Samantha (and Amanda's) personal and moral faults, medical practitioners immediately moved to a position of intervention and surveillance. On the other hand, Samantha spent just enough time in therapy to satisfy professionals that she was really an 'okay' mother, so that she could push for a more appropriate intervention. A number of theorists have noted that professional intervention and surveillance is more onerous and imbued with presumptions about the pathology of women who are disadvantaged (Knowles, 1996; Baines et al., 1991; Abramowitz, 1996; Arnup, 1994; Fraktman, 1998; Fraser, 1994). Caroline Knowles, for example, states that 'not all families lead equally scrutinized lives, but the lives of the poor are much more open to observation and intervention' (Knowles, 1996: 72–3). Other theorists, building on the work of Bourdieu, have argued that some women are able to draw on cultural capital, comprising material resources, educational qualifications, available time, information about the educational system, social confidence, and a sense of entitlement and assertiveness to mitigate maternal–professional oppression (Reay, 1998).

Samantha's reactions complicate these claims, providing more in-

---

9 Perhaps this is why the teacher–mother relationship ultimately becomes more stridently adversarial than with most other professionals. Unlike pediatricians, psychiatrists, speech therapists, occupational therapists, or psychologists, teachers must rise to the responsibilities of providing day-to-day care to these children, and they thus are less able to absolutely leave mothers to bear the full burden of discipline or responsibility. In addition, teachers, who hold lower status in the hierarchy of professionals that manage children and children's problems, are more open to challenge by mothers as they interact with their children's teachers on a day-to-day basis.

sight into how poor and marginalized women are not only victims of
professional scrutiny, but how they also might act to obtain meaningful
assistance while avoiding professional mistreatment. Samantha is the
young (twenty-five years old) mother of Jordan, who at the time of our
interview was eight years old. She has been divorced, is remarried, and
works full-time as a house-cleaner. Her roots and her present socioeconomic status are firmly working class. When Samantha told me her
story, I was struck by how, despite her youth, lack of education, and
family background, she managed to avoid professional censure and to
obtain services and treatment for her son that other, more socially
advantaged women in the study were not able to access. Not only was
Samantha one of the few women in the Canadian study who managed
to get her son into a private school for children with special educational
needs, but she was the only one who was successful in her appeal to
have the government pay his tuition.

A fourth theme that this chapter foreshadows is the ambiguity of
what can be termed 'normal' or 'natural' in developing children and
what professional understandings of those two terms are. When initiating mothers went to professionals, they were told that behaviour that
was troubling was within the range of 'normal' busy-ness for the age of
the child or 'normal' masculine behaviour for boys. However, when
professionals did the initiating, the litany of milestones and markers
that constitute 'normal' development in early childhood came to operate as evidence of an exceptionally broad range of pathological characteristics. Indeed, often those presumed pathological characteristics not
only became the temporary focus of medical and psychiatric intervention, but they involved some quite invasive procedures (actual or threatened surgery) and diagnoses (mental retardation or cerebral palsy) that
were ultimately of little or no value to the child.

A final theme that we can draw out of the stories in this chapter
relates to the relationship of professionals to mothers, and to one another. More often than not, pre- and playschool staff alerted mothers to
differences between the children and their peers and suggested that
mothers have the problem checked out by a physician. In turn, the
family physician would then send mothers and their children to a
pediatrician, a physiotherapist, a psychiatrist, or a psychologist. Often,
mothers found themselves under the care of several professionals at
the same time. This route of identifying a problem and initiating
interprofessional follow-up, we will see, was repeated again and again
for the women in this study. Inevitably, mothers acted in these sce-

narios as interlocutors between professionals, conveying day care workers' suspicions to medical personnel, psychologists' assessments to pediatricians, and specialists' findings and suggestions to educators and family doctors. As already shown, however, the role of interlocutor was neither straightforward nor rewarding; mothers in these scenarios often found themselves unwittingly caught in the cross-hairs of interprofessional conflict and competition.

In Britain and Canada alike, then, most mothers reported that, even as infants and toddlers, their children were 'different' – energetic, active, difficult to settle, difficult to manage, destructive, or socially problematic. As well, many of these mothers began, even when the children were young, to encounter difficulties in their communities, their families, and with medical and psy sector professionals. Nonetheless, most mothers in Canada and Britain indicated that these problems really only escalated to the point of being burdensome or cause for concern as their children entered into more formal day care and educational settings. The following chapter conveys the experiences of mothers as their children entered the school systems and their children's problems began to deepen.

In this chapter, mothers' narratives have been used as a first step towards developing a feminist discursive ethnography of mothering a child with AD(H)D. In this chapter, I also outlined some of the connections between mothers' experiences and professional and lay discourses of maternal blame, discursive claims about the legitimacy of professional over maternal knowledge, and the truth claims that operate within the controversy that surrounds AD(H)D. In the following chapter, I will examine mothers' stories against professional discursive materials, drawing direct links between the operations of texts and the experiences of mothers in identifying and assessing children who are deemed to be problematic.

5 Ideals and Actualities in Identification and Assessment

Research has shown that a skillful investigation usually involves a team approach which typically includes the parents and child, school personnel (e.g. teacher, learning specialist, resource teacher, counselor, etc.), the child's physician, a psychologist, and relevant individuals (e.g. social workers, occupational therapists) ... [and] ... involves observations, interviews, rating scales, questionnaires, checklists, classroom observation, and formal and informal testing.

Pat Young, Psychologist
'Childhood Assessment of AD(H)D'
Alberta Parent Quarterly, Spring, 1997

Diagnosis should be based on a timely, comprehensive assessment conducted by a child/adolescent psychiatrist or a paediatrician with expertise in ADHD. It should also involve children, parents and carers and the child's school, and take into account cultural factors in the child's environment.

'Guidance on the use of Methylphenidate for ADHD'
National Institute for Clinical Excellence
National Health Service, 2000

Each of these quotations, one from a Canadian professional working in the field of ADD who is directing her comments to parents seeking services, and the other from National Health Services guidelines provided to U.K. health and psy sector professionals, offer an idealized depiction of how assessment for AD(H)D should unfold. As well, each implicitly responds to criticisms that occur in both professional and lay discourse about AD(H)D. In short, these texts argue against a number of circulating critiques and assumptions in both professional and lay discourse relating specifically to AD(H)D and more generally to the psychiatric labelling and medication of children.

The following sections first examine some of the discursive problems that are argued against by idealized assessment discourse. Following a feminist approach in understanding the discursive fields attached to AD(H)D, I then examine mothers' narratives about their children's assessments. In this way, I play women's lived experiences and their readings of the discursive practices related to AD(H)D against the truth claims of professionals.

Realness Issues

The first problem that the idealized assessment truth claims respond to is what I will call the 'realness' issue. By this I mean that with the category of AD(H)D, physicians, psychologists, specialists, and educationists must do more than matter-of-factly diagnose the disorder and prescribe treatment in order to convince mothers of the legitimacy of an AD(H)D diagnosis for their troubled child. Rather, because there is no physical test that can be reliably used to diagnose AD(H)D, because the diagnostic criteria themselves are simply 'abnormal' levels of 'normal' childhood behaviour, and because of the controversy over Ritalin in both Canada and Britain, practitioners must present their diagnostic strategies as incontestable. As the quotations above exemplify, this incontrovertibility is accomplished through reliance on discourses of interprofessional consensus and scientific objectivity in the 'typical' identification and assessment of AD(H)D.

Interprofessional Consensus

In professional accounts that address the 'realness' issue, not only is the idealized diagnostic procedure portrayed as the site of seamless interprofessional agreement on the diagnostic *criteria* but, the claim goes, a good assessment must also include interprofessional agreement on the diagnostic *process*. Thus, members of multiple disciplines must be seen not only to agree on the problematic nature of a broad range of symptoms in a child who will be diagnosed with either ADD or ADHD. In addition to being observed (and observable) by a wide array of professionals, these symptoms must also be seen to occur across all aspects of the child's life. Finally, reaching consensus on the child's condition must be accomplished through the use of standardized and objective measures.

As discussed throughout this chapter, this idealized form of assessment – legitimated by a representation of assessment as interdisciplinary, consensual, and concerning all aspects of the child's life – is largely a fiction. Nonetheless, it is a fiction that serves as a counter-narrative to various critiques occurring within professional discourse and in the lay literature about AD(H)D.

In the professional discourse of both countries, tremendous controversy persists over the foundational question of AD(H)D's legitimacy as a diagnosis. For example, the British Psychological Society has warned its constituent members 'not to follow the Canadian and U.S. practice of applying the label attention deficit hyperactivity disorder (ADHD) to such a wide variety of behaviors in children' (cited in McConnell, 1997). The report goes on to say, 'The idea that children who do not attend or who do not sit still in school have a mental disorder is not entertained by most British clinicians' (ibid.). An examination of the archives of the government-sponsored SENCO Forum (http://forum.ngfl.gov.uk/majordomo-archives/senco-forum/), an on-line discussion list for British special education coordinators,[1] provides evidence of considerable scepticism among these educational professionals regarding ADHD.

In 2001, fewer than ten articles or threads specifically relating to ADHD were run on the SENCO list while literally dozens occurred concerning dyslexia, oppositional defiant disorder, and conduct disorder. Of the relatively few postings relating to ADHD, almost all were sceptical, offering comments to the effect that vision problems, emotional and behavioural problems, or discipline problems are the 'real' diagnosis and that the ADHD label is unnecessary and to be avoided.

In the Canadian context, although most relevant professional groups *officially* accept the 'realness' of AD(H)D, a number of individual professionals have made it clear that they are unconvinced of the legitimacy of the label. Canadian psychiatrists Felix Yaroshevsky and David Schatsky contend that the disorder is more often than not simply the

---

1 A Special Education Need Coordinator (SENCO) is an education professional who works at the school or local education authority level to organize the assessment and treatment of a child who requires special assistance in learning. Hence, they act as the interface between teachers, school psychologists, administration, and parents in dealing with special needs children.

behavioural problems of children whose families are in crisis in one way or another; their remedy is family therapy and education (Foss, 1999; Schatsky and Yaroshevsky, 1997). Still more polemical is the campaign of the Church of Scientology's Citizens Commission on Human Rights, who used a number of medical practitioners' testimonies in a brief presented to the Canadian federal government in its investigation into the use of Ritalin. This group's position is in keeping with the antipsychiatry movement: they propose that the AD(H)D label is neither overzealously nor inappropriately applied, but that it 'is a total, 100 percent fraud' (Baughman, 1999).

Again, the legitimating deployment in professional discourse introduced in this section – that a 'good' diagnosis will involve interdisciplinary assessors – responds in many ways to the above controversies in professional discourse over AD(H)D. By presenting the 'typical/ideal' diagnostic procedure as a consensual process, the actual intraprofessional scepticism over the label is elided. Instead, the image of multiple professionals agreeing on the legitimacy of the label of AD(H)D for a *particular* child operates to obscure the reality that, in both Canada and Britain, many professionals fail to agree on the legitimacy of the label of AD(H)D for *any* child.

Standardized Measures

As we have seen, AD(H)D is a diagnosis that many people, both lay and professional, believe is little more than a fabrication. Thus, a great deal of clinical discourse focuses on ways to shore up diagnostic legitimacy through attempts to contain the label to a discreet and undeniable group of symptoms and to avoid the sloppy or inappropriate assessment of children with AD(H)D. The call for a multidisciplinary assessment can be seen as a response to this scepticism about AD(H)D. It can also be seen as an example of a more historical and macro-level tradition within the helping professions of shoring up claims to diagnostic and professional legitimacy through the ongoing search for 'better' (more accurate, reliable, standardized, and irrefutable) instruments of measurement.

Historians of the psy sector have noted that the attempt to perfect assessment techniques is part of a long-standing and continuing strategy of mental health professionals in rebutting critiques of psychiatric categorization. David Armstrong (1983) describes how psychiatry in

Britain during the late nineteenth and early twentieth centuries relied on broad-based categories of 'abnormality' that derived from surveys of large populations. In response to critiques of the resulting population-level (and often class-based) diagnostic categories, he notes, there has been an increasing trend within psychiatry towards the personalization and particularization of the patient's problems. He clarifies that in earlier times 'the psychiatric judgment of normality or abnormality had been a function of external criteria'; however, now the ideal psychiatric assessment is one in which 'the psychiatrist could freely enter the mind of the patient and judge what "normality" might look like for the individual patient' (1983). Thus, he concludes, psychiatry's earlier reliance on nosographic categories has given way to more individualistic and intimate ways of determining the normal from the abnormal, typically through psychotherapy.

Conversely, in psychology, in response to the vagueness that arises from the lack of physical indicators in most behavioural or emotional problems, standardized technologies in the form of pencil-and-paper testing have become the preferred method of choice for selecting and identifying individual problems (Rose, 1985). In psychology, then, standardized testing devices, inter-rater reliability, and universal categories are now held to be the 'gold standard' where assessment is concerned. Finally, in special education, the tradition of psychology has been maintained; with learning difficulties in particular, a long, complex battery of assessment tools have been devised during the twentieth century to identify 'the exact nature of the problem ... as precisely as possible' (Sigmon, 1987: 51).

Regardless, however, of the subdiscipline of the psy sector, the push for professional legitimation has resulted in the construction of increasingly 'improved' tools and methods to 'properly' assess and label a widening range of human behaviours and attributes. In this sense, the call for a multidisciplinary assessment for AD(H)D can be seen not only as a call for caution in performing an assessment, but stands also as an example of the use of 'improved assessment technology' discourse in legitimating the psychiatrization of difference (Castel et al., 1982). It also provides an intimation of interprofessional conflict in managing personal problems – although the call for multidisciplinary assessments portrays a seamless face between the subdisciplines, a great deal of friction exists between these fields in terms of both methods and philosophy.

A final consideration relating to 'realness' and the idealized assessment procedures described above concerns the recommendation that professionals' observations should include the home, the school, the family, and the culture. This recommendation indirectly addresses a central critique of the anti-AD(H)D argument – that AD(H)D is not a biological, neurological, or psychological condition, but that it is merely a problem of poor parenting, poor teaching, or a culture that is overly stressful and demanding of children. By offering an idealized assessment that presumably encompasses all aspects of the child's life, the critique that AD(H)D is really just a 'local' problem in the home or in the classroom is effaced. In short, the truth claims embedded in idealized assessment discourse present a hidden argument that AD(H)D is a 'real' rather than a 'social' problem.

In the above section, I outlined some ways that the idealized assessment process responds to controversies over the 'realness' of AD(H)D and, hence, to the legitimacy of assessing and treating it as a disorder. I would also argue that idealized professional discourse concerning identifying and assessing ADD is constructed in such a way as to allay parental concerns about the disorder's legitimacy and, thus, to preempt parental concerns about professional overreadiness to both label and medicate children who are different. The following section examines how the idealized assessment form speaks to internal professional debates concerning 'ownership' of AD(H)D in each of the national contexts. Here my analysis focuses not so much on whether AD(H)D exists, but rather which professionals are most legitimately positioned to handle its assessment and treatment.

Ownership Issues

As mentioned above, professional claims to legitimacy rest on interprofessional consensus and on discourses of scientific, objective, and standardized assessment tools. In addition, the legitimacy of AD(H)D as a diagnosis relies on claims of clinical legitimacy. In other words, professionals who handle AD(H)D must also convince patients and their guardians that their professional status entitles them to make judgments about the child and about the disorder. This requirement of 'good practice' leads to a second recurring professional and lay problem, which I will call the 'ownership' issue. The 'ownership' issue can be broken down into two related concerns: the first relates to controversies over who 'drives' the exponential growth of AD(H)D, and the second questions which profession is best positioned to diagnose and treat AD(H)D.

Driving the AD(H)D Machine

Lay literatures in both countries frequently and virulently hold parents responsible for children's AD(H)D-related problems. The implication is that, because they are overburdened by conflicts between paid labour and family labour in dual-income homes, leading stressed lives, or are simply incompetent as disciplinarians and caregivers, parents 'drive the ADD machine' (Anonymous, 1999a, 1999b; Browne, 2000a, 2000b; Foss, 1999; Jenish, 2000; Rees, 1998c, 1998d).

These criticisms are also located within professional discourse on AD(H)D. In Britain, where acceptance of the diagnostic category of ADHD is more tenuous, there is considerable professional discourse that holds parents and teachers as culpable for these children's differences. Even in Canada, however, where ADD is theoretically understood to be a neurobiological disorder, some Canadian professionals continue to blame parents and teachers for children's ADD-related problems. For example, Canadian pediatrician Gabor Maté has written a book and undertaken a nation-wide speaking tour to promote the notion that although ADD does indeed have a biological basis, inadequate infant bonding and poor early childhood parenting results in underdevelopment of the frontal cortex and decreased production of dopamine (Maté, 2000a, 2000b). His suggested treatment, again reflecting a presumption of deficiency or pathology in parents, is retooled parenting skills, a more child-centred lifestyle, and marriage therapy (ibid.).

Presumptions about who 'drives' the diagnostic rates of AD(H)D is not only limited to whether parents 'cause' it. Rather, it also involves the suspicion that some professionals are prone to push the diagnosis. Media coverage in both sites has offered competing claims about the 'culprits' behind their country's increasing rates of AD(H)D diagnoses and Ritalin prescriptions. Some have blamed teachers who push for medication in the classroom in lieu of adequate staffing and discipline in the schools (Cohen, 1999; Mack, 2000; Rees, 1998a, 1998b), or because an increased focus on academic excellence has reduced opportunities for children to 'run off some steam' during play times in the schools (Anonymous, 1998c). Other claimants note that physicians and psychiatrists, because of their medical education and their symbiotic relationship with pharmaceutical companies, are too ready to prescribe psycho*pharmaceuticals* when psycho*therapeutical* interventions would be more appropriate (Anonymous, 1999b; Foss, 1999). As discussed in the introductory chapter of this book, such criticisms of the professions are not limited to popular media. Indeed, antipsychiatry professionals and critical social researchers have also provided fuel for the debates that circulate in the lay literature.

In the claim that a good AD(H)D assessment will necessary be the result of a cohesive and flawless intraprofessional process, the very public debate over who is responsible for the increasing rates of diagnosis in both cultures is somewhat effaced. If a wide range of professionals can agree on symptoms, and can further agree that these symptoms have little to do with the specifics of school or of home, the question of whether parents, teachers, pediatricians, psychiatrists, special educators, or psychologists are the 'source' of burgeoning diagnostic rates becomes moot. Rather, the conception of AD(H)D as a disorder that is 'caused' by, or is a label that is 'sought' by, one group of another is repositioned; AD(H)D instead becomes a set of characteristics that, without regard to context, would be clinically recognized by any parent or professional as pathological.

Intraprofessional Conflict

In addition to eliding the question of who is 'behind' the increasing rates of AD(H)D labelling, the call for interdisciplinary agreement in assessment also addresses the larger question of which kind of profession should be involved in assessing *any* childhood problems. AD(H)D is conceptualized as a disorder of childhood and is also a psychological and psychiatric diagnostic category. However, the professionals who are involved in both Canada and Britain in assessing (let alone treating) children with AD(H)D are limited neither to childhood specialists nor to psychiatric and psychological specialists, and include educators, educational specialists, special needs professionals, and general medical practitioners. As a result, considerable friction exists between the professions as to which kind of practitioner is best positioned to understand and assess problems of behaviour and learning in children. Further, it is apparent that professional struggles over 'ownership' of the labelling process of these children differ between Britain and Canada.

Intraprofessional Relations in Britain

In Britain, the Nation Health Service (NHS) has funded a major study and provided guidelines to professionals on the use of Ritalin for children identified with ADHD (NICE, 2000). This report has been circulated by the government to a wide array of professionals, including medical and nursing directors in hospitals, all general practitioners in England and Wales, all consultant child and adolescent psychologists in England and Wales, chief pharmacists, NHS directors in Wales and England, community health councils, representative bodies for health services, professional organizations, and royal colleges (including psychiatry). It should be noted that educators, SENCOs, school psychologists, school administrators, and teachers are not included in this distribution.

Researchers have noted that there is a historical rivalry between medical and educational professionals in England with particular regards to children with special educational needs (Cooper, 1998). Specifically, with the 1993 Education Act, 'educationists (teachers and psychologists) gained legal ascendancy over medics in the decision making process with regards to the treatment of children ... with EBD [Emotional and Behavioural Difficulties]' (Cooper, 1998: 128). This victory by 'educationists' is evidenced in the DFEE's Code of Practice, which clearly places the assessment and labelling process in the hands of educators, who are only encouraged, rather than mandated, to seek medical advice to assist them in making their assessment decisions (DFEE, 1994a: 52–67). Additionally, the children's conditions that the Code of Practice presumes medical personnel should provide input on are, quite simply, medical, and include such things as heart disease, rheumatoid disorders, hemophilia, and diabetes. Conversely, such concerns as learning problems, emotional and behavioural problems, perceptual problems, and specific and non-specific learning disabilities are clearly laid out in the code as falling under the bailiwick of the teacher, the school psychologist, or a private specialist in psychological and/or learning problems (DFEE, 1994a). Thus, the first level of intraprofessional conflict in Britain is seen between 'educationists' and medical personnel, and this conflict is supported through official policies relating to the assessment of children with special educational needs.

In Britain, there are additional arenas of intraprofessional conflict relating to the assessment and treatment of ADHD. These occur between general medical practitioners and pediatric and psychiatric specialists. Again, the NICE report guidelines specify that treatment with

Ritalin 'should only be initiated by child and adolescent psychiatrists, or pediatricians with expertise in ADHD [while] continued prescribing and monitoring may be performed by a general practitioner, under shared care arrangements with specialists' (NICE, 2000: 3). Thus, the second level of British intraprofessional conflict occurs within the various branches of medicine, with child psychiatrists and pediatricians holding ascendancy, and general physicians' roles limited to writing prescriptions and doing maintenance work once the initial assessment and treatment has been made.

A third level of British intraprofessional dissonance occurs between psychiatrists and psychologists. In Great Britain, the psy sector follows a psychoanalytic tradition whereas in North America, psychology enjoys ascendance (Cooper, 1998; Burman, 1994). As noted earlier, the psychological model of understanding difference centres on measuring and testing within established categories of normal and not-normal, while the psychiatric tradition leads to understanding the traits, idiosyncrasies, fears, and repressions of individuals (Armstrong, 1983; Burman, 1994; Castel et al., 1982; Rose, 1985). Thus, the British psy sector climate favours psychiatry's idiosyncratic and therapeutic interventions over psychology's testing and labelling strategies.

It is apparent that pre-existing bifurcations between educationists and medical practitioners, medical specialists and medical generalists, and psychologists and psychiatrists in Britain occur at the level of the individual professional, the professional association, and public policy. As a result, this may explain how British arguments for an ADHD assessment process that would rely on interdisciplinary agreement are almost destined to fail.

Intraprofessional Relations in Canada
Perhaps because in Canada AD(H)D is a more or less accepted diagnostic category, or perhaps because of differing special needs policy between Canada and Britain, there is little discourse at the professional association or public policy level to illuminate intraprofessional conflict. However, a lack of official acrimony does not mean that cooperation reigns between the professions in Canada. At the very least, the assessment scene in Alberta can be characterized by intraprofessional confusion. In fact, a recent governmental review of special education in Alberta, contributed to by educational, mental health, and health and welfare officials, as well as a wide range of advocacy groups from across the province, has revealed several problems in special needs

identification that relate to intraprofessional miscommunication (Alberta Learning, 2000d). These problems include fragmentation of services between different agencies, lack of information between different professionals relating to a particular child, and lack of communication between provincial ministries of Health, Education, and Mental Health concerning policies for special needs identification and intervention. Thus, intraprofessional miscommunication is seen as endemic from the level of local practitioners and agencies right up to the provincial ministerial level.

Canada, influenced by its proximity to the United States, is strongly immersed in the legacy of developmental and behavioural psychology, where tests, measures, and classification systems have emerged to organize and regulate populations (Armstrong, 1983; Burman, 1994; Rose, 1985, 1990). One might expect, then, that ADD assessments in Canada would fall primarily under the auspices of psychologists. Indeed, a great number of AD(H)D-related service providers in the Calgary area do include staff psychologists or learning specialists. On the other hand, because the primary treatment is medication, professionals who are able to write prescriptions continue to fill a central role in the assessment procedure. In Canada, only psychiatrists, pediatricians, and physicians are able to write prescriptions for methylphenidate (Ritalin). Thus, despite the psychology-based 'culture' of assessment in Canada, the prescription-writing requirements of treating AD(H)D mean that pediatricians, general physicians, and psychiatrists must be involved in the AD(H)D assessment process. Additionally, even though educators (including teachers, resource specialists, and school psychologists) might see themselves as ideally equipped to provide children with assessments that relate to learning concerns, restrictive school funding and staffing shortages mean that, more often than not, medical practitioners 'own' the process.

In Calgary, as noted earlier, CBE policy asserts that the school principal or her or his designate must ensure not only that children are identified, but that they will be assessed and appropriately placed within the system (CBE, 1999a). Hence, one might reasonably expect that, unlike the United Kingdom, where 'educationists' are automatically excluded from 'owning' the assessment process through NHS policy, Canadian teachers, resource specialists, and school psychologists might play a central role in student assessments. In practice, however, many barriers exist to the educational management of assessments in Calgary. As Sally Peters (a pseudonym), a school psychologist on the CBE's centralized system resource team, which coordinates CBE assessments, acknowledged: 'I think it's a struggle. Policy recognizes that teachers and specialists need to identify Special Needs students, but because we no longer have the resources, we have to make compromises between the ideal and the interests of kids. So, we'll send a family to a pediatrician or a private clinic in order to speed things along' (personal communication, 2001). Hence, although the *ideal* assessment (in light of CBE policy) involves the work of a teacher, a resource specialist, an educational psychologist, or a school psychologist, the typical assessment is done by an outside professional and may not even include consultation with educational professionals.

Although there is no official CBE policy on referrals, according to Dr Peters, parents are usually sent to outside professionals for assessment in this order of preference:

1 A pediatrician specializing in AD(H)D.
2 The attention clinic at the Calgary Learning Centre, which, although a private fee-for-service clinic, is housed in a CBE school for children with learning difficulties. The clinic offers a multidisciplinary team that bases their assessments on data from school specialists, teachers, and parents.
3 For more complex cases, to Alberta Children's Hospital, which also operates within a multidisciplinary framework, involving data and observations relating to child, family, and school.

Dr Peters acknowledges that for pediatricians specializing in AD(H)D, and for the Children's Hospital, the time on a waiting list can be well over a year. She also notes that the $90 per hour costs (averaging $1,000 to $1,200 per assessment) of centres like the Learning Centre are prohibitive and that, even though the centre does offer some sliding-scale consultations, many parents are dissuaded by the costs and the waiting time. Further, she acknowledges that the move from idealized assessment to simple medical advice does occur, noting that 'in the interests of the child, we may move to "but *your* family doctor can do this, too" if all that is needed is a competent medication trial' (Peters, personal communication, 2001).

Thus, although educationists might prefer to refer to a pediatrician with AD(H)D expertise, or to a multidisciplinary clinic or hospital team, pragmatism often results in referrals to less 'expert' medical practitioners, for the very reason that they can administer Ritalin trials and titration. As a result, Calgary AD(H)D assessments are often handled by (at best) a pediatrician specializing in AD(H)D, or simply any pediatrician. In either case, consultation with teachers, other educational professionals, or psychologists rarely occurs.

Not only do assessments often occur without professional collaboration; sometimes interprofessional disagreement plays a role in the Calgary professional scene. I have spoken with a number of psychological assessment providers in Calgary about their views on assessment and treatment for Canadian children, and some expressed criticism over the 'typical' Calgary assessment.

Pat Young, for example, is a chartered psychologist who heads up Alberta Attention Deficit and Learning Disabilities Services, a private clinic offering assessment and intervention. She claims that fully one-third of her clientele are patients who, upon her reassessment, have been improperly treated with Ritalin. Young claims that physicians, who work under the umbrella of public health care (and hence are more likely to be seen by parents with limited budgets), do not assess adequately, because they do not go into the classroom, examine school records, observe in the home, or consult with other professionals. Further, she states that medical professionals, because of their pharmaceutical and medical training, tend to see medication as the best (or only) solution and thus tend to medicate too readily and too heavily. In short, she finds the medical approach to AD(H)D assessment is not only inadequate, but sometimes downright incorrect. Her criticsm is not limited to medical professionals, however. She also believes that educators shortchange girls when it comes to assessment referrals, because female children do not pose the same behavioural or disciplinary problems in the classroom that boys do. In other words, she feels that educators and medical professionals both fail to provide adequate identification and assessment services for troubled children (Young, 1997; personal communication, 2000).

Conversely, medical specialists in the field of AD(H)D assessment may not be ready to count psychological service providers as part of the AD(H)D 'team.' The developmental clinic at the Alberta Children's Hospital, for example, provides parents with a handout on attention deficit disorder that includes a list of Calgary area community resources relating to AD(H)D. The list includes telephone numbers, addresses, and a brief outline of services provided by a number of medical professionals and parent support groups (Alberta Children's Hospital, 1993). However, it offers only terse reference to psychological assessment providers, under the rubric of 'private therapists,' stating that interested parents can 'consult the yellow pages or contact the Psychologists Association of Alberta' which incidentally is located in another city (Edmonton) in Alberta.[2] Interestingly, the hospital's list provides no listing or association contact for psychiatrists.

In Calgary, then, although there is no official policy that would necessarily privilege one group of professionals over another in the handling of children's AD(H)D assessments, funding arrangements, intraprofessional fragmentation and lack of communication, and interprofessional competition operate to create considerable confusion in the AD(H)D assessment process.

In the above sections, I outlined how an idealized identification and assessment process operates to discredit both professional and lay criticisms of AD(H)D, and how professional discourse and practice in each site can complicate the probability of achieving an assessment along the lines of the idealized recommendation. As mothers' stories will show, there were considerable gaps in children's actual assessments in each country. Finally, I show how these discrepancies between the ideal depiction and the actual assessment played out in ways that are specific to each site. The balance of this chapter, discusses mothers' descriptions of how diagnosis actually occurred for the children in this study.

Identification and Assessment in Practice

As noted in Chapter 3, although a number of children evidenced physical or behavioural differences prior to entering school, for the vast majority of the children in both countries, these differences were only formally investigated once the children entered school. In each instance, the child's classroom teacher was the professional who made the first suggestion for a general assessment because of classroom-related problems.[3]

Ideally, it would be helpful to provide the reader with information on how old each child was when first identified, how long the assessment took, and at what age the final diagnosis was conferred. Ideals, how-

2 In itself, the use of the term 'private therapists' is somewhat elitist, and could be a deterrent to individuals for whom payment of fees not covered by medicare would be a barrier. In fact, many psychologists' services are covered through employer plans, and are not 'private.'
3 Some teachers (particularly in Canada) went so far as to suggest that assessment should focus on ADD.

ever, rarely find their way into practice. In this group of children, the range for receiving an actual diagnosis was between five and fourteen years of age. However, the length of time it took between the child first being identified as requiring AD(H)D testing and the receipt of an actual diagnosis is very difficult to guess at because of the uncertainty of professionals themselves over the label and over its application to a particular child. Indeed, trying to 'fix' the actual identification of AD(H)D for the children in this study was itself no straightforward matter. In some children's cases, despite receiving an official diagnosis, the mothers remained ambivalent as to whether their children 'really' have AD(H)D. In other situations, the mothers were convinced that their children have AD(H)D but have in fact only received 'official' confirmation that their children are 'borderline.' Even using a child's Ritalin prescription as evidence or disconfirmation of AD(H)D was problematic. In both the Canadian and the British group, there were a small number of diagnosed children who had actually been coded or 'statemented' as special needs students because of their AD(H)D and who had nonetheless never been on medication.[4]

The following section provides insight into the varied ways that the legitimating concerns, such as interprofessional consensus on the diagnosis, interprofessional communication and cooperation in the diagnostic process, observations of the symptoms across multiple settings, and standardized testing procedures, actually played out in the labelling process of Canadian and British children.

Canadian Mothers' Experiences of Interprofessional Consensus

Even in Canada, where theoretically AD(H)D is a well-established and accepted diagnosis, mothers and their children encountered lengthy and complicated assessment procedures, conflicting opinions from various professionals, miscommunications about their children's problems, and a pervasive professional presumption of family pathology as the basis for children's symptoms. A number of children were told by one

---

4 The reader might recall that in describing the sample, I claimed Canadian children averaged less time in obtaining a diagnosis than did British children. This claim was based on parents' self-report: at the beginning of each interview I asked parents how long their children had been diagnosed and at what age their children had first been identified by professionals as problematic. However, when analysing the transcripts, it becomes less clear exactly how those numbers are derived.

professional that they had AD(H)D, only to attend a second or third professional for difficulties, and be told that their problems were not the result of having AD(H)D after all. Pat's story provides a good example of a lack of professional consensus on a child's diagnosis.

Pat's daughter Chloe was diagnosed with ADD at seven years of age. Her diagnosis was confirmed throughout her repeated medical interventions by the follwoing individuals: a pediatrician, a child psychiatrist, a developmental psychologist, a multidisciplinary medical and psychiatric team as an outpatient to the psychiatric care centre of the Alberta Children's Hospital, and ultimately, by a community psychiatrist, who managed her ongoing care. When Chloe was eleven, she had a mental health crisis of such concern to the multiple professionals who knew her that she was admitted late one night into a residential program in the psychiatric unit of the Alberta Children's Hospital, called 'W Cluster.' The next morning, Pat arrived back at the hospital. She described what she encountered:

> So now, what's the next battle? They said, 'This child is very bright, we don't understand why she is here. It must be because she had too much Ritalin. We are going to take her off everything, then everything will be fine. Maybe she's not ADD after all.' And so they did.
>
> So I suggested to this particular psychiatrist that he should perhaps speak to the other one (in the community) that had been treating her for the past three years. He did not do that for one month. We were in the hospital full time for two months. It took four weeks before the hospital psychiatrist called the other one for a consult. And with flippant comments like, 'Well, we don't really see any ADD.' And eventually he did diagnose her. So now we're talking five diagnoses of ADD. Always wanting to see behaviour. Always not recognizing the complexity of things that can also be the result of ADD.

Chloe thus, despite receiving at least four previous confirmations of an ADD diagnosis, under observation in a new setting with a new set of professionals, had yet again to 'prove' the appropriateness of the label. Further, as Pat's last comments intimate, with each new professional encountered, the focus once again is on the child's behaviour, and as a result, falls back on the assumption that the child's problems are 'really' the manifestation of psychological (read: familial) problems.

Another example of professional lack of consensus, and the professional tendency to fall back on psychiatric and familial explanations for children's problems, can be seen in the experiences of Samantha and her son Justin. In October, when Justin was five years old and in kindergarten, his teacher noticed that he did not seem to be hearing her. She suggested he have his hearing checked and set up an assessment with the school nurse. When no hearing problems were found, his vision was tested. In March, the teacher suggested, because Justin seemed to be withdrawing further and further from classroom activities, that Samantha should take him to the doctor for a full physical examination. The family doctor found no gross physical or neurological deficits, so referred him to the behavioural clinic at a local hospital, even though Justin had not been having behavioural problems in class or at home. She said: 'That scared me – the name itself scared me, because I'm thinking – this child is a golden child. He doesn't hit. He doesn't talk back. He doesn't – he just sits there, but doesn't pay attention to what's going on – he lets the world revolve around him, and he's off on his own.'

As so often happened for these women, the lack of a physical problem to explain Justin's difference led to the evaluation of Samantha's character: 'They had me fill out a bunch of papers about birth, and was he slow talking, and was everything normal. There was nothing – no alcohol, no drugs, I mean – I'm totally no drugs when I'm giving birth. But they wanted to know that stuff, and whether I drank, and if I breastfed him. You know, did you take drugs? Are you a drug user? How about your husband? Any abuse? Everything. Every aspect of my life was covered.' This assessment occurred in Canada, within a supposed climate of medical and psychological professionals' acceptance of AD(H)D as a diagnostic category, and within a culture of psychological rather than psychoanalytical traditions. Still, Samantha encountered professionals who did not consider AD(H)D as a problem until all else had been ruled out, as well as a professional insistence on focusing on presumed maternal and familial problems rather than specific testing of the child's difficulties.

Although she realized that this line of inquiry was neither relevant nor appropriate, Samantha said she cooperated, because 'I guess if it was just something asked about me I would have been more upset – but because it was something asked about my child – it gave me a little bit of, "Okay, I'll tell you anything you want to know – just tell me why my child is like he is."' Unable to locate any behavioural problems, or to identify any obvious family pathology, the behavioural clinic decided that they could offer little support, and they referred Samantha and Justin to the Learning Centre for further investigation.

Even in situations where AD(H)D was the suggested diagnosis from the outset, where professional communication was open, and where the professional who did the investigation was known to be sympathetic to the label, the process was not necessarily expedient. Jenny is one of the Canadian mothers in this study. She is divorced and remarried to a successful professional; she has an undergraduate degree, and although she used to have a successful career, she is now a stay-at-home mother. When Jenny's son was first identified, the teacher suggested she see her family doctor and ask for a referral for assessment with a pediatrician specializing in AD(H)D. The teacher even suggested a specific pediatrician for Jenny to see, because of his reputation as an 'AD(H)D-positive' specialist. When Jenny and Mark saw this doctor, however, they were told: 'I really believe that before we do anything you need SCOPE with your family. You need some help through SCOPE. It's an organization where you go and you learn how to parent, and if you need some mediation at the school, they'll help you.' Thus, even when a professional (in this case a teacher) made a tentative diagnosis, and the child saw a pediatrician known to be 'ADD-friendly,' the first step was again a ruling-out of familial problems.

Although Jenny refused to go to the remedial family group, the pediatrician continued to press for alternative approaches. He sent Jenny and Mark together to a psychologist for private counselling, and Mark was sent alone to a private psychologist for anger management training and to the Learning Centre for a social skills course. When Jenny could no longer afford to pay the private psychologist's fees, she was sent to Alberta Mental Health Services, who eventually provided her with a psychiatrist (who she did not like) for family counselling. During the two-and-a-half years that the ruling-out process continued, Mark's teachers continued to press Jenny for an AD(H)D assessment. Jenny, caught in the middle, finally called a halt to ruling out alternatives. She explains:

> Dr G did not want to put him on medicine. He said he wasn't totally convinced that he was ADD. He said, 'Yeah, I can see where he kinda fits in here and there, but you need to do this first, you need to do that.' So we saw Alberta Mental Health and saw the psychologists, on and on. He said, 'You need to have his behaviour under control.'
>
> Well, finally when Mark was in Grade 3, I just got sick of fighting with the teacher over when he was going to get a Ritalin trial. I went back to Dr G and I said, 'We need the medicine. We've done everything you asked us to, and I'm not leaving until you give me a prescription!'

Only at this point did the pediatrician agree to an AD(H)D assessment. However, despite hearing from the teacher that the child had attentional problems in the school, and despite little supporting evidence for suspicions of familial problems, it took over two years before the 'AD(H)D friendly' pediatrician was willing to consider an AD(H)D label.

Thus, despite media and professional discourse that voices concerns about overmedication and overreadiness to label children with a psychological disorder in Canada, it is apparent that the AD(H)D label was not the first suspected diagnosis for many of the Canadian children. Rather, a lengthy process of ruling out occurred – even when the routes of investigation were not supported by the children's symptoms. Thus, children were sent to psychiatric clinics, to psychologists, and to hearing and vision specialists, extending the process and increasing the scrutiny of the child and her or his family. It is arguably quite laudable that these professionals' first reaction to the children's problems was not to medicate, but instead to rule out any possible physical, social, or mental problems prior to medication. Nonetheless, the ways that professional ruling out of alternatives occurred often seemed ineffective at best, and pejorative at worst. In the end, these investigations did little to foster maternal–professional collaboration and sympathy. Mothers were both frustrated and alienated by professional uncertainty, which they often interpreted as incompetence. Further, mothers expressed feeling anxious and angry, because the lengthy waits and circuitous procedures they had to put their children through did not reflect the urgency of their children's problems. For children who wait, but whose educational and social demands continue, the result is an ever-increasing gap between the child and his or her peers. Finally, mothers were painfully aware of professional readiness to presume that family or mothering problems, rather than neurobiological ones, were the 'real' cause of the child's problems. Ultimately, this led to maternal suspicion of professionals' motives and undermined professional–maternal collaboration.

Canadian Mothers' Experiences of Teamwork and Communication

A central claim in discourse relating to AD(H)D identification is that interprofessional communications should be open and should include a multidisciplinary forum where all members of the child's 'team' (e.g., teacher, mother, father, doctor, psychologist) can share information and insight about the child. In practice, however, communication between professionals was spotty at best, and not all members of the 'team' (particularly mothers and fathers) were included as legitimate communicators. Professionals failed to read children's records properly, resisted contacting other professionals who may have already been involved with the child, refused to accept other professionals' judgments about the child, and were singularly loath to accept mothers' information at face value.

A common problem that Canadian mothers described stemmed from barriers to interprofessional communications. An example of this occurred in the case of Chloe's hospital psychiatrist, who refused to consult with her previous, community-based psychiatrist when Chloe was admitted to W-Cluster. Chloe's mother Pat believes the reason the hospital psychiatrist would not consult with the community psychiatrist was not only based on interprofessional competition or conflict, but was the result of financial considerations. She claimed that there are actually disincentives to interprofessional collaboration, because, when such a consultation occurs 'only one gets to bill. There is no – it's an Alberta Medical Association thing. So that means that information is not passed easily. So parents have this incredible role of facilitation that's not clear to you from the beginning.'[5]

Pat raised an important point. Because AD(H)D assessments and interventions typically do involve multiple professionals across disciplines, coupled with the fact that interdisciplinary communication and agreement is often poor or non-existent, mothers in particular are placed in the role of interlocutor. Often the maternal role of interlocutor is not only complex, but professionals make mothers' work as interpreters more difficult because they do not see mothers as legitimate knowledge brokers. When a mother says, 'Yes, but my child has ADD' or 'I would like you to perform an assessment for ADD,' the professional she says this to is as likely to discredit that information as to accept it as true or worthy of follow-up.

Samantha learned this when, on instruction from the behavioural clinic she and her son had attended, she phoned the Learning Centre to set up testing for AD(H)D. She explained:

Apparently you're not allowed to just pick up the phone and call the learning centre. Apparently there's somebody – and I don't know who has

5 Pat is not merely speculating here. She is a member of a government-appointed board whose mandate is the streamlining of mental health service delivery in the city of Calgary – a position that she took on as a result of personal frustrations.

to send them there, or how these kids get there, but they just assumed that the hospital should have done it.

And that was the question they asked me – how come they didn't send me to the Children's [Hospital] because the Children's does that?

I said, I don't know. At this point, I didn't really know what I was supposed to do or where I was supposed to go – I just knew there was something wrong. So they [the Learning Centre] sent me back to the behaviour clinic so they could send me to the Children's Hospital.

Samantha's experiences were not unusual and in fact reflect thematic experiences other mothers encountered. Very often one professional told mothers one thing, only to have that 'truth' challenged by another professional. In the end, these actions are not only confusing, they are frustrating, alienating, and frightening. Mothers who encountered these situations expressed again and again how the events left them believing that the professional 'team' did not value their opinion, did not care about what other experts had to say, and perhaps most worrisome of all, seemed to have no idea what they were doing. In short, mothers not only felt sidelined, but their faith in medical competence was sorely shaken through these experiences.

Canadian Mothers' Experiences of Standardized, Objective Measures

Maternal confidence was not bolstered once the hurdles leading to assessment had finally been jumped. In the Canadian context, there were three routes by which women and their children finally came to receive the diagnosis, and each posed problems for mothers in terms of acceptance of the label and confidence in the professional process. In the first group, mothers described their children's labelling as 'too easy'; in the second, the label was conferred 'serendipitously'; and in the third, the process amounted to ruling all else out, then finally falling back on a diagnostic process that a colleague of mine has likened to 'witch dousing.'[6]

6 In AD(H)D medication trials, children are provided the medication, and if it works, they have AD(H)D; if it does not, they presumably are then investigated for other condi-tions. The parallels to dousing, an assessment process used in medieval Europe and Puritan New England are uncanny. Dousing was used to determine whether an accused person (typically a woman) was a witch. In this test, the woman would be tied to a dousing chair and submerged in water. If she drowned, she was not a witch.

In the following sections, I will discuss each of these problems in turn.

Assessments as Too Easy

Amanda provides an example of a labelling process that she felt, was too easy. Her son Michael came to be assessed as a result of behavioural problems identified in the classroom by his Grade 1 teacher. She complained to Amanda about Michael's disruptive qualities and suggested that Amanda should get some parenting help from a support group for mothers of children with behavioural problems, a government-funded group that uses the school for its meetings. According to Amanda, the support group worker Louise (a pseudonym) 'works mostly with kids with ADD or behavioural problems.' Even though Louise works as a consultant, because she works out of the school and is in fact paid by the CBE for her services, she is also a colleague to school staff. Amanda describes how Louise facilitated Michael's identification: 'The teacher gave me a flyer from Louise that asked if you thought your child had ADD, or problems in school – like, with behaviour. So I called her and asked what to do. So she said she'd come to my place and meet with me and talk with me, and then if it's okay, she'd meet my son. So she came over one day and we talked for a while, and she met with Michael, and she said, "I really do think he could be ADD."' Louise suggested a pediatrician, and within a week Amanda and Michael met with him. Amanda describes how the pediatrician applied the ADD label: 'So I went in to this doctor and he just basically asked some questions, then he gave me uhm, kinda like a questionnaire thing that I could give to his teacher so she could mark it in. There was a whole bunch of things about the classroom. Did he need direct one-on-one attention? Could he work by himself? So she did that, and I took him back a week later, and he said, "Yeah, you know. I think he is ADD."'

Perhaps at a stretch, this could be construed as an interdisciplinary consult. It does, after all, involve a pediatrician, a social worker, and a teacher. However, the 'standard criteria' for labelling – that the child's behaviour should be observable across situations and over time, in consultation with professionals from different disciplines, who are working together with the family – were not even minimally present in Michael's diagnostic process. Instead, a teacher identified the initial

---

If she survived, she was found guilty, and punished 'appropriately.' (My thanks to Sandra Rastin for this analogy.)

problem and tentatively suggested AD(H)D assessment. Then, two professionals (Louise the support worker and the pediatrician she sent Amanda to) who were virtual strangers to Amanda and Michael were able, in the course of a brief visit, to make the initial determination. Finally, their determination was confirmed by feedback from the professional who first suggested the diagnosis, his teacher. Thus, a perfect circle, in which teacher-as-initiator to teacher-as-confirming-assessor was enacted. The structure of the assessment, and the exclusion of Amanda's insight, was not lost on her. As she notes, 'I didn't fill out anything. And I knew him better than anyone, his teacher included.'

Amanda, like many of the mothers in this study, was a good record keeper, and she was able to provide me with a copy of the assessment form the pediatrician provided to her to pass on for teacher observation and completion (see Appendix 6a). As is apparent, the forms have little to say about Michael's activities at home or with friends; rather, the focus is on tasks, group activities, and disciplinary problems such as turn-taking and social skills. Thus, in Amanda and Michael's case, there was no attempt to include all aspects of his life. Rather, reflecting the criticisms of AD(H)D assessment noted above, Michael's problems, from first identification to final assessment, were driven by the concerns of the school.

While Amanda characterized Michael's assessment as 'too easy,' at least it involved some observation outside of the doctor's office, if only by the referring teacher. In comparison with the stories some mothers recounted, Michael's assessment, as described by Amanda, was quite rigorous. Glenda, one of the Canadian mothers in the study, divorced, remarried, and now a stay-at-home mother of two children; her husband works in upper management. By way of comparison, Glenda described how her son, on suggestion from the teacher that he be provided an assessment for ADD, was diagnosed:

> The teacher sent me to my family doctor, and he referred us to a pediatrician who is supposed to be an ADD specialist. And naive little old me, we're sitting there talking away – Kevin's looking around, and we're having a chit-chat for over an hour, and this poor kid's probably bored out of his blessed mind. Of course he's wriggling around and not paying attention.
>
> Then he says, 'Okay Kevin, I want you to go out in the hallway for a while, your Mom and I are going to talk for a bit.' So, Kevin went out and sat in this hallway in a metal chair for a half hour while this doctor asked me stuff. And then, he dismissed me to the hallway so Kevin could come

in and talk to him. So we did that. And that's how he determined a person is ADD.

No observation, no tests, just a letter from the school, and I brought his report cards. And he just said, 'He's ADD for sure. Just go back to your family doctor. I suggest Ritalin.'

Both Amanda and Glenda responded to the assessment not only with incredulity, but with refusal. Neither woman agreed to medicate her child, because in the first place the assessments themselves had been unconvincing, second, because the assessment process seemed to be school-driven rather than child-focused, and finally, because each had negative feelings about Ritalin. Thus, despite receiving diagnoses, in both cases nothing really changed in the children's lives. They were not put on medication and, despite being diagnosed as AD(H)D, received no discernible treatment or benefit from the label in their schools.[7] In fact, school–mother relationships deteriorated for these mothers once their children received the label. Because neither mother would agree to Ritalin, they were seen by teachers as uncooperative and as 'in denial' about the 'real' nature of their children's disabilities.

The question of 'who drives the ADD machine' remained a backdrop for some mothers against which these 'too easy' assessments were played out. Glenda, whose son's teachers first identified him and then pushed for the ADD label, illustrates the ambivalence a number of Canadian mothers expressed, saying, 'The school wanted the label. Let's be honest – they wanted it so they could have a scribe for my son for their blessed Grade 3 exams [the provincial standard examinations]. Other than that – and maybe to throw him on Ritalin to perhaps make it easier for them.' In Glenda's discussion of her child's assessment, there is profound disaffection: not only did she suspect the school of driving the machine, but she saw that the motivation stemmed from financial and institutional demands rather than from any concern over her child's problems. Finally, Glenda's scepticism about labelling reflects discursive claims of professionals (Mate, 2000a, 2000b; Schatsky and Yaroshevksy, 1997) and in the media (Bongers, 1997; Chisholm, 1996; Hough, 1997; Rees, 1998a; 1998c) that many Canadian professionals are

---

7 As we will see in the next chapter, many children (regardless of whether they were on medication or not, and regardless of their location) did not receive any benefit from the label in terms of services or understanding on behalf of teachers and school officials.

too quick to label Canadian children. Ultimately, when mothers like Glenda took seriously the discourse of doubt relating to ADD, labelling, and the 'ownership' question, they obtained little comfort in the label, and expressed little confidence that the diagnosis was appropriate, or that it would make their children's lives any easier.

Lengthy and Contradictory Assessments

While Amanda and Glenda's experiences were swift, seemingly teacher-directed, and anything but thorough, other mothers experienced interventions that were lengthy, invasive, and although not always accurate, broad-ranging and detailed. Still, the actual assessment for AD(H)D, in the end, often seemed to occur haphazardly or through serendipity.

For example, Daphne had been through numerous assessments for her daughter Melanie. At various points, Melanie had been diagnosed as hard of hearing, visually impaired, developmentally delayed, and had at one point scored 60 on an IQ test. She had been placed in special classes, refused access to programs, undergone eye surgery, and seen innumerable therapists – all to no avail. Daphne described how Melanie first was 'diagnosed':

> So that summer, I'm talking to my neighbour and telling her how terrified I am, that I just don't know what I'm gonna do, and what does she think about home schooling? And she looked at me and said, 'She's not re-tarded.' And I said, 'well, I don't think so either, but that's what everyone keeps telling me.'
>
> And bless my neighbour's heart, she said – she said, 'Well, I can see it from here – I've seen her on the deck. That kid's got ADD!' and I said, 'Well, she's not hyperactive.' She said, 'She doesn't have to be. That kid's got ADD. I can tell.'

Despite many years of interventions, observations, and assessments performed by a wide array of medical, psychiatric, educational, speech, occupational, and psychological professionals that took place in hospitals, doctors' offices, clinics, classrooms, and learning centres, not one professional had previously suggested that Melanie might have ADD. Instead, someone who really barely knew her, watching her play at a distance in a public place, identified Melanie's problems (correctly, it turns out). The irony of the situation was not lost on Daphne, who immediately went out and bought a book about AD(H)D. She explained her reaction:

It was like the whole book was written about my daughter! Everything! It was textbook! And I was so angry with myself that I hadn't figured it out. That I hadn't read it. That I didn't know. Because if I'd read this book, I woulda known. (crying)

And not just me! What about all those so-called experts who saw her, who said she was visually impaired, that she had severe motor defects, failure to thrive, retarded, [that she had] cerebral palsy? Where were their heads? And now, having read the book, knowing that's what she had, and watching her – it was so obvious (crying again). And I was so angry.

Daphne's anger and self-blame are not unique. The broken trust mothers experienced when professionals proved themselves to be fallible resulted in anger over their incompetence and rage at the wasted time and the invasive procedures that had been for naught. Hence, mothers expressed an obvious sense of betrayal when professionals clearly failed to deliver on their promises of care and solutions. In addition, however, mothers' anger and disappointment were often directed at themselves, because they had been too trusting of professional knowledge claims despite the obvious weaknesses in professional practice, and – reflecting common understandings of what good mothers should do – because they themselves felt they should have known better and sooner what their children's problems were.

In the end, once Daphne was convinced that ADD was the right diagnosis for her child, she abandoned the system of 'helpers' she'd been working with over the years and headed straight to the Learning Centre, the private clinic that Samantha had so much difficulty accessing. Perhaps because by this time she was so frustrated that she had become a force to be reckoned with, or perhaps because unlike Samantha she is an upper class, educated woman, Daphne prevailed and her child was accepted for assessment.

Although for Daphne the diagnosis came as a relief, others who shared the history of a lengthy, complex, ruling-out process felt incredulity when the diagnosis finally was conferred. Pat's daughter Chloe, for example, had been involved in psychiatric and medical interventions from the time she was three years old. With each intervention and each new yet unsatisfactory diagnosis, Pat's confidence in medical and psychiatric infallibility became shakier. Thus, when Chloe was seven and a psychologist said to her, 'Do you suspect ADD?' she replied with: '"I can't accept it. I can not accept it." Because I felt that she just had to be stressed out by this stuff – the intervention – that was occurring. I just felt that it was too easy, that I would go a long way before I accepted that. And I did. I spent a year not accepting that diagnosis. And we both had to wait through that whole year – through all those issues – until we got to a place where I could accept that.' Pat's comments raise several important points. First, as noted, because professionals were not always able to show themselves as competent judges, mothers learned over time to be cynical about any new labels or interventions. Second, the spectre of iatrogenic illness is raised here: Pat implies that the interventions Chloe had to tolerate were themselves so stressful as to cause psychological problems. Third, and perhaps most importantly, the notion that Pat found the ADD label in and of itself to be 'too easy' reflects 'common knowledge' understandings of ADD as label of last resort. Recall that in popular discourse and some academic critiques AD(H)D is often described as a label that professionals and parents alike fall back on when a child's 'badness' or 'troubledness' cannot be explained by other means. In critical popular and academic discourses, AD(H)D is also constructed as a fictional category that excuses medical incompetence and parental ineptitude. That Pat was unwilling to accept this label reflects yet again the dilemmas of maternal choice when those choices occur within the culture of ambiguity that surrounds AD(H)D. Her refusal also belies critics' claims that mothers 'drive' the AD(H)D machine and use the AD(H)D label to absolve themselves for poor parenting: for Pat, ADD did not come as a godsend, but as yet another brick in the wall of doubt and concern surrounding her child.

Assessment by Medication – Dousing

By far the most common labelling process – for over half of the children in the Canadian group – occurred through being prescribed Ritalin and being observed for improvements. Although physicians in these instances stated prior to medication that they suspected the child's problem was ADD, they also clarified that the only way to really know would to be to gauge whether or not the medication brought any 'improvement' for the child being assessed. Typically, this involved a double-blind Ritalin trial. In this process, the child was provided with a supply of date-coded medication that would be either Ritalin or a placebo, and the child's teachers and (sometimes, but not always) parents were provided with forms to complete that asked questions about the child's behaviour over a brief observation period.[8] In effect, if the child showed 'improvement' on non-placebo days, then a diagnosis of AD(H)D was confirmed.

A copy of a typical assessment checklist is attached (see Appendix 6b). As can be seen, the behaviours that are to be assessed are almost exclusively activities that would be important to the classroom teacher: sitting still, taking turns, attending to tasks, working in groups. Typically, this is the form that parents were asked to complete as well. Mothers acknowledged that these forms had been frustrating for them to fill out, because they provided little opportunity for them to respond with their own concerns about medication, and also because the structure of the assessment forms bore little relevance to their lives with their children. For example, on the days the children were receiving Ritalin (and all mothers felt that they had been able to tell whether it was a 'Ritalin day' or a 'placebo day'), some experienced side-effects that made them weepy or feel ill during the day. Others experienced profound rebound effects that made them irritable or argumentative at the end of the day when the medication wore off. Hence, mothers' concerns about their children's problems with medication, or their worries that their children's problems were 'really' mainly school and/or teacher problems, were not relieved by the structure of this assessment process. Thus, the notion of whether Ritalin 'improved' the child's life was not entirely unproblematic, because even though the child's school life might have become calmer, the child's home life became worrisome.

A second problem raised by these assessments was the forms' focus on children's overt activity levels. As we may recall, for many of the Canadian children, problems of attention were not related to hyperactivity, at least outside of the school setting. Hence, these were often children who simply drifted away from the classroom activities, and who became problematic only when it was noticed that they weren't achieving to their expected levels, or when they began to encounter social problems in the school setting. The assessment forms, perhaps from necessity, focus on overt and observable behaviours rather than on simple inattention or withdrawal. Thus, the contradictions between criteria assessed in the forms and the children's personal qualities were highlighted in particular for children whose problems stemmed from being inattentive or impulsive rather than hyperactive. As well, mothers expressed some incredulity that teachers, in a classroom with twenty-

---

8 For most children who were diagnosed by double-blind trials, the duration of the trial was two weeks; in two cases, however, the trial was only over a one-week period.

nine other children and routines of coming and going in the classroom that were often chaotic in and of themselves, would be able to observe accurately how their children were faring each day. Again, this doubt was fuelled by mothers' encounters with claims like those of anti-Ritalin activist Peter Breggin, in which Ritalin is represented as the 'sit down and shut up drug' (Bongers, 1997).

Mothers' descriptions of their children's assessment processes provide direct evidence of the contradictions between the discursive promises and the discursive practices as they relate to AD(H)D in Canada. In fact, the call for interdisciplinarity, observation across all aspects of the child's life, and the use of standardized, even scientific, measures was little more than a fiction. Children were rarely observed in ways that were direct or systematic across all aspects of the child's life: instead, observations in the classroom were the central consideration in assessments, and these observations were not made by professionals other than teachers. No mother described, for example, that a medical or psychiatric professional actually observed the child in the classroom, either before prescribing medication or during the medication trial. Neither did any medical or psychiatric professional confer directly with the child's teachers and explore their concerns about the child. Instead, children's problems were at best represented by teacher letters, by parents providing report cards, or by teacher-completed reports of blind Ritalin trials.

Again, these problems in assessments – the haphazard or invasive or seemingly teacher-driven quality of the process – did not give mothers ground for trusting professionals' claims to expertise, to infallibility, to consensus within ranks, or to necessarily having the right to judge or name their children's problems. Further, this lack of trust ultimately made Canadian mothers' 'choices' about treatment particularly painful.

British Mothers' Experiences of Assessment

British women's experiences in many ways mirrored those of their Canadian counterparts. As occurred in Canada, British children's assessments were not confidence inspiring, included multiple and often conflicting opinions on the part of professionals, did not include observations across all aspects of the children's lives, and did not include mothers as knowing experts on their children's problems. On the other hand, British mothers reported significant differences in their encounters, and these relate to the discourses of professional incredulity in Britain over ADHD and to a general antipathy towards labelling children. Rather than reiterate the experiences that British mothers shared with Canadian mothers, the following sections develop an argument of how mothers' experiences, when enacted within a discursive field of professional and lay scepticism over ADHD, differed from those enacted within a field of professional and lay 'acceptance.'[9]

British Mothers' Experiences of Interprofessional Consensus (Labelling)

It is tempting to take at face value the claims of ADHD activists and specialists in the United Kingdom that ADHD is underrecognized and in many instances unknown by the general population, educators, psychologists and psychiatrists, doctors and pediatricians, and other professionals. Indeed, most of the mothers in the British portion of the study did indeed have to search harder for assistance, go further afield of local professional services, pay privately rather than rely on the National Health Service, and spend more time in obtaining an ADHD diagnosis than did their Canadian counterparts. In fact, most mothers described ultimately locating a sympathetic and 'ADHD-friendly' professional, not through interprofessional referrals or through a professional's suggestion that ADHD be investigated, but through less formal means. In England, more than in Canada, mothers drew heavily on information provided by grass-roots support groups about ADHD and about professionals who provide services related to ADHD. Often mothers learned about local 'ADHD-friendly' pediatricians, schools, specialists, and psychiatrists through the website of ADDNET, the national umbrella organization for support groups and services related to ADHD in the United Kingdom. In addition to electronic sources, mothers also reported gaining information about 'which specialist' to see from friends and through actually attending support groups to gain local information. Hence, in the British group, it was more typically mothers who 'drove' the specific ADHD diagnostic process. Mothers would locate information about the disorder, locate information about a professional who might support applying the label, and find some way to bring their children under that professional's care, often outside of traditional avenues of referral.

9 In the world of AD(H)D, such terms as 'acceptance' and 'scepticism' are not easily applied in either context. I am arguing that, although AD(H)D is highly criticized in both contexts, at the time of the project, it was less known, 'understood,' and 'accepted' in Britain than in Canada.

In some ways, the British mothers' narratives about the difficulties in obtaining information on services related to ADHD lend support to claims that ADHD is 'misunderstood and underrecognised in Britain' (Kewley, 1998). Indeed, mothers themselves often complained that 'nobody here understands ADHD' (Evelyn) or that 'there's only one fellow in the district who knows about ADHD' (Amy), or 'they just don't seem to have heard of it over here' (Rosalind). However, from an examination of mothers' narratives, it seems that professionals actually do *know* about ADHD, but the helping professional culture in Britain makes pursuing it as a diagnostic category very difficult.

British professionals often clearly articulated their negative feelings about the label. Penelope, for example, had heard about ADHD through her friend Moira. Feeling she had discovered an important clue to her son's problems, she went to an educational psychologist at his school to ask whether ADHD would be an appropriate avenue to investigate. The educational psychologist, who in Britain would typically be the appropriate professional to get the school assessment and statementing process rolling, had heard of ADHD, but he told her 'that he doesn't believe that you should ever put an ADHD label on a child.'

Tacit knowledge about ADHD was often expressed in such a way that, even while professionals claimed not to have heard of ADHD or refused to accept it as a legitimate label, they nonetheless drew on some aspects of ADHD discourse as a 'real' category in suggesting treatment. For example, both Cassandra and Corrine, whose children are in their teens, have been struggling for many years with teachers, educators, and medical personnel to obtain an appropriate diagnosis for their children. Each described being approached by their children's teachers early on because of behavioural concerns in the classroom. Although for each of these women it would be several years before their children would actually receive an ADHD label, at this early stage in the journey, they were each told to 'make sure not to give him any sugar, refined or prepared foods, or fizzy drinks.'

This suggestion stems from claims in popular discourse that AD(H)D is caused by poor nutrition. These speculations date back to the mid-1970s, when American physician Benjamin Feingold posited that processed foods, additives, and sugar were the 'real' culprits behind hyperactivity (Conrad, 1976; Feingold, 1975). In the intervening almost thirty years, Feingold's theories have been more or less discredited; however, the discourse that nutrition is somehow connected to hyperactivity remains quite virulent, particularly in alternative therapy texts (Efamol,

1998;[10] Enrich, 1996; Stordy, no date; Swartz, 1997). Thus, the suggestions of Conrad and Feingold, in response to concerns about children's classroom behaviour, indicate some acceptance of long-standing 'knowledge' about treating ADHD, despite hesitancy to apply the label.

Although British professionals, outside a select group of 'ADHD-friendly' experts, were reluctant to label children, this is not to say that British children did not receive professional attention. Rather, in most cases, helping professionals had been active in directing children's assessments for other presumed problems for many years before women finally 'stepped outside the box' and sought the ADHD label. As occurred in Canada, these professional interactions were far from coordinated or collaborative. Rather, the interactions were fraught with uncertainty, fragmentation, and sometimes even unprofessional or harmful approaches to understanding the problems of children who are different.

Many mothers reported being sent for treatments that were inappropriate, or to specialists who seemed to have little insight into their children's challenges, or in how to help children and their families. Evelyn, for example, was sent to family therapy, to occupational therapy, to speech therapy, and finally to a child psychologist. Harry's diagnoses have been variously poor muscle tone, behaviour problems, and dyslexia. At age three, a child psychologist administered a Wechsler Intelligence Scale for Children (WISC-R) intelligence test that identified Harry as a child with an extremely high verbal IQ coupled with an extremely low non-verbal IQ. In giving Evelyn this news, she told her, 'Well, of course, he'll probably never be able to write. This will always be a problem because his brain works so fast, and he will never be able to write it down.' Evelyn described her response to this:

> She said it 'of course,' and la-di-da. I mean, I was so – staggered – I couldn't say anything. I was completely gob-smacked. I remember I came out of that hospital. I got back to the car, and I just sat down and cried ... I mean, for a child of the intelligence that he had – at three – to just say, 'Well, he's never going to be able to get over this, and he will just always be frustrated.'
>
> No label. None. Nothing. Not learning difficulties, nothing. And I don't

10 Efamol manufactures a blend of evening primrose oil and fish oils that it promotes as contributing to children's ability to pay attention and learn; ironically, the company's headquarters are in the United Kingdom.

think she did see him again. I think she said that she would, sort of –
counsel me. And again, this really riled me deep down. I thought, 'Why is
it that I am the one that's being offered psychological counselling?'

Evelyn's experiences highlight several recurring themes in the British
context. First, British mothers described professional demeanours that
were even more high-handed and dismissive of women's insights and
feelings than those of Canadian professionals. From the reports of the
mothers in this study, it is possible to surmise that British professionals
continue to enjoy high levels of prestige and professional privilege
compared with their North American counterparts. This is not to say
that British women's feelings, perspectives, or suggestions were actually dismissed more than Canadian women's – it is simply to say that
when British professionals dealt with mothers, they were much more
overt in their devaluation of women's knowledge claims and in their
scepticism over women's motives. In a sense, the experiences of British
mothers reflect attitudes of professionals in which mothers (unlike in
Canada where the rhetoric belies the reality) are not even *rhetorically*
included as partners or members of their children's assessment and
treatment 'teams.'

The second issue Evelyn's story highlights is the strong tendency of
British professionals to presume maternal lack or maternal pathology.
Although Canadian mothers also recounted professional assessments
that were as much about the mothers' behaviours and attributes as they
were about the child's, in England, the tendency to quickly shift the
focus from family problems to maternal problems was remarkable and
consistent. In fact, the tendency to blame mothers was almost universal, and it occurred regardless of the professional involved, regardless
of the 'presenting aspects' of the child, and regardless of the socioeconomic, racial, or marital status of the woman involved.

A third concern that is raised in Evelyn's narrative relates to a great
reluctance by British professionals to confer any kind of psychiatric
label on children and a strong cultural antipathy towards labelling
generally. Repeatedly, mothers recounted interactions with professionals in which they acknowledged the symptoms the children presented,
yet drew short of supplying a name for those symptoms. Instead,
mothers were told that their children had 'low muscle tone' (rather
than dyspraxia), non-specific learning problems (rather than dyslexia),
behavioural problems (rather than ADHD), or focus and organizational
problems (rather than ADD).

Often, professional reluctance to label meant delays in children's assessments because referring letters and interprofessional communications were couched in terms that were vague and that left the next professional with little concrete information to go on. Thus, achieving interprofessional consensus over British children's problems, without an organizing position (like a diagnosis) upon which such consensus might converge, seemed to be virtually impossible. Penelope provided a comment that illustrates maternal frustration over this reluctance to label and the lack of clarity that resulted:

> I don't know why schools can't refer to a doctor and say, 'We think this child's got some kind of hyperactivity that needs assistance' and I don't know why when you go the doctors, they can't send you on to a pediatrician and say 'Please assess this child for dyslexia, or hyperactivity.' Why? Why this?
>
> Instead, we went to the school, and they said, 'No.' We asked our doctor, and the health visitor if they would support us in having Morris assessed, and they said, 'No, it would be worse for Morris. He would be labelled.' And we didn't even know what the label was gonna be. No one said what the label was.

In retrospect, Penelope noted that the process of assessment, enacted within a frame of refusing to assign categories, was almost designed to confuse. At the very least, it made obtaining any diagnosis difficult. Instead, the numerous professionals that she and Morris saw remained focused on dealing with Morris's 'presenting attributes' and avoided any global category or label that might contain those attributes.

Although professionals eschewed a label for Morris, Penelope recounts, 'Everyone just said, "Give him structure. He needs structure."' Interestingly, the instruction to Penelope that Morris's problems could be treated by 'creating structure' is indeed a standard suggested treatment for AD(H)D. In a similar vein to the physicians noted earlier who suggested diet, these British professionals expressed some understanding of what appropriate responses to AD(H)D symptoms should be and were prepared to suggest those treatments in hopes of helping the child. It seems, however, that what British professionals typically were not prepared to do was apply a psychiatric label to categorize children's problems.

It must also be noted that British mothers – in the assessment phase at any rate – were themselves often ambivalent about labelling. Penelope noted, for example, that she was reluctant to push for an assessment because 'as a parent I thought, "well, I don't want my child labelled."' Mothers' reluctance to push for a label led, in retrospect, to regrets that are expressed eloquently in Kate's comments. Kate is married, has four children, and works on a consultancy basis as a coach for children with ADHD. She said:

> I've done my best. I know I have – with the information that I've had, and I feel that I couldn't – if I'd had just an inkling more information – he wouldn't have gone through this. If just one person had said, 'get him tested for dyslexia, or have you heard about ADHD or attention problems. Or, you know – *anything* – yes, push harder, go and see if you can get a diagnosis. See if he has got the condition.'
>
> But I've taken them as knowing what they're talking about. I've believed them as professionals. And they just wasted so much time.

Here Kate makes a nice point. Kate believed professionals because of their claims to possessing knowledge that is both superior and incontrovertible. She believed them because they claimed to know best, and because there was no other knowledge available to her at the time. Her belief in professionals, she now feels, caused her son harm.

Perhaps even more than for Canadian mothers, British mothers' responses to the actual labelling process were constituted within the discourse of antilabelling sentiment. As a result, even though British mothers might in fact have pushed for the label, and have gone to extraordinary lengths to locate someone who would be willing to apply it, they often remained profoundly ambivalent towards the ADHD category. When I asked British mothers whether they had found the ADHD label to be helpful or comforting, a surprising number expressed misgivings. Dolores, for example, said, 'I'm worried about it that it's actually going to be detrimental for him, in that he's going to be looked at differently now. I worry that people don't know what it is and they will judge him.' Dolores's answer can be viewed as a reading of the discourse of antilabelling movements – that children will come to be seen as their label rather than as individuals (Kiger, 1985; Leifer, 1990).

Another thematic response to the label was expressed by Gloria, who said, 'It really gets me down and I think – whatever it is, he's like it, and he's gonna be like it forever. And I just – when I sometimes think that this is *who he is* it just makes me very down' (emphasis mine). This notion, that the label is a permanent marker that will not only provide information about someone, but that will define who they are and what their limits will be, is another central tenet of antilabelling discourse relating to AD(H)D (Kiger, 1985; Slee, 1994). Thus, in maternal feelings of remorse over the presumed permanence and stigma of the label, and over the totalizing effects of the label, we can see how mothers themselves take up circulating knowledges that delegitimate the labelling process, even while seeking the label on a personal level.

A third response that British mothers provided to this question was shared by Canadian mothers as well. This response had to do with feelings of guilt – that ubiquitous maternal emotion. Here, mothers expressed sorrow at the label because of its genetic component, saying things like, 'I feel bad because it's probably me who gave it to him' (Diane). Here again, mothers can be seen to take up discourses of maternal responsibility for all of their children's problems, even when those problems have no direct bearing on the women's mothering (or necessarily on their genetic contributions either). Mothers' continuing claims to guilt feelings, even after receiving a diagnosis, challenge the popular criticism that the AD(H)D label is really a way for mothers to obtain some kind of absolution for their poor parenting practices. In- · deed, rather than feeling themselves to be 'taken off the hook' for their children's behavioural and learning problems, mothers simply took information about the neurobiological and genetic causes of AD(H)D as one more reason to feel guilty.

In the end, however, both British and Canadian mothers alike agreed that their feelings about the label rested primarily on the level of supports and services that resulted from the labelling process. If women had been able to obtain special educational supports in their children's schools, or if they had been able to secure a disability allowance, or simply if they felt that the label had made professional and community supporters more tolerant of their children's difficulties, mothers expressed satisfaction with the label. As Gloria succinctly stated: 'I don't think the ADHD label was helpful at all, except it got me a way to get him into a private school for kids with learning problems. It was no help in the regular school at all. But my attitude is, if the label can be useful to me, then – certainly – I will use it.' Gloria's comments reflect a sort of pragmatic acceptance evidenced by many mothers from both sites in the study. Rather than cling to normative positions about labelling, Ritalin, medicalization, or even mainstream versus segregated schooling, mothers repeatedly evidenced a 'whatever it takes' attitude towards obtaining solace for their children.

British Mothers' Experiences of Standardized, Objective Measures

As we have heard, British mothers and children experienced delays and barriers to obtaining a diagnosis that were qualitatively similar, but that took longer and were more difficult to negotiate than those experienced by Canadian mothers and children. Ironically, however, once British women did hear about ADHD, and learned of a specialist who might be willing to provide an assessment, British assessments were typically very swift, remarkably straightforward, and bore little resemblance to the idealized interdisciplinary, multi-faceted assessment protocols set out in professional discourse.

Moira, for example, had seen innumerable professionals in attempts to find solutions for her son before she finally located a pediatrician known to specialize in ADHD. Her comments exemplify a typical assessment and response:

> She was brilliant. She looked at Teddy, spoke to him. She did a pretty thorough medical examination of him. She tested reflexes, got him to walk along the floor, looked at him all over very thoroughly. And she spoke to us about Teddy without him being there as well, so we were able to talk freely. And then she had a talk with Teddy, and then sent him out again. And she said to us 'Have you ever heard of a thing called attention hyperactivity disorder?'
>
> We went right to heaven. She said she thought Teddy was showing a lot of signs of having this condition, and that she would like to try him on Ritalin, which she gave us a prescription on the spot for it, and he started the next day.

Moira's comments are interesting for a number of reasons. First, the assessment process she described is cursory at best: it involved only one visit and a number of tests that have little to do with attentional difficulties. Then, having ruled out any glaring physical anomalies, the doctor not only conferred a diagnosis, but wrote an immediate prescription for ongoing medication. Indeed, in British practice, the notion of a double-blind trial or of a tentative period on medication to be followed up in a subsequent doctor visit was quite rare.

Interestingly, although Moira's experiences were similar to those of the Canadian mothers who characterized their children's assessments as 'too easy,' she expressed very little scepticism over the diagnosis or the treatment. In practice, once the 'right' professional had been found, there was considerably less scepticism among British women about assessments that were often swift, involved only brief observations, and included absolutely no interprofessional consultation. Instead, most British mothers, by the time they actually found someone who would 'give them a diagnosis,' were too relieved to question the methods of their specialists, their readiness to apply the ADHD label, or their readiness to go forward with Ritalin.

Most British children, once diagnosed, were put on Ritalin without testing for efficacy or without titrating an appropriate dosage. Further, many of these children were prescribed doses that were significantly higher than those provided to Canadian children of similar ages. Indeed, almost half of the British mothers noted that their children had suffered severe side effects, such as anxiety, lack of sleep, weight loss, tics, and Tourette's-like symptoms.[11] However, perhaps because they were hesitant to alienate the one professional who gave them a label to cling to, or because of a more deferential attitude on the part of British mothers towards professionals in general, British women stayed with the label (and with the dosage) faithfully once it was applied.

One other possible reason for this dogged acceptance of the label and its treatment is offered by Kate, who said: 'Yes, I had heard about it (Ritalin). There was a lot about it in the book I got about it, so I knew exactly what to expect. I knew that it was very controversial. But I also know that if things continued as they were – uhm – there was going to be something more. Perhaps far more serious than a side effect that we read about with Ritalin. Which was either a suicide or a murder, to put it bluntly. My suicide, or his murder! Or both! [laughs].' As Kate implied, by the time she located a professional who would offer an answer to Colin's problems, who would name it, treat it as real, and promise to resolve it, Colin's problems had become so grave, and the family's relationships so strained, that she was willing to tolerate almost anything rather than relinquish that answer and its promised solution.

Perhaps because it took so long in Britain to find anyone who would provide any label for a child, British mothers and children reached levels of desperation that transcended the Canadian experiences. Or perhaps because children with hyperactivity are more likely to receive the ADHD label in the United Kingdom, the children in the British

11 Tourette's syndrome is a psychiatric category that is characterized by involuntary physical spasms, verbal outbursts [often obscene], tics, and extreme impulsivity.

portion of the study might have had more 'hyperactivity' problems while the Canadian group contained children with 'inattention' or 'impulsivity' problems. For whatever reasons, it seems the British mothers as a group just seemed happy to have something – anything – to hang their hopes on. Nevertheless, as we will see in the chapter on treatment, once the first blush of excitement over receiving a label had passed, many of the British mothers began to have second thoughts about the benefits of labelling their children, even if they did not necessarily question the appropriateness of its application.

Conclusion

In discussing the strengths of a feminist Foucauldian discourse analysis, Sara Mills (1997) notes the importance of employing an analysis of absence. Here, the researcher should consider who is excluded from texts and what unacknowledged dissents or controversies the text argues against or attempts to silence. A feminist Foucauldian discourse analysis reads instructional texts about an idealized assessment of AD(H)D with particular attention to the absences. Reading these texts in this way reveals implicit responses to controversies over the 'nature' of the disorder, over the overreadiness of the psy sector to apply psychiatric labels to behavioural problems, and over who is 'driving' the AD(H)D machine. Thus, idealized assessment texts argue indirectly against circulating critiques on the part of some academics, professionals, and media over the legitimacy of AD(H)D by offering a narrative of infallibility, objectivity, and a depiction of the typical assessment as one that occurs within a system of checks and balances.

However, in addition to taking a discursive analysis of professional texts that idealize assessment and identification techniques, I have also contrasted mothers' narratives of their embodied experiences of labelling against the professional truth claims and the circulating controversies in both lay and professional literature. I thus have demonstrated how discursive practices and truth claims operate at a personal level by asking mothers to describe a number of fissures in the intersections of discursive practice and personal experiences. On the one hand, idealized claims about the proper identification and assessment of ADHD children depict professional understandings of the problem as consensual, involving standardized, universal, and objective measures. On the other hand, the lay and professional controversies over the realness of AD(H)D and over labelling in general are discursive fields that mothers are also well aware of. Hence, when discrepancies arise between ideal-ized practice and actual assessments, mothers are left with lingering doubts not only about the immediate problem of receiving an adequate assessment, but also about the larger problem of whether the diagnosis is at all legitimate.

When mothers were happy about the label, it was because it pro-vided hope that their children would receive assistance, because it provided their children an opportunity to be seen not as bad children but as struggling children, and finally because mothers hoped that they could learn to understand their children better. As we will see, how-ever, each of these hopes was problematic once the assessment hurdle was passed, and mothers and children entered into 'treatment' for AD(H)D.

A final level of uncertainty relates as much to treatment as to identifi-cation and intervention. As we will learn in the following chapter, treatment suggestions for AD(H)D include not only medical protocols, but also behavioural and educational ones. In fact, many of the children in this study, long before they were identified or assessed as AD(H)D, received some of these treatments from parents and teachers who intuitively seemed to know what to do. Thus, many of the children experienced ebbs and flows in their difficulties, depending on what was being done for them outside of the bounds of an official diagnosis. Many times, indeed, these differences resulted in deferred assessment processes. For example, many mothers in both sites used star charts, reward programs, and positive reinforcement protocols to manage such problems as getting ready for school or getting homework done. These behaviour modification protocols that mothers employed informally are often prescribed formally for AD(H)D once the diagnosis has been conferred. Hence, mothers, in doing all they could for their children, were treating AD(H)D (although perhaps not conceptualizing it in this way) prior to their children's diagnosis.

A troublesome aspect of this 'pretreatment' occurred within the schools. Again and again, mothers told stories of how, for a year or two, their children experienced terrible chaos and interpersonal problems in the classroom, falling behind peers, suffering devastating social isola-tion, losing things, forgetting their homework, failing tests, and ending up at the principal or headmaster's office on a regular basis with one particular teacher. Then, for a year or so, these same children found themselves in a classroom managed by a teacher who *intuitively* taught in the ways that AD(H)D children respond to. In these classes, children thrived on the teacher's use of structure, one-on-one attention, making eye contact, and above all, ensuring the classroom was a safe and supportive place for children who were different.

Mothers' claims about good teacher / bad teacher effects were often shored up in interviews when mothers provided me with copies of children's report cards. Very often, a child might experience several years in which she or he might be described by a teacher as 'inattentive, disruptive, and defiant' or 'well behind age-appropriate levels in reading and mathematics.' However, there often seemed to be shining years, in which a teacher would report the child as a 'joy to teach,' and the child's grades would reflect learning successes. During these quiet years, parents, teachers, and children alike would ease up on the assessment and intervention process, because the need was simply not so pressing: professionals and parents alike would believe (or hope) that the child had simply 'grown out of it,' and all concerned would heave a metaphorical sigh of relief.

This inconsistency in the very 'nature' of the child's problems, of course, caused mothers to feel cynical about the diagnosis when it finally was conferred: they recalled that the child's problems disappeared during years of 'good teaching' and became exacerbated during times of 'bad teaching.' Thus, this ebb and flow in educational 'competency' undermined mothers' confidence in the AD(H)D label as 'real.' Instead, these mothers were left with suspicions that AD(H)D – as many public critiques claim – is 'really' a problem of poor teaching and a teacher-driven phenomenon. Further, as we will see in more detail in the next chapter, it left them feeling less than confident in the ability of their children's schools' to *consistently* deliver an appropriate education to their child.

6 Challenges and Conflicts in Treating AD(H)D

Teachers need to develop a reward and consequence system ... Classroom rules and expectations should be clearly defined, posted and monitored regularly ... Highly structured routines are important ... Allow students to have an extra set of books for home ... Behavior management may include ignoring minor, inappropriate behaviors, increasing immediacy of rewards and consequences ... allowing students to take frequent 'seat breaks' ...' Through the use of relatively simple interventions and accommodations ... teachers can adapt to the strengths and weaknesses of the ADHD child.

Karen Sealander et al.
'Attention-deficit hyperactivity disorder:
An overview for elementary school teachers'
Early Childhood Education 28, no. 2, 1995

A comprehensive treatment programme should involve advice and support to parents and teachers, and could, but does not need to, include specific psychological treatment (such as behaviour therapy) ... Current treatments for ADHD include a range of social, psychological and behavioural interventions, which may be focused on the child, parents or teachers. They may vary from the provision of information and advice through to formal psychotherapeutic interventions.

'Guidance on the use of Methylphenidate for ADHD'
National Institute for Clinical Excellence
National Health Service, 2000[1]

1 Distributed to medical personnel at a wide range of service institutions, pediatricians, and psychiatrists across the United Kingdom, but not to parents, teachers, educational psychologists, or SENCOs.

The above quotations, one from a North American journal for elementary school teachers, and the other from a recent policy document generated by the British government on ADHD and methylphenidate (Ritalin), offer idealized portrayals of treatment protocols for children with AD(H)D. As with professional knowledge and hegemonic truth claims deployed over the assessment of AD(H)D, these quotations also offer arguments against unspoken criticisms that recur about the treatment of AD(H)D, both in lay and professional or academic discourse. The truth claims embedded within these idealized treatment portrayals include assurances that the typical response to an AD(H)D diagnosis might include a variety of educational, social, and psychological strategies that would assist the child who is different to fit in with 'regular' classroom and social demands. In addition, AD(H)D-specific education and training of the professional and personal caregivers in the child's life is portrayed as typical. Here, parents, teachers, and med/psy personnel are portrayed as communicative, mutually supportive adults who are willing to learn about and able to implement programs that will serve the needs of special children. Thus, the argument goes, 'typical' AD(H)D treatment is multimodal, involving interprofessional communication and parent partnership, and is child-centred rather than focused on the needs of teachers or parents for 'teachable' and 'trainable' children (Anonymous, 1998d, 1999d, no date; CLC, 1997a, 1997b; Chisholm, 1996; Cooper, 1998; Cooper and Ideus, 1998; Cosgrove, 1997; Gilmore et al., 1998; Alberta Children's Hospital, 1993; Minde, 1987; Murphy and LeVert, 1995; NICE, 2000; Scott, 1987; Sealander et al., 1995; Taylor, 1997).

The claims in these texts are not only positive statements about what educationists, physicians, and psy sector professionals can and will do to provide remedies for children who are different. These texts also offer a tacit argument against the controversy over Ritalin.[2] Although the word 'Ritalin' is never mentioned in either of the texts that introduce this chapter, following on Mills's (1997) insight that discursive silences should be read as arguments against circulating counterclaims, I believe a central function of these professional treatment texts is to take on anti-Ritalin criticisms. Particularly, treatment discourse takes on anti-

---

2 In practice, most texts generated by medical, educational, or psy sector professionals – and particularly those directed towards parents – that offer suggestions for AD(H)D are extremely coy about using the word Ritalin. Instead, 'medication' or 'medical interventions' are used.

Ritalin critiques, pervasive in popular media, professional discourse, and critical academic disciplines, that position medication as the primary (and often sole) treatment for children identified with AD(H)D.

Anti-Ritalin Discourse

Wrapped up in the anti-Ritalin discourse are two recurring problems. The first is the claim that too many children are identified with the disorder, and hence Ritalin is being used inappropriately to serve the needs of parents and teachers. In this argument, Ritalin is seen as a drug used to create 'zombie-like' states or 'robotic behaviour' in large numbers of children who in fact have nothing more than childish high spiritedness 'wrong' with them (Atkins, 2000; Breggin, 1998; Flynn, 2000). Thus, it is argued, 'normal' children are being drugged into an unnatural state of submission, becoming 'docile bodies' upon which parenting and particularly educational discipline can be more easily inscribed (Berry, 2000; Bongers, 1997; Browne, 2000a; Breggin, 1998; Cohen, 1999; Hough, 1997; Kiger, 1985; Merrow, 1995; Palmer and Bongers, 1997; Rees, 1998a). In this critique, rising rates of Ritalin prescriptions are seen not as a reflection of the increasingly sophisticated ability on the part of professionals to understand and recognize abnormal attributes in children or to understand the relatively new category of AD(H)D. Rather, in this stream of anti-Ritalin discourse, Ritalin is seen simply as a medical means of social control. By questioning the actual labelling of AD(H)D for many or most of the children who are medicated, this discourse not only criticizes professional competence in appropriately identifying 'real' cases of AD(H)D, but it also poses an implicit challenge to the very 'realness' of AD(H)D itself.

A second argument expressed within anti-Ritalin criticisms is that, although psychological differences are problematic for children, treatment with psychotropic medication is inappropriate for *any* child. In this criticism, although AD(H)D is accepted as a legitimate disorder, the concern is expressed that Ritalin is used in place of more conservative treatments because it is quick, cheap, and easier to deliver than educational, behavioural, and psychological treatments for children with attentional problems. In this criticism, while the ontological category of the disorder is not challenged, the willingness of medical and educational personnel to medicate children rather than deliver appropriate educational and social support is seen as a response that is tied to economic pragmatism rather than compassionate humanism. Included in this body of criticism is a vast array of textual material related to alternative therapies for AD(H)D,[3] as well as arguments from a number of educationists, psychologists, and psychiatrists that AD(H)D intervention should be psychotherapeutic rather than psychopharmaceutic (Adduci, 1991; Armstrong, 1993; Baughman, 1999; Berry, 2000; Bowles, 2000; Mack, 2000; Schatsky and Yaroshevsky, 1997; Ullman and Ullman, 1996).

Folded into these criticisms of Ritalin as the first-choice treatment of AD(H)D are hegemonic concerns over which profession ought to maintain control over the treatment of children with behavioural and psychological problems. In this strain of anti-Ritalin discourse, psychiatrists argue that psychiatric interventions (talk therapy) are the preferred way to approach attentional and behavioural problems in children, psychologists argue that behaviour modification and training protocols are the most effective treatment, alternative therapists argue that nutritional, massage, and vitamin regimes are what these children need, and special educationists argue for learning aides and specific classroom interventions (Breggin, 1991, 1998; Schatzky and Yaroshevsky, 1997).

In the second anti-Ritalin argument, while it is understood that labelling children who are different is a necessity, the treatment of these children with Ritalin (which is often characterized as 'speed,' 'kiddie cocaine,' or 'an addictive substance') is seen as an abuse of innocent children. In these accounts, the spectre of addiction and drug abuse is frequently invoked. Ritalin is described as a drug with street value (Anonymous, 2000; Browne, 2000a, 2000b; Cohen, 1999), as a drug that is often abused recreationally (Merrow, 1995), and as a drug that has long-term implications for the mental health of children who use it, whether recreationally or medicinally (Armstrong, 1993, Breggin, 1991, 1998). In these arguments, Ritalin is framed as dangerous and risky – in an ironic contrast to protreatment arguments that frame children who are not treated 'properly' as being simultaneously at risk for personal and social problems and potentially dangerous or burdensome to society if not treated 'properly.' Obviously, these competing discourses of danger and risk create tensions for mothers who must decide what, if any, treatment to consider in helping their troubled children.

In practice, there is considerable overlap between these two streams of anti-Ritalin discourse, and it is not always clear from reading criticisms of Ritalin whether the writer is in fact arguing against the treatment or

---

3 I have written elsewhere on the discursive strategies contained in alternative therapy texts, and their reliance on discourses of science, medicalization, standardization, and mother-blame (Malacrida, 2002).

against the diagnosis. It must also be noted that anti-Ritalin discourse is present in a wide range of discursive fields. Hence, one can encounter discourse about the 'problems' of Ritalin use in the popular press, on radio and television, in opinion columns by medical, educational, and psy sector professionals, on the Internet, in parenting books and magazines, and in materials from alternative therapy providers.[4]

One can also locate anti-Ritalin and overmedication criticisms (either directly stated or embedded within antipsychiatry, antimedicalization, and antilabelling arguments) in academic journals in the disciplines of education, psychology, psychiatry, sociology, and anthropology (cf. Bernier and Sigel, 1994; Brooks, 1994; Conrad and Schneider, 1980; Conrad, 1992; Cosgrove, 1997; Cotugno, 1993; Kiger, 1985; Slee, 1994). These academic arguments, although more subtle and theoretically sophisticated, nonetheless reflect similar content to less academic anti-Ritalin discourse.

Texts that argue for the treatment of AD(H)D in general and Ritalin treatment specifically, positioned against this backdrop of controversy, are in a similar position to texts offering truth claims about the proper assessment and identification of AD(H)D. Again, treatment claims must do more than simply announce that Ritalin is the 'proper' intervention for a child identified with AD(H)D. Rather, treatment suggestions must be made in contrast to circulating counterclaims about the realness of AD(H)D, about professional hegemonic struggles over treatment, about lay concerns over professional competence, and about circulating criticism of the drug itself.

Claims about AD(H)D treatment are put forward discursively against these criticisms through statements that treatment occurs with the collaboration of numerous professionals, across a wide array of disciplines, and (when necessary) it involves a diverse palette of educational, psychological, and medical interventions. Further, the idealized treatment includes not only a broad spectrum of services (of which Ritalin *might* be one), but it also occurs within a system of checks and balances against medical zeal. In this argument, Ritalin, while acknowledged as an important element in the treatment of a child identified

---

4 There is a large industry of alternative service providers offering therapies for AD(H)D. These include health food distributors, vitamin and food supplement manufacturers, neurofeedback and behaviour modification therapists, massage therapists, nutritionists, homeopathic practitioners, chiropracters, and rapid eye movement therapists. This industry produces a vigorous anti-Ritalin critique in its advertisements and in its promotional materials distributed through retail outlets, on-line, and at educational conferences and info-fairs.

with AD(H)D, is also positioned as only one possible element in a multimodal, multiprofessional arsenal of treatments that are deployed in helping the troubled child.

Another theme in the treatment discourse is the use of team metaphors. Here, parents, teachers, physicians, and psy sector works are positioned as equal members of the treatment team; each providing input, feedback, and participating as informed equals. A final theme is not necessarily explicitly stated. However, as occurs in all truth claims relating to any kind of treatment or remediation, AD(H)D treatment discourse offers implicit guarantees that the child will be helped. In short, AD(H)D treatment discourse is the discourse of hope.

In the following sections I continue my strategy of employing a feminist Foucauldian discursive ethnography to examine the ways that mothers themselves experienced their children's treatment. In particular, I highlight mothers' narratives as they intersect with discursive claims about AD(H)D treatment occurring within a multimodal system of checks and balances. I also compare women's stories with treatment discourse that positions Ritalin as only one of many social, educational, and psychological interventions designed to help children identified with AD(H)D, and against claims that AD(H)D treatment is typically handled through collaborative professional (and maternal) teamwork. Furthermore, I discuss how the promise of hope and resolution offered in treatment discourse played out in practice for these mothers and their children. First, however, I review the ways that discursive practice relating to AD(H)D treatment had an impact on mothers' abilities to decide about their children's care and to feel comfortable with those decisions.

The identification and assessment of children with AD(H)D differed considerably between Canada and Britain, primarily because of the presumed lack of exposure British professionals and parents had to the category of AD(H)D. However, once children in both sites were identified as having AD(H)D, they and their parents faced similar concerns and challenges in obtaining appropriate treatment and support. Thus, the balance of this chapter discusses the experiences of British mothers and Canadian mothers together and draws inferences about similarities and differences in experiences in the two sites.

Mothers' Choices and Anti-Ritalin Discourse

Because anti-Ritalin discourse is extensive across disciplines and pervasive throughout a wide range of media, it would be difficult for anyone interested in AD(H)D to avoid encountering these arguments. Thus, it is likely that professionals who handle children identified with AD(H)D, and mothers who must decide whether or not to accept Ritalin treatment for their children, will have had some contact with the claims that Ritalin is an inappropriate, dangerous, or overused treatment. Even in England, where the claim is made by mothers and pro-ADHD activists and professionals that AD(H)D is little known or understood, well over half of the British mothers had encountered anti-Ritalin discourse prior to their children's diagnoses. The uncertainty and doubt that these mothers felt about Ritalin is eloquently expressed by Moira, a British mother who discussed her feelings about her son's diagnosis and treatment:

> I'm not happy that – the only reason he's been diagnosed as ADHD is the Ritalin's working. I've got documentation now that says that Ritalin works on a normal person – you don't have to have ADHD for Ritalin to work. What does that mean?
>
> Of course, some of this information is quite contradictory. And I don't know – as a parent – don't know what is right. There is so much anti-Ritalin material out there. And it's very damaging. Because it's certainly helped – while I don't like it – it's certainly helped Teddy to – uh, I don't like the effects it has on him – but it's the first time he's realized that what he's doing is affecting other people, and that they are reacting to him. With Ritalin he started to get an understanding of things.

Moira's comments reflect some of the ambivalence expressed by other British and Canadian mothers. Many mothers grudgingly admitted that Ritalin had been helpful in school and in public places, and even in the home. However, they still had concerns about whether or not Ritalin was a 'good' treatment. Further, Moira clearly articulates that her doubts have been fuelled by a variety of discursive practices, by research that is contradictory, by the unconvincing nature of her son's 'dousing' diagnostic process, and by the anti-Ritalin discourse she has encountered. Thus, although her son's embodied experiences of treatment, seemed to have been beneficial, the immediate evidence of his improvement was clouded by doubts raised through discourse and practice in the ambiguous handling of his assessment, the lack of rigour in his treatment and the controversy over Ritalin.

Moira's account provides a clear example of the ways that critical discourse relating to Ritalin can impact a mother's own perceptions of the treatment on her child, shedding doubts even on apparent success.

Her concerns reflect the experiences of other mothers as well. Penelope also provides insight into the ambivalence that mothers in Britain and Canada described when their children were first prescribed Ritalin, offering us evidence of the connections between maternal subjectivity and anti-Ritalin discourse: 'We didn't want him to go on Ritalin, but what we wanted – have always wanted – was to try to teach him with different strategies first. And, to be honest, when I handed it over to his teacher – the Ritalin – I just burst into tears. I've never wanted drugs as the – I've heard of people who've used Ritalin to subdue their children, you know, and I've never wanted that for him [crying].' Penelope's comments speak directly to two elements in anti-Ritalin critiques. First, Penelope's opening comment – that what she in fact has always wanted for her child is that he be treated first through educational interventions rather than solely through medical interventions – speaks directly to the anti-Ritalin discourse that positions medication as the cheap, simple, and easy alternative to more humane but complex educational, psychological, and behavioural interventions. Second, Penelope's comment that she had heard about parents who administer Ritalin to their children simply to make them placid, emotionally flat, and submissive subjects speaks directly to claims that are embedded within anti-Ritalin, antipsychiatry discourse. She clearly has thought about this discourse, and understands that it has made her own choices more difficult to live with. Although she has agreed to medication for her son, she clarifies that she has never simply wanted to be like those other 'people who've used Ritalin' to numb their children. Instead, Penelope positions herself as a mother who has chosen to medicate, despite her own misgivings, because she has in fact had very little choice.

Indeed, many mothers spoke in these terms about treatment options for their children. These women report that despite the promise of multimodal interventions, for many of the children in this study indeed, pharmaceutical treatment was de facto the sole option provided to children and to their mothers.

In contrast to Penelope and Moira's reports, a little over a third of the English mothers did, at least in the beginning stages, seem to have had little exposure to anti-Ritalin discourse before encountering Ritalin as their child's treatment. Further, this group of mothers indicated that their lack of negative perceptions about Ritalin had been beneficial, because it allowed them to feel comfortable with their treatment decisions. Gloria described her reactions when her son first was prescribed Ritalin: 'I had never heard of it – my friends in the States had told me to get Keith looked at for ADHD and that I should ask for Ritalin – but other than that, nothing. The first quarter of a tablet he had, he was a different child. Totally different. I mean, my husband and I just sat down and cried. There was a little boy in there. The monster was gone.' Gloria's reaction to her son's medication was clearly celebratory. For her, the problem had been named, the answer had been found, and the solution looked to be nothing short of a miracle. Her decision to put Keith on medication was untroubled by doubts as to the legitimacy of using medication or by concerns raised in anti-Ritalin discourse. As we will see, however, in the long run, Keith's problems were not completely resolved by medication alone. For Gloria, the first blush of relief that Ritalin brought was soon to be followed by strife with Keith's school over administering Ritalin and, ironically, over problems in obtaining any treatment or services outside of Ritalin.

Indeed, in both Canada and England, mothers who initially saw Ritalin as the answer to their prayers typically came to a more complex long-term assessment of Ritalin. Further, it must be acknowledged, the ambivalence that mothers described over using Ritalin was not solely predicated on doubts raised through discursive practice: rather, material concerns left mothers doubting the wisdom of relying on Ritalin to solve their children's problems. These mothers found that, although Ritalin did help their children pay attention and interact socially, there were often problems with side-effects. Further, they noted that few, if any, services in addition to Ritalin were provided to their children so that they might make up for lost ground and learn appropriate social and educational skills. I discuss each of these concerns below. However, it is important here to point out that discourse was not the only contributor to maternal ambivalence over Ritalin. Rather, embodied effects and material practices often eroded mothers' early optimism at finding a single answer to their children's problems.

Accepting and Refusing Ritalin

In the British group, every child who had actually received an ADHD diagnosis[5] was using some sort of medication, with most using Ritalin.

5 At the time of the interviews, three British children were in the process of being assessed for ADHD, although in each case the mothers were convinced that the child would be labelled as ADHD. As well, one Canadian child had just been diagnosed as having ADD, and was to begin taking Ritalin the week after our interview took place.

In Canada, however, several mothers, despite being told that their children had ADD, refused to accept Ritalin as a treatment. The alternative treatments these mothers used included 'vitamins, essential oils, whole foods, and massage' (Clarissa), 'gingko biloba, evening primrose oil, no refined foods or sugars, and lots of structure' (Sheila), 'pure love' (Glenda), 'love and understanding' (Belinda), 'blood, sweat and tears' (Teresa), and 'work, work, and more work with the school' (Lucille).

Perhaps not surprisingly, all Canadian mothers in the study described having encountered anti-Ritalin discourse both before and after learning that their children were diagnosed with ADD. Further, for those mothers who opted for alternative treatments to Ritalin, negative discourse about Ritalin had a direct impact on their treatment decisions. For Clarissa, who is a trained naturopath, the decision was based on a general mistrust of the medical profession and on an affinity for homeopathic rather than pharmaceutical interventions. For the other 'refusing' mothers, however, the treatments they described using for their children were not necessarily based on a mistrust of the medical system globally, but on mistrust of Ritalin, of the diagnosis of ADD, and of the assessment and treatment experiences of their children.

Reading what those mothers who refused Ritalin had to say about their decisions provides insight into the connections between mothers' refusal and anti-Ritalin criticisms. Glenda, for example, after a great deal of struggle with the public school system, has placed Kevin in a special school for children with learning and attentional difficulties. For her, this has ultimately proved to be a satisfactory treatment. However, from the time Kevin was diagnosed, Glenda refused to medicate him. She said:

I had such a hard time with this – I mean we don't know what Ritalin is, we don't know what this is all about, we don't know what it's doing to the body. I don't know what it's going to do with Kevin in the long term – or the short term. You know, there's huge drug and alcohol abuse problems in my family – I don't want to put Kevin in that situation – to set him up to taking pills to solve his problems. I think that's a bad idea.

Besides, they don't know enough to label kids with ADD. How dare they? If I have diabetes, you can tell that, and you can label that. Go ahead. But diabetes is provable! And I don't see ADD as a disease. It's something else – a teaching disability, or whatever – but it's not enough to convince me to fill my kid up with a bunch of drugs!

Glenda's comments connect to circulating truth claims about the inappropriate and irresponsible use of Ritalin, about med/psy sector overreadiness to medicalize children's problems, to doubts about psy/med professionals' ability to actually identify AD(H)D, to discursive claims that connect Ritalin with recreational drug use, and to doubts about the legitimacy of the disorder itself. Each of these claims contributed towards Glenda's uncertainty about using Ritalin, and ultimately persuaded her to forego medication because she became convinced that the risks of this 'treatment' are too high.

Other Canadian mothers, despite initial misgivings similar to Glenda's, ultimately accepted medication. Nonetheless, that acceptance came with some struggle. Samantha's route to acceptance was quite complex. She at first accepted Ritalin, then spent several months trying alternative and nutritional therapies, and finally put her son back on Ritalin. She explained some of the reasons for her ambivalence:

I didn't know what Ritalin was, first of all. But then you hear all this stuff on TV, you see it in the doctor's office, 'No Ritalin on Premises.' Well, then you start to think this must be a bad thing. And then I'm hearing from people that some people are selling Ritalin at $30 a pill because they mix it with another narcotic on the street and they make it a cocktail. And I think, 'Oh, my God, I don't want this stuff in my house. This is something scary.'

So I hid his medicine. I didn't want anyone to know he was on it. Like, when you get your prescription for Ritalin it's in triplicate. You have to sign for it. I've never signed for a prescription in my life.

Then I started going on the Internet and finding out stuff about it, because the other things weren't working. And I began to think, 'This isn't that bad.' Okay, there were side-effects, but the side-effects I saw were good-side effects. It helped him.

For Samantha, discourses of danger and risk that tie Ritalin to drug abuse were contributors to her decision to stop treatment. Her comments about Ritalin as a street drug are a telling argument – Ritalin is *not* a narcotic, but has taken on the status of one in this mother's mind, as a direct result of her encounters with anti-Ritalin discourse. In addition, the actual mechanics of caution relating to the distribution of Ritalin (the triplicate prescription and the requirement to sign for the pills) served to reinforce her presumptions about Ritalin's dangerousness. In deciding to reintroduce Ritalin, she drew not only on the evidence of her own son's improvement, but again sought out discourse that provided information supportive to Ritalin use. In short, like for other mothers in the study, outside knowledge had as much to do with Samantha's decision to accept or reject medication as did the immediate evidence of her child's improvement.

Lydia told a slightly different story to explain her ambivalence. She had initially been quite unhappy with the idea of medicating her child. After many years of seeking answers through behavioural and psychological interventions, and under continuing pressure from her child's teachers and school administrators, she and her husband did agree to put Karla on Ritalin. She said:

> Eventually, we said, 'Let's just do it.'
>
> We had already done all of the soft issues. We had put the white board in her room, with the list of 'get up' and 'brush your teeth' and 'make your bed.' We'd done all of that. We had done token economies. We had been there. We had done the structured homework. We had the timelines. We had the special pencil grip, and the math manipulatives. We had strung the macaroni, brought in private tutors, dragged her to Kumon and Sylvan Learning Centre.[6] We'd had the special glasses, and the family therapy, and the parenting courses, and, and, and!
>
> We had done all of that, and it hadn't helped her.

In Lydia's response, we hear the frustration at having worked long and hard to implement almost any kind of protocol *except* Ritalin. Indeed, many mothers shared this reaction, particularly in Canada where the anti-Ritalin discourse is perhaps more firmly entrenched than in Britain. Repeatedly mothers spoke of how, even after receiving an ADD diagnosis, they continued to explore and implement behavioural, physical, and educational strategies in hopes of be able to avoid 'drugging my child.' In these mother's narratives, the recurrent sense is that, by having agreed to Ritalin, they have, in a sense, surrendered. Having tried the alternatives, with little to show for their efforts, these mothers gave in to the pressures (spoken or unspoken) to use Ritalin for their children's problems.

Daphne also spent considerable time exploring alternative treatments

---

6 Both of these are private tutoring services for students having academic difficulties, and much of their advertising is directed specifically towards children with attentional and learning difficulties.

for Melanie's ADD-related problems. Eventually, she placed her daughter on medication. She provides us with some information about how she came to terms with her decision:

> I'm a medical person. And I believe in pharmacological therapy. I believe that if there is a need, and it's used appropriately, that's why the drug is there. It's not an optional therapy.
>
> And over the past few years, I have come to believe that there is a need. *This is something.*
>
> If your child were diabetic, you wouldn't insist on diet management only, and refuse the insulin. If your child was epileptic, you wouldn't say, 'well, seize away, I'm not giving you a drug.' So why would I, with attention deficit, say 'I'm not giving you that medication that would give the ability to focus, to able to put the structure in your life that you need?'

Daphne's response offers insight into the arguments that some mothers engage in with respect to the 'realness' critique about ADHD and Ritalin. In Daphne's comments we can read not necessarily only resignation, but also defiance against criticisms of ADD and Ritalin. Daphne's description of her surrender frames ADD as analogous to diabetes, and Ritalin as analogous to insulin. Through using the metaphor of a 'real' and 'accepted' disease, Daphne makes a simultaneous claim to the realness of AD(H)D and to the appropriateness of medical treatment. The diabetes metaphor was, incidentally, echoed by many women in both study sites, and seemed to be a compelling way for women to justify their use of a medication that is as controversial as Ritalin.

Veronica is a Canadian mother in this study. She is thirty-seven years old, working class, and the mother of four boys; she is married and an active community advocate for special needs educational policy. Veronica provides us with an explanation that, like Daphne's, sheds light on how mothers can come to accept Ritalin despite the conflicting information they might receive about it:

> When I first put him on it, I hadn't heard of it before. Well, since then, I've heard that it doesn't work for some people, and that some people take it even when they don't need it. My husband gave me a hard time about it for a while, and my mother-in-law, too.
>
> But it works for my son, and – I'm not gonna take him off of it because it doesn't work for somebody else, or because somebody else doesn't need it. I've seen him not on it, and I've seen him on it. I can see when the medicine

is wearing off. I see him at night when he's not on this medicine, and you know, he really does need it.

Veronica's response shows how some mothers are able to use embodied experiences to counter discourses and controversies over Ritalin. Despite the discourse, despite the opinions of others, Veronica sees her son's needs, and the way that Ritalin provides him help, and this is enough evidence for her.

A final response taken by mothers pertaining to Ritalin was neither acceptance nor refusal, but an almost grudging compromise. Over half of the Canadian mothers and a little over a third of the mothers in Britain ultimately decided to provide Ritalin to their children only during school times, and on rare occasions that might place high demands on their children's attentional and behavioural capabilities. Dolores explained:

> During weekends and holidays we do give him a break. If we're going out anywhere, then we do give it to him because he can get carried away. He plays football and cricket – and when he goes to football we give him a tablet because he'll kick the ball and end up kicking someone and he gets carried away.
>
> We do it just to give him a break, really from the tablet. We don't want him to have it all the time. We don't want him on this tablet forever. We would like him to come off it – slowly, so we don't give him a tablet in order to see how he's reacting, and we hope eventually he can forget about it. We try and wean him off of it when we can, we don't want him on it forever. And he's a lot better – doesn't have it as often. He still does need it, but we try.
>
> We was [sic] actually told that he won't be on it forever. So I know they don't need it all the time. They said he can't keep having tablets forever. So I suppose that's stuck in my head to try. The psychiatrist told me that – that it's not something he's gonna be able to use forever, he'll need to learn how to control himself.

Dolores's explanation illustrates how, in some cases, Ritalin is seen more as a necessary evil than as an answer to a mother's prayers. As an indirect response to criticisms of Ritalin as a substance that *makes* children behave compliantly, as a drug that masks normal human behaviour, and as an addictive substance, Dolores frames Ritalin as something to be weaned off of, to take a break from, and to learn to live without.

Dolores's comments not only provide us with some insight into the ambivalence that many mothers experience in accepting the use of Ritalin for their children, but they also provide considerable information about the ways that mothers can take up the ambivalence that professionals express about AD(H)D and Ritalin. From the moment of being provided a Ritalin prescription, Dolores has been forewarned that her child will not be able to 'lean on' Ritalin indeterminately to solve his problems. Instead, she is told, Aaron will have to learn how to 'control himself,' to which she responded: 'I find that hard to accept, because I think, "If he could control it, he wouldn't be in this state. He wouldn't need it at all."' Dolores's response is insightful. She intuitively understands that the doctor's warning contains within it a hidden statement of ambiguity about AD(H)D. Embedded in the physician's instructions is the implication that indeed AD(H)D is simply a matter of lack of self-control and that medication is not something either to be relied upon nor to be continued with. With professionals directly providing these ambivalent framings of AD(H)D and Ritalin, and within the larger framework of anti-Ritalin/anti-AD(H)D criticisms, it is no small wonder that so many mothers in both sites struggled to limit their children's exposure to Ritalin.

There are some final considerations I would like to put forward relating to the experiences of those mothers who chose the 'compromise' response to Ritalin. Many of the mothers who chose to curtail the child's exposure to medication, while optimizing the child's ability to pay attention and behave appropriately in public settings, expressed considerable resentment. For these women, there was an overwhelming sense that they were medicating their children 'for the school.' This was expressed in two ways: first, that teachers were the ones who most benefited from the effects of Ritalin, while mothers had to put up with rebound effects in the evenings or deal with their children's problems without the benefit of medication, and second, that the school itself was the 'driving force' behind the need to medicate the child at all. The logic was that if the child could (and did) cope with life outside of school without medication, then perhaps there was some truth to the anti-Ritalin/anti-AD(H)D claims that children are simply being drugged to facilitate poor teaching and inadequate classroom discipline. Ironically, then, making this compromise often left mothers feeling not better about their child and Ritalin, but even more confused about whether the Ritalin was even necessary at all.

Interprofessional Teamwork

As noted earlier, one of the truth claims attached to treatment discourse over AD(H)D is that multiple professionals will not only agree objectively that a particular child has AD(H)D, but that there is also consensus among professionals about the proper way to treat AD(H)D. In practice, however, mothers in both sites encountered significant disjunctures between this discursive promise and their actual experiences.

Med/Psy Sector Disjunctures

In England and Canada, these disjunctures were most apparent between regular family physicians and the ADHD-friendly pediatricians or psychiatrists who had prescribed Ritalin for diagnosed children. British mother Evelyn, for example, after extensive research, managed to locate a pediatrician with a reputation for understanding ADHD. This specialist's office, however, was almost a two-hour drive from Evelyn's home and, more importantly, he was a private consultant whose services were not covered under the British National Health Service. Once Evelyn's son Harry had been settled on a dosage that seemed to work for his attentional problems without creating any side-effects, Evelyn sought assistance in having the prescription handled by her family physician. This doctor was not only Harry's regular physician, but his office was located closer to Evelyn's home, and his NHS affiliation would mean that the prescription costs would be covered by public health insurance. Evelyn described how her request was received:

> The GP actually wrote one prescription, but then he wrote on the bottom that he would not fill it again until he'd seen us. Which I did – make an appointment ... we sat down and the doctor said, 'Oh, well, how are things?' in a sort of vague way, and then he said, 'Well, of course this isn't my field. Really I don't know much about it at all, and so I suggest you should really go back to your specialist for this from now on.'
>
> And I said, 'Yes, well you don't think you can carry on managing Harry? I mean, all the specialist ever does when we go see him is measure him and weigh him and that's about it really.'
>
> 'Oh, no!' he says, 'I wouldn't be competent to do that. I wouldn't know anything about that.'

In the end, Evelyn did convince this physician to write the prescription for her. In fact, she said: 'He can't say "No, I'm not going to prescribe this for the National Health." But he's not going to be easily willing to accommodate someone looking for Ritalin. And, because he says he doesn't know anything about it, you cannot say he's negligent – it just isn't his field. I mean, you get a parent like me who sort of pushes through and insists – and he can't say no. But not everyone would get that from him.'

Evelyn's comments raise an important point. Had she not persevered in requesting the prescription from the publicly funded local physician, she would have found herself again paying from her own pocket to obtain Ritalin for her son. Thus, Evelyn's story not only highlights the fissures among medical professionals in Britain over ADHD and the lack of uniformity in British services relating to ADHD, but it also highlights the fact that, at present, ADHD service delivery is centred in the hands of private specialists rather than National Health Service physicians.

Finally, as Evelyn perhaps rightly asserted, not every woman would have the educational, class, or social skills to persuade an NHS physician to comply to her request. As she said, 'In this country there is still a huge feeling of "doctor knows best." And you think that if it's what the doctor says, they must be right. However, I basically turn on the computer to get my information before I even go to the surgery.' Evelyn's comments also highlight the notion that mothers' ability to dispute medical knowledge depends not only on their comfort with challenging authority but also on their ability to obtain alternative information outside the doctor's office.

In Canada, mothers encountered med/psy sector disjunctures as well. Despite the assumption (and criticism) that acceptance of ADD and Ritalin is universal and enthusiastic among Canadian professionals, a number of Canadian mothers also chose to obtain treatment through private rather than publicly funded services. Daphne, for example, experienced such frustration with publicly funded medical, psychological, and psychiatric assessment and treatment that she no longer uses those services in the ongoing management of her child's treatment and monitoring. When I asked her if anyone had ever given her any grief about using Ritalin, she said:

Family doctor. That's why I won't leave my safety net of Dr P at the learning centre. Because I went to the family doctor to have the baseline blood pressure, height, weight, and get the prescription, and he just said, 'Ritalin! She doesn't need to be on Ritalin! She's not hyperactive!' As Melanie's sitting lovely all quiet.

Of course! It's a white room, there's absolutely nothing to distract her, not even a window. And he's just saying, 'There's absolutely nothing wrong with this child!'

And I'm thinking, 'You're stupid. You are a stupid man. So just do what you need to do – take her blood pressure, keep her chart, and let me deal with someone who knows.'

While Daphne's story provides another example of how mothers opted to use privatized services, it also highlights the lack of consensus among Canadian professionals about Ritalin and about ADD. Even though Melanie had received her diagnosis and had been taking Ritalin for over a year, and was by this time attending a school for children with attentional problems, she once again had to deal with a professional who did not believe that Ritalin should be given to a child or that she has ADD.

In Daphne and Evelyn's narratives we can also see how, although both Canada and England enjoy government-funded health care and educational services, many mothers in both sites moved their children's care outside of the public systems as a result of frustration and worry. The implications of social class, knowledge, and personal and/or cultural qualities on mothers' ability to obtain services will be discussed more fully in the following chapter. However, it is worth noting here that mothers' ability to move outside of the system was not solely predicated on their ability to pay for private services. In Canada, a number of private institutions and services do keep at least a small portion of their client load open for sliding-scale and subsidized treatment (S. Young, personal communication, 2000; Foothills Academy, personal communication, 2000; Calgary Learning Centre, personal communication, 2000). Indeed several of the Canadian women in this study did have children who were being provided private services through subsidized means. In Britain, as well, a number of mothers had managed to obtain full financial support from their local education authority in moving their children into specialized, private schools for children with learning and attentional problems (see Appendix 3). Still, many of the mothers in both sites whose children were being managed by private consultants or attending specialized educational settings were able to provide their children with these opportunities because of their class positions.

Medical and Educational Disjunctures
In England, the difficulties and disappointments relating to Ritalin were further complicated by contentions over actually administering

Ritalin as treatment. We might recall Gloria's celebratory reaction when her son was first prescribed Ritalin and my comment that her elation would prove short-lived.

Keith was one of the lucky children who not only responded positively to Ritalin, but who experienced no negative side-effects. His teachers were delighted with his new behaviour in class and called Gloria regularly to comment on Keith's positive attitude. On the other hand, the same teachers refused to administer the medication for Keith's noon dose, while the school administrators appeared ambivalent about Keith's treatment. Gloria explained: 'He has to have it at lunchtime, so – but because the school had said they were agreeable to the ADHD diagnosis, they couldn't really refuse. So the way they found round it was to have me take his tablets in every day. Now, I'm classed as severely disabled with my back, and so I cannot go in every day to take him a half tablet. So I put it in his lunchbox – which caused quite the panic! So eventually his teacher agreed to give it him.' Not only did Gloria and Keith run aground of the school regarding the dispensing of medication, but the school seemed to object to the notion of the diagnosis and the medication regardless of who administered it. Indeed, the school psychologist, the SENCO, and the headmaster pressured Gloria to take Keith off medication because they felt the drug was not beneficial. She explains how she ultimately convinced these professionals that Keith did indeed need his Ritalin:

At the three-month review, the head, the Ed Psych and the SENCO called me in for a meeting – and the SENCO didn't want him to have Ritalin. She said they didn't have any ADHD in that school. The SENCO had heard of ADHD and she didn't think it existed. She said, 'If he's got ADHD, then a good 20% of the children in this school have ADHD.' So they said they were going to write to the doctor saying they hadn't noticed any difference, and recommending he be taken off it.

So, that week, I just didn't give it to him. On the Monday morning I didn't give him his 8 o'clock pill and I didn't go in with a lunchtime one. And at 2 o'clock that afternoon I had a call from the teacher asking what was wrong.

I said, 'Oh, I'm sorry. Did I forget to tell you? I've taken him off the Ritalin, because the school feels he doesn't need it.'

The teacher said, 'Who said that? I notice a tremendous difference!'

And I said, 'I'm sorry, but because the Ed Psych and the SENCO and the head haven't noticed any difference. He's got to be off for the next week. And she said, 'Well, I don't think we can manage him for a week!' And I said, 'Well, can I have that in writing please? Because unless you write and say it makes a difference, he will not be put back on it!' I was lying through my teeth, but I was trying to make a point! (laughs)

Gloria's story provides a glimpse into an almost comical lack of consensus among professionals. In this case, all the professionals involved were educators and worked at the same institution. Still, they shared little agreement as to the 'proper' treatment for ADHD, and in fact the administrators and specialists acted not only against the interests of the teacher, but without her knowledge.

In addition to the struggle over who would administer medication, there were other instances of disjunctures between medical and educational perspectives on AD(H)D treatment in England. For example, Rosalind provided the school with a list of strategies and information from the child's pediatrician about ADHD, as well as offered to put the teacher in touch with her son's attending consultant for more information. Nevertheless, she says said:

The teacher still will phone me up and say, 'Robbie won't sit down in his chair, and he doesn't manage his homework.' And I'd say, 'Well, you know that's part of his condition.'

While he's taking Ritalin, it doesn't solve everything. He can't sit down all day, and he can't organize himself all by himself. They know that that is his condition, but they don't seem to take it on board at all. It just sort of goes in one ear and out the other. It's like they don't care.

Yeah, they think I'm a neurotic mother. They just think that I'm making excuses for him all the time. I try to make them understand that this is why he takes Ritalin, that this is a condition, not just an excuse, and they can help him.

From Rosalind's comments we can speculate that perhaps Robbie's teachers do not believe that ADHD is a disorder, and hence they do not take the materials Rosalind provides seriously. Or perhaps Robbie's teachers do believe that ADHD is a legitimate disorder, but they refuse to accept Ritalin as a reasonable treatment for a child with this diagnosis. In either case, the suggestions provided by Robbie's pediatrician and psychiatrists that Rosalind has passed on to his teachers and school administrators for treatment beyond medication have simply been ignored.

The refusal of educators in Britain to understand ADHD as a disorder that would require more than a simple tablet for its remediation was evidenced in other mothers' stories. In Canada, Veronica described an incident that occurred when her child was in Grade 4, two years after his original diagnosis for ADHD, and after numerous consultations with teachers and administrators about her son's diagnosis and treatment. Frustrated with the school's seeming inability to provide treatment for her son, she brought in a well-known private ADD consultant whose specialty is both designing educational supports for children with ADD and facilitating communications between parents and educators. Veronica described her school's response:

> I had brought the psychologist – our psychologist and Dr Ricketts in Grade 2 to give the school an in-service for Jason's ADD. So we did strategies then.
>
> Uhm, I also brought in Carol Johnson ... Jason was in Grade 4 ... The resource teacher at the time – she went on to be a principal of a school, she said to Carol, 'Oh, you're here. You only deal with ADD kids. Why are you here? Jason's not ADD! Why are you here?' (laughs) We had such a reputation of being such bad parents that they refused to see that Jason had any need for help.

At the point when this event occurred, Veronica had been working together with the school's resource teacher to coordinate special needs services for Jason for over three years. For two of those years, Jason had been diagnosed with ADHD and had been taking Ritalin. Still, as Veronica perhaps rightly surmises, the specialist chose to believe that a child who is being medicated, and who still continues to have problems, is not a child with ADD but is a child with emotional and behavioural problems.

Mothers and the AD(H)D Treatment 'Team'

As noted earlier, truth claims about the treatment and management of children with AD(H)D rely on rhetorical claims of a collaborative team of parents and medical, psy sector, and educational professionals who together share knowledge and insight in constructing a suitable program of care for the troubled AD(H)D child. However, mothers' experiences with medical and psychiatric professionals and with educators cast suspicion on claims that parents are important partners in the child's treatment or that maternal knowledge is a valued element in decision-making over the AD(H)D child's treatment regime.

As shown above, mothers experienced considerable distress when they saw how, on the one hand, Ritalin allayed the child's 'problem' symptoms, yet on the other hand, new difficulties arose because of the drug's side-effects. The stories these mothers recount about trying to have medication changed, or about having dosages decreased, shed considerable light on the role of mothers as knowledge brokers in the treatment 'team' or 'partnership.' Corrine is one of the British mothers in this study. She is educated, middle class, works as a computer consultant, and teaches Yoga part-time; she is married and an active community advocate for special needs educational policy. Corrine provides an example of how medical professionals operated in distinct contradiction to one another over her son's treatment and how mothers can find their own attempts to bridge communications delegitimated. She had been expressing concerns for several months to her son's pediatrician about the side-effects that Aaron was suffering with his Ritalin dose. She noted that on Ritalin days Aaron would be awake until 2 or 3 o'clock in the morning and that she would often 'have to hold his hand, he was that frightened, he'd say his heart was racing. And I thought, "What am I doing?"'

Corrine went to her family doctor, who said he could not change the dosage, because the original prescription had come from a pediatrician. She then called the pediatrician who insisted that the dosage was the correct one 'according to Aaron's weight,' and that she should continue with the medication. When she went back to her family doctor explaining that her son was in quite a severe state, he again refused to counter the pediatrician's advice or even to see her son. She said: 'I've just been disgusted with it. And when it began to look like Aaron was going over the edge, when I really began to believe he might go suicidal, I just stopped him. I couldn't get anywhere with the pediatrician. Even though Corrine complained to two physicians that her son was suffering severe side-effects and that she was profoundly concerned about him, neither doctor took her concerns to heart. While the first physician demurred because of concerns of interprofessional hegemony, it must be noted that there is no legal ground for this physician's refusal to see the child and withdraw medication, as physicians, as well as pediatricians, are permitted to prescribe Ritalin and to monitor children with AD(H)D in the United Kingdom. The second medical specialist, the child's pediatrician, also refused to take Corrine's concerns seriously, adhering instead to the 'truthfulness' of his weight charts over the 'truthfulness' of the mothers' claims that her child was suffering side-effects from the medication. In both cases, professional concerns and beliefs superseded maternal ones, reflecting the professionals' devalued assessment of maternal knowledge.

In Canada, Veronica shared a similar experience. In Veronica's case, however, there was no possibility that interprofessional courtesy or hegemony was the problem because only one professional was involved. Instead, it was quite clear that the attending professional simply discounted the concerns Veronica expressed about her son's problems. She explained:

> Dr K is a psychiatrist, so he can write the prescription, and I've gone to him and asked him to change the medication to Dexedrine so that Jason can be on it longer so he can do it late at night. He's on the slow-release Ritalin, but it wears off by 3:30–4:00. It goes through his system really fast. But I've asked for the Dexedrine so maybe he can have some benefit – like, for doing his homework in the evening. But Dr K says, 'No. The Ritalin's working really well for him, we'll just keep him on it.' He doesn't want to change it. Jason's on 40 milligrams a day. That's a lot, and I worry it might even be too much, but no, he won't look at it.

Veronica's experiences illustrate how a mother's concerns take second place to the concerns of the professional. Veronica worries about the high dosage her son is on and also asks that her son be provided help to concentrate for his outside school activities. Her psychiatrist, however, is satisfied – Jason experiences no side-effects, his reports during the school day are good, and so to the professional, there is no need to reconsider treatment. The child remains on the Ritalin regardless of the mother's concerns.

Some mothers' experiences seemed to support the idea that professionals not only devalued maternal input, but that they felt profoundly uncomfortable hearing that Ritalin treatment was not a cure-all for their young clients. Gloria explained: 'We do actually see the psychiatrist every so often, and he checks his height and makes sure he's physically fine. But even the psychiatrist – he never wants to hear anything negative about what Keith's doing. If I say, "Keith is still not like this, or not able to do that," he says, "Well, I don't want to hear that. I only want to hear what's positive about Keith."' In this case, the medical professional seems to be unwilling to hear a mother's information about her son's actual response to treatment. Rather, he prefers to have his perspective upheld, despite maternal evidence to the contrary. Further, Gloria noted, this particular professional appeared to have difficulty in dealing with women at all: 'And when I used to speak, he'd tell me to be quiet. I found him to be very – he didn't like women. I don't think he liked women very much. It wasn't just me – it was other people as well. I talked to other mothers who said they wouldn't go see him any more, because that's the way he treated them. A few times I've nearly walked out of there – raging! And it's just the way he used to undermine you. You know. He used to make me feel that I wasn't putting in any effort into Keith.'

In Gloria's narrative we can read how little she felt her insight into her child's response to treatment was valued by the professional responsible for his care. It is also clear that Gloria felt not only discredited and silenced in her interactions with the psychiatrist, but she also understood that any failure on her son's part to respond 'appropriately' to the doctor's treatment was interpreted by him to be a result of her failings. In short, if Gloria were to offer any counternarrative to the professional's truth, she ran the risk of being found blameworthy for the very concerns she brought forward. Small wonder she felt uncomfortable with this helping professional!

Not only was maternal knowledge about the child's condition or response to Ritalin not taken seriously, but a number of mothers also pointed out how little their children's input had been considered in managing children's treatment. Amanda, for example, described typical interactions for her son's ongoing Ritalin monitoring in the following terms: 'The doctor at the pediatric clinic – when I would take him there, he would have Jordan stay out in the waiting room and I would sit and talk with him about how he was doing, how school was, what were his teachers' concerns. And I'd think, "Bring my child back here – he can answer these questions better than I can. I mean, I know what's up, but shouldn't you ask him how he feels on his medication? I don't know how he feels."' Amanda is insightful. Her concerns about receiving her child's input about his condition stem not only from a genuine desire for her son's inclusion, but also from a desire for accuracy. Who could better provide insight into the effects, positive and negative, of treatment than the patient? However, it seems that the insight of children, and of the women who live most intimately with them, was of passing interest at best to the educators, psy sector, and medical professionals many mothers in Canada and England described in their interviews. Ultimately, the idealized 'team' imagery that is deployed in professional truth claims about the treatment of AD(H)D is little more than that – an image, bearing little resemblance to the practices mothers encountered when they tried to express their knowledge about their children and their concerns about their care.

Multimodal Treatment

In addition to claims that proper treatment and monitoring of the AD(H)D child should involve the collaborative and caring interactions of parents, teachers, medical, and psy sector professionals, idealized treatment claims include the notion that Ritalin will be just one of many interventions provided for the benefit of the child and her or his family. For most of the children in this study most of the multimodal interventions they experienced occurred prior to diagnosis. However, for over half of the children in both sites, multimodal interventions did continue after diagnosis. These included family therapy, individual psychotherapy, social skills classes, private lessons and tutoring, special camps for children with learning and attentional problems, and occasionally occupational therapy. As with assessment issues, mother's narratives about multimodal treatment are rife with stories of poor interprofessional communication, professional disjunctures about the child's 'real' problems and 'best' treatment options, pejorative treatment of children, families, and mothers by professionals, and frustrating evidence that professionals are not always as insightful as they claim to be.

Here, I will not repeat the stories about disjunctures, disagreements, blame, and questionable competence among med and psy sector professionals in providing multimodal treatment options to children, because in many ways treatment stories among these professionals mirror what has already been said in the previous chapter on assessment. Instead, it is important to explore the most critical place of disjuncture, disbelief, and blame that mothers encountered once a diagnosis had actually been obtained, namely, the school. Thus, for the balance of this chapter, I will discuss the stumbling blocks mothers who were dealing with treatment options for their children encountered in their children's schools from teachers, special educators, and administrators.

As we have seen, the ambiguities of the 'ownership' of AD(H)D include struggles for professional hegemony over the processing of children who are different and claims about what kind of professional knowledge and expertise is best positioned to understand these children's problems. In the assessment and identification phase, these struggles occur primarily between medical, psychiatric, and psychological professionals. However, although AD(H)D might in many ways be conceptualized as a medical problem, in the end, it becomes more an educational concern. This is because the child's problems typically begin in school, and teachers are often the professionals who bring things to a head and demand that mothers 'do something' (either through direct requests for an assessment or through ongoing disciplinary and exclusionary problems). As problems continue, and as assessment is taken on, teachers play a central role as evaluators of the efficacy of medical interventions. Finally, because so much of the child's treatment – at least ideally – rests in educational strategies, educators are positioned as part of the treatment 'team.' Thus, although educators as neither medical nor psy sector professionals, they play a role as initiators, evaluators, and treatment providers in the AD(H)D child's medicalization and/or psychiatrization process.

A central claim of the multimodal treatment discourse is that, once children are stabilized on an appropriate dose of medication (and it is often asserted that this may in fact be *no* medication for some children), the focus should shift from medical intervention into the educational and psychosocial realm. Educators are implicated as central treatment providers for children identified with AD(H)D – as the child becomes medically stable, educators should then implement remedial strategies in the classroom to help the child integrate socially and achieve his or her full academic potential. Remedial strategies include the following: behaviour modification protocols that reward positive behaviours and discourage negative ones, preferential seating to ensure the child is engaged in classroom and teaching activities, using teacher–student eye contact with consistent follow-up to ensure the child has fully understood instructions, pairing the child with another child to ensure the child is included socially, teaching the child specific planning and management skills, providing structure, avoiding punishment and instead focusing on consistent consequences for inappropriate actions, providing frequent breaks, providing directed and/or structured rather than 'discovery' learning opportunities, modifying tests and examinations to accommodate children's attention spans, modifying the amount of (home)work to be completed, ignoring some disruptive behaviours, and – in yet another 'teamwork' metaphor – maintaining good communications with the family.

Rarely, however, did mothers in either Canada or England describe teachers who seemed to understand or implement appropriate educational protocols for the AD(H)D-identified children in their classes.

Instead, mothers described ongoing friction between themselves and children's classroom teachers, situations that can only be described as educationally neglectful at best and abusive at worst, and interactions that indicated teachers had little insight into or interest in learning about the special educational needs of children with AD(H)D. In England, Penelope summed up her interactions with educators in the following terms: 'What we're finding is schools today – children are not – teachers are not allowed to show care to any particular child. They have to teach them all the same. And so, what we notice is that Morris, if you give him something to do, you know, in the classroom, he could, you know, sharpen the pencils, and he'd love doing things like that. He likes to please. But in a class of thirty-five children, he is not given those – do you understand? – those opportunities.'

Penelope's comments stand in contrast to experts' truth claims in which the ideal treatment plan is set out as one that will include 'relatively simple interventions' in the classroom that might 'adapt to the strengths and weaknesses of the ADHD child.' In Canada as well, simple strategies that ought to be easily implemented were not taken up by educators. Daphne provided an example: 'Stuff like, I would ask her to be sat in the front of the classroom – and they wouldn't because she's too tall. They put her in the back, by the door! Why don't we just put her in front of the TV!? Stuff like that really angers me. The disbelief of the diagnosis. Of the strategies. Of what it means. Of what it needs.' From Daphne's description, we can see that such a small accommodation as placing the child in a more appropriate position in the classroom is not readily incorporated into the AD(H)D treatment plan. Perhaps this is because such interventions are too 'trivial' to seem worth pursuit, or perhaps teachers (as Daphne speculates) generally disbelieve the diagnosis, and hence fail to accept the importance of such measures. For whatever reasons, however, very frequently mothers in both Britain and Canada complained that the educational interventions that mothers suggested, often basing their requests on materials provided by psychologists and special educationists to help their AD(H)D children, were rarely implemented in the schools.

One effect of the apparent resistance by teachers to implement simple behavioural and classroom management techniques into children's treatment regimes is that mothers begin to see teachers not as allies, but as adversaries in managing their children's problems. Lydia provided a nice account of this, in describing her opinion of teachers:

These people see it as a behaviour, not a learning problem. So once the behaviour gets dealt with – they don't have to do anything.

They assume that medication is the cure. Medication is *not* the cure. Medication is what allows the children to develop the strategies to help with their learning. But it's not gonna fix it. And if they don't wanna fix it – you could just give the kid a truckload of Ritalin and it won't make a difference ... It frustrates me that teachers don't get that – makes me really angry.

These people say they can teach. They say they know what to do. And they're lying.

Lydia's closing comment provides insight into another response of mothers to the inability or unwillingness of educators to provide appropriate educational interventions for AD(H)D; identified children. Lydia's response illuminates how mothers come to believe that teachers are not only not part of the treatment 'team,' but that in fact they are not competent.

British mother Diane, for example, has learned a great deal about behaviour modification through parenting classes provided by her local support group and through a local psychologist's clinic. She described the kinds of protocols she uses, the ways her son has taken them up, and the ways that she has tried to share these tools with her child's school:

I mean, we've tried all kinds of things. I've tried with his classroom teacher to show her about the star chart that we have at home. It says, '7 o'clock – get out of bed. 7:15 – take the sheets off the bed, because he still wets his bed. 7:30 – get in the bath. 8 o'clock – get out and get dried.

It's like every single thing is there. He likes doing it. He checks and ticks in his boxes himself. So we've got several systems like this – a card system for weekend duties, etcetera – like, cues to help keep him on track. And of course, we had this system of rewards – like he can save up points and he'll get a toy that he's been wanting, or a privilege, like playing on the computer, or whatever.

Diane's description of her home strategies covers very nicely the key elements to behaviour modification: that the tasks demanded should be small, manageable, and immediately rewarded, and that the individual should find the rewards desirable. Professionals who deal with AD(H)D also recommend the strategies she outlines as treatment protocols for use within the classroom. As she noted, the program has made life a great deal simpler at home, because Andrew 'is great with it.' However, when she has tried to pass her successes with Andrew on to the school, she said:

> I've told them what we do with him, and they say that it is good, but they seem to be, uhm ... Like, I mean I've told them what works, and they seem to agree with me, that shouting at him, for example, absolutely doesn't work. I find, however, that even though the school says it does these things, and they agree with me, they do shout at him a lot, and he gets sent out of the classroom on a daily basis. I've been told this by other mothers who volunteer at the school. And I've seen it myself.
>
> Oh yes – one week he had been absolutely perfect with the chart, and so he used all his points to buy himself an action man. And the teacher actually wrote a note, she actually wrote down on his report, that I buy him toys to make him behave, to make him be good. I saw the notes, and I was absolutely furious. She wrote it as though I was spoiling him, as though this was what made him behave badly.

From Daphne's reports of the teacher's actions and comments, it is clear that the teacher either does not understand the fundamentals of behaviour modification or that she simply disagrees with behaviour modification in principle. In either case, she fails to implement the simple but effective protocols in the classroom. Further, her assessment of Daphne's use of behaviour modification is not that this is a mother who is doing an excellent job of responding to her child's difficulties; rather, this teacher interprets Daphne's efforts as *causing* the child's problems by 'spoiling' the child. Clearly, there are serious gaps in this teacher's understanding of how and why to implement the 'simple classroom interventions' that are recommended for AD(H)D children. Instead, as Diane indicated, the teacher falls back on old standbys in dealing with the situation – first, she shouts at the child and when all else fails, she blames the mother.

Shouting at children, handing them detentions, making them stay inside during recesses and lunch hours, giving them extra work, and ultimately excluding them were tools that teachers in both sites used with alarming frequency for children with AD(H)D. Repeatedly, mothers expressed dismay that, for example, a child whose natural levels of activity made it difficult to remain seated and concentrating would not be provided with frequent breaks or would even be denied access to regular school activities that might permit them to 'let off steam.' Instead, and in contradiction to idealized treatment claims, rather than understanding that these children require time to 'let go' and opportunities to experience success in 'non-academic' subject areas, teachers often punished these children by refusing them playground time or participation in elective classes such as art, music, or physical education.

Penelope provided an example of how ineffective these sorts of informal and formal exclusions were in terms of teaching children desirable classroom behaviours:

> Morris had been made to stand outside the deputy's office for a week. On arrival at school, at playtime, and at lunchtime. And I had to take him to the doctor's because he had a wound – he'd been standing there outside the office since Monday, and he came to me at 10 o'clock at night on the Thursday, and said, 'Mom, I've got a sore toe.' And I looked at it and it had an open wound, and he said, 'Can I wear trainers today? Because I think I'm going to have to stand outside Mrs P's office today.' So he'd been standing there for hours all week, rubbing his feet, kicking his toes, and he'd caused a wound.
>
> So my immediate reaction is, because I know he can cause problems and all the rest – so I say to him, 'Oh, Morris, what have you done?' He said, 'Well, I don't know, mom.' I said, 'Well, you must have done something to be standing outside Mrs. P's office. How long have you been standing out there?' He said, 'Well, since Monday lunchtime.' And I said, 'Well, what have you done, Morris? Come on, tell me what you've done. We can straighten this away.'
>
> And he couldn't remember. He could not remember. To this day, neither of us knows why he stood there all those hours.

It is hard to imagine that punishing a child who cannot understand or remember what he has done wrong will be an effective strategy in teaching him to correct his actions. Further, while Morris did not apparently understand why he was being disciplined, he did understand that he was being treated badly. Penelope described the way that Morris was behaving during this time: 'I took him to the doctor's – not just for the wound on his toe, but because I'd noticed that he had not been able to sleep that week, wasn't eating properly. He hadn't told me what the problem was. I didn't know what the problem was. But when he told me about the standing out in the hall, I just knew what was going on then. You know? This teacher has been using discipline as a tool against children – and not only Morris – to get rid of children who are too difficult for him to teach.'

These are the effects of teacher practices that fail to live up to the promises of idealized treatment strategies. Not only do children who get punished inappropriately fail to learn how to improve their behaviour but they suffer emotional and psychological turmoil. Additionally, in situations like this, any belief on the part of mothers that educators are competent or even *humane* becomes undermined.

A second effect of educational treatment practice that is ineffective or inappropriate is related specifically to children's problems of social isolation. While the idealized treatment discourse stresses that teachers need to provide avenues for marginalized children to become integrated into the classroom and the playground, mothers repeatedly told stories that indicated teachers did not see this as an important aspect of the child's care.

In situations like this, where children are reportedly badly treated by teachers, when they are made examples of, isolated, and ostracized, not only do mothers not see teachers as part of the solution, but in fact, they see teachers as *creating* problems. Becky provided us with some insight:

> It's got to the point that, whenever anything happens, the teacher blames Anton. And now the children do it as well. There'll be like a group of them laying on the carpet fiddling and fiddling, and the teacher will ask what's happening, and the other children will lay still or say Anton was doing this or that. So it's often, 'Anton, out!' You know? He's taken on this role, and the kids have learned that it works, because he's an easy target.
>
> A seven-year-old. To be thrown out for being disruptive. He has to stand out in the corridor, or go to the head teacher to be told off. Or, often, in the classroom, they have this little carpeted area where they go to have group talks. And the teacher will pull him out, to sit on the tiles, away from the classroom, with his back to the room, because he isn't very good at sitting still and waiting his turn. Things like that.

This story stands as an example of how a teacher's classroom management techniques not only fail to address social isolation, but indeed seem to contribute to it. Through formal and informal exclusionary techniques, the child's difference is not minimized but accentuated. Further, the child's peers learn that the child who is different is one who is easily scapegoated in the school setting.

In Canada, working-class mother Marlene was so concerned about the social isolation her daughter was experiencing in the school that she approached the classroom teacher over it, asking her to help Leanne socially. She described the teacher's response:

> Leanne never complained about it – never told me a thing, but I heard it from other mothers, so I started going to the playground, just to keep an eye on things. And I saw it – running away from her on the playground, calling out to her that she was crazy, making fun of her, viciously, isolating her.
>
> And I asked the teacher if there was anything she could do about it. Was there anything in Leanne's behaviour that she saw that we could work on?
>
> And she said to me, 'Well, you know, let's face it. Leanne *is* different. She is tall for her age. She's slow. She can't really follow what's going on in the classroom, and she needs a lot of special attention. The kids pick up on the fact that she's different. I have a class full of children who have very low self-esteem, and unfortunately it makes them feel very good to pick on someone who they feel has lesser ability than they do. Unfortunately, there's really not much I can do about it.
>
> I just stood there, and I thought, 'What do I do now?'

Marlene's petition to the teacher for help is not out of line with idealized educational, social, and psychological treatment texts that suggest teachers have considerable power and ability to help children become a part of their social circle. Further, Marlene was careful to ask for help with an attitude of deference and with an openness to learning from the teacher how she could help her daughter to ease integration. She did this to avoid alienating the teacher, and also to indicate that she, as a partner in her child's education, was more than willing to meet the teacher halfway. Nonetheless, Marlene clearly came away from this exchange convinced that the teacher was not only uninterested in making efforts on Leanne's behalf, but that she actually found Marlene's isolation convenient in the classroom. As she said: 'I thought to myself, "You're *promoting* this!" Because it's good for everyone else. They all need someone to pick and she's a good choice. She doesn't fight back, she walks away, she doesn't complain about it, and she is different. I think it actually helped this teacher out in managing the other kids to have my daughter in this position!'

Whether Marlene's assessment of the teachers' motives is correct is not my main concern in this book. Rather, my concern is how mothers perceived the treatments their children were provided and how poor treatment responses had an impact on mothers' opinions not only about teachers and other professionals, but about AD(H)D treatment in general. In Marlene's case, the effect of this teacher's poor treatment response was that she believed the teacher was not only incapable of helping, but that in fact, she 'profited' from her child's problems.

A third effect of teachers' lack of understanding and expertise relating to AD(H)D was that mothers came to suspect that teachers really had little interest in actually treating the problem. Mothers believed that while teachers might want to identify problem children for assessment, and might be relieved to think that medication would help the child to fit in with classroom regimes, they actually chose not to learn how to deal with AD(H)D in any way. In other words, while teachers might 'drive the ADD/Ritalin machine,' they had little interest in 'owning' it. Again and again, mothers described providing information to teachers about their child specifically, and about AD(H)D children in general, only to be ignored. Jenny provided an example:

> It's their choice not to be educated. I went to the school and said, 'You have a professional development day coming up. I will pay Dr P. I will pay the fee of having Dr P come to your school to run an information session on ADD.' And she was willing to come, because to her Mark is an example of what should *not* happen to a child.
>
> I said, 'Look, three kids in each classroom – statistically – have attention deficit, and the earlier it's treated, the more – you know, you can *save* these people. You can save them. You can help their self-esteem. You've gotta do this.'
>
> I gave the teacher a book. At the end of the year she gave it back. I said, 'Did you read it?' she said, 'No. I didn't have time.' I read that book in one night! One night, and she couldn't give that much! God! I just hit my head against the wall.

In the end, teacher responses like this left mothers feeling betrayed, disappointed, and angry. As well, the apparent lack of interest of teachers to take on an active treatment role for troubled children led to suspicion. Here, Daphne offered a succinct example of maternal suspicions, saying, 'I think that a lot of the teachers don't know what is it is they're dealing with. It's something they don't understand, or know about. Or they think that once it's identified, that once this kid just gets put on meds all will be well. We're gonna calm him down. And we're gonna titrate up the medication until they're stuporous, because it'll be easy to have this child in my class.'

We will recall that Daphne, in part because of her medical background, was quoted earlier saying that she supported the use of Ritalin and saw it as necessary, likening its use to that of insulin for individuals with diabetes. However, even a woman like Daphne who accepted Ritalin as a reasonable treatment option struggled with the ways that Ritalin was used as the only intervention, while other strategies were left unused. Further, because of her unsuccessful struggles to obtain educational interventions for her child (and not simply because of anti-Ritalin discourse), Daphne came to believe that often Ritalin use *is* a teacher-driven phenomenon, employed by educators and administrators as a quick, cheap, and dirty way to control children.

Conclusion

This chapter examined the truth claims contained in the professional discourse over idealized AD(H)D treatment, where Ritalin is positioned as only one element in a wide array of medical, psychological, social, and educational options for troubled children. Additionally, it explored the elements of anti-Ritalin criticisms and speculated on the effects of these criticisms on mothers' decisions about treatment. Finally, by reporting the frustrations of mothers over their children's actual treatment, I have conveyed the disappointments and doubts that mothers continued to live with, even after their children were supposedly being provided with treatment.

As we have seen, when the children in this study finally received a label or a name for their problems, their mothers generally described feelings of relief. Often, they spoke of how, when their children were first provided with a Ritalin trial, they felt hope that they and their children would finally receive the help they needed. However, once that first blush of optimism wore off, mothers encountered discursive and material practices that left them feeling ambivalent at best and cynical at worst about the medication their children were asked to take and about the helping professionals in their and their children's lives. For some mothers, this meant refusing medication under any circumstances, while for others, the answer was to curtail medication at every possible (non-school related) opportunity. Finally, for many of the mothers in both sites, the ambiguities of AD(H)D treatment led to anger, suspicion, and – as shown in the following chapter – resistance to medical, psy sector, and educational professional truth claims and practices about AD(H)D, Ritalin, and mothers themselves.

7 Resistance, Risk, and the Chimera of Choice

I am a mother whose child is on Ritalin, as well as a family physician who has several young patients on the medication ... I would dearly welcome an alternative to giving my daughter drugs. In fact, my husband and I spent three years with her going through play therapy, behaviour counseling, paediatric consultations and tutoring. At the end of all that, we still had an unhappy kid who was going to fail Grade One. So I had her seen by a specialist, who prescribed Ritalin. We worked very hard to give her the best start in life. So why do I feel so guilty?

Dr Val Bayley

Letter, *Maclean's*, Canada, April 1996, p. 4

I started a support group with another mother, Christine Spice, last year because we were not getting any help and did not want other families or children to suffer like we had. The group now has 30 members and we listen to problems and do not reject people as neurotic because we have been rejected in the same way ourselves. We also aim to make professionals and academics more aware of this condition and the problems parents and children face.

Helen Peters, Founder

Herts & District AD/HD Support Group, U.K.

http://www.disability.now.org.uk

One of the concepts I wished to explore in my discussions with mothers was the Foucauldian understanding of knowledge as a form of power and of power as available to all actors through resistance based on an appropriation of knowledge and discourse. As noted earlier, my interviews were undertaken with the assumption that mothers are not simply objects of medical, psychiatric, educational, and helping professional discursive practices. I also assumed that mothers of AD(H)D children are active subjects who interpret, interface, advocate, and care for their children both in conjunction with, and in opposition to, these multiple professionals. Thus, I expected that maternal narratives would not only offer a critical insight into professional discourse and practice attached to AD(H)D, but that mothers would have a great deal to tell us about how women in relatively subordinate positions tread the terrain of compliance and resistance. Thus, my examination focuses on how maternal experiences in both sites are constrained by the deployment of professional truth games that include normative discourses of motherhood, knowledge, and risk, and how in turn, mothers enacted their own strategic truth games in countering professional practice.

This chapter examines the ways that these mothers' stories open up the Foucauldian concept of resistance and show us how mothers' modes of resistance are necessarily enacted within relationships that must be sustained, even though they may not be ideal or even tolerable to mothers. In short, these women's narratives provide evidence not only of the ways that women are able to enact resistance, and use knowledge and power to their own ends, but also show the limits women encounter in their attempts to appropriate discursive power for themselves.

The introductory quotations to this chapter, from women who mother children with AD(H)D, reflect shared concerns: the compelling need to provide care at all costs, the struggle to find appropriate assistance for one's child, the ambivalence of dealing with professional authorities, and the feelings of stigma attached to parenting a child deemed problematic. These quotations also provide insight into the ways that some women take up circulating discourses of risk, responsibility, and blame as personal failings and the ways that others use discourse to construct a counternarrative about themselves, their children, and professional knowledge. This chapter examines the strategies that mothers in this study used in dealing with professionals. These strategies ranged from apparent compliance through to active resistance; however, each was deployed by mothers in hopes of keeping the situation under some sort of control, and each can be seen in terms of mothers exercising power and resistance to professional truth games about AD(H)D, motherhood, and normativity.

Bad Children Have Bad Mothers

Mothers in this study were acutely aware that they were judged as lacking or worse when their children began to encounter problems. Repeatedly, women described picking children up from day care settings, school yards, church groups, and children's activities, to be met with the glaring looks and negative comments of teachers, activity leaders, day care workers, and other mothers. The mothers were also aware that the public censure they encountered went far beyond the specifics of the situation: the negative judgments included not only the immediate situation, or the child itself, but extended more generally to the mother and her personal character. As Deanna described: 'Other parents, who don't have kids with special needs, can be a pain. I've had some negative comments about kids being on Ritalin, and how it's drugging kids because Moms are too lazy to raise their kids properly. ... And when they don't realize who they're talking to, I've had people make comments like, "The mother must have been drinking when she had the baby." Just really ignorant!' Deanna raised an important point. Often mothers learned of the judgmental and derogatory beliefs of others through general social discourse. In shopping lines, in casual conversations at work, in school yards, in church, and at home, mothers often encountered thoughtless comments about children on Ritalin and AD(H)D. Often, the speakers did not realize they were talking to someone who came from 'those kinds of families' or who had 'those kinds of children.' Nonetheless, even though the messages were not directed at the women personally, mothers clearly perceived them as hurtful.

In professional interactions, the judgments were also evident. Women who pressed too hard to achieve a diagnosis, or who insisted that there was something that their children needed in order to achieve their full potential, were named by teachers, psychiatrists, psychologists, and physicians as overprotective, or overachieving, or simply in denial of their children's true limits. Women who were reluctant to have yet another assessment or therapy session, or who were loath to medicate their children, were accused of being negligent or in denial of their children's difficulties.

Women whose children appeared unruly in shopping line-ups, playgrounds, classrooms, or churches heard in both direct and indirect ways that their mothering was questionable. Constantly, they encountered questions from family members, friends, and professionals about their disciplinary practices, their parenting skills, and their personal lives. Women were told by professionals and informal supports alike that their marriages, their employment, their moving homes, their divorces, their other children, even (as in the case of Clarissa's Argentine-born son Julio whose behavioural problems were speculated to stem from second-language issues, or in the case of Daphne who as a Canadian was presumed by British professionals to be less adept at parenting than a British mother), their foreignness was 'really' the cause of their children's problems.

For example, in Grade 3, after much intervention and assessment, Samantha's son Justin was diagnosed with ADD, and he began taking Ritalin. As so often happens, because he had missed out on crucial elements in his early schooling, and because Ritalin was pretty much the only intervention that was offered at the school, he had significant gaps in his knowledge base and in his ability to learn new materials. Samantha described the problems that arose:

> He has an older brother and a younger brother and they're both picking up stuff he cannot grasp. And the younger one is five years younger! That, for him, was rough.
>
> And the Ritalin was helping, but he still was having trouble picking these things up, especially in school. And that's what they brought up – maybe it's just – he's jealous because he's been the baby for all that time and suddenly now there's a new baby. And they wanted to know – like – do you get along with his Dad. It was – me. All about us – first. But, and that's what I said to them – no, this was long before the baby ever came. But they never made that connection that it was school – to them, it was still about stress at home, and the new baby, and my relationship to his Dad.

In this case, Justin's professional 'team' initially perceived Ritalin to be a godsend – he was able to concentrate and attend to his learning for the first time. However, when it failed to 'fix' everything, the gaze of professional scrutiny returned once again – not to teacher practice, medication levels, or remedial work that might need to be done, but to maternal and family-centred pathology.

Repeatedly, regardless of the specifics of the mother's life: whether she lived in Canada or England, whether she was married or single, whether her family was large or small, rich or poor, professional or working class, foreign or native, each mother described similar experiences of censure and distrust, particularly at the hands of helping professionals. Further, this occurred whether the child was just beginning to present problems, only at the early stages of assessment, or diagnosed for some time. Professionals' attitudes towards mothers were judgmental, discrediting of maternal opinions and claims, and assumed some measure of maternal culpability. Conversely, and perhaps understandably, mothers' attitudes towards helping professionals were characterized by suspicion and anger.

Presentation of the Family as Emotionally Normal

Mothers' understandings of themselves as scrutinized and judged led them to find ways to represent themselves and their families in a positive light. Sheila is a First Nations woman who is divorced, raising her daughter, and working full-time as a health professional; she describes herself as 'working poor.' She summarized a typical teacher-mother interaction: 'Oh, they were always calling from the school. You know. "We've been having problems in class. Sheryl's homework is not getting done, her agenda's a mess, she's forgetting things." And always it was, "*Is there something wrong at home?*"'

In this comment, it is clear that, although the child's problems take place outside the home, the first assumption is that home life, rather than classroom practice or the child's capabilities, is at fault. The AD(H)D child's inability to rise to a standard of what is 'normal' in the classroom is seen by teachers as a reflection of a home life that is not 'normal.'

Professional blame of mothers was, in both sites, almost universal. In turn, mothers struggled to refuse that blame. Sheila provided an example: 'I just got to the point that I learned to smile and say, "No, home life is pretty good these days. Is there something wrong at school? Can we work on that?"' In her refusal, Sheila consciously positions herself as a normal woman engaging in healthy family practice. Home life (regardless of the professional's insistent question) is, in fact, good. Further, she turns the tables of blame, placing the responsibility for classroom problems onto the teacher.

Moira is a British mother of two adoptive children; she possesses two graduate degrees and is married to an academic. Numerous medical and educational professionals had accused her of being overly ambitious for her 'retarded' child and of protecting him too much from the 'real world' of school demands. She found another way of refusing pathology and attempting to present her family as normal to professionals: 'When I went for an appointment with the Director of Education, I invited parents of other children – like Penelope and her husband Lawrence – to give their stories on one or two sides of A4[1] that I could take, bound, to give to him, to say, "Look. It's not just me having difficulties with my ADHD child. Here are other people's stories."' In the end, Moira produced a bound, fifty-page document to present to the school staff and administration. Moira's decision to represent her case as one of many similar others is more than an attempt to show that her family is numerically normal. In Moira's document, ADHD children are children who come from 'good' families: she strategically chose to include parents, 'like Penelope and her husband Lawrence,' who are married, heterosexual, middle-class, and 'respectable' couples. Her presentation of a group of idealized parents who simply share a common, but not totalizing, problem is offered as an implicit counternarrative to the institutional story of her (and any ADHD) family as a site of pathology.

Another battleground for the struggle to be seen as normal concerned family structure. Women in this study who were single mothers, experiencing divorce, or part of blended families intuitively knew they were being judged. In fact, very often educators, psychologists, and physicians stated that these personal attributes were the probable cause for their children's problems, which often led to serious delays in receiving appropriate assessments or treatment. Thus, in both sites, family therapy often became the first suggested step in attempting to help children in these families.

Glenda, a Canadian woman who went through a divorce during the course of her son Kevin's assessment, experienced strong pressures from helping professionals to assume responsibility for her son's problems because of the presumed upheaval her divorce was causing. She explained, 'I'm really, totally responsible for Kevin's learning disability because I was a divorced woman ... The feeling I got from them was that I just refused to accept my son the way he is, and I refused to accept what a marriage breakup might do to someone like my kid.' As an attempt to deflect some of that responsibility, Glenda provided professionals with several reports from a male psychologist who led a Parents and Kids Working through Divorce workshop that she and Kevin attended. She did this to show that any divorce-related problems were being dealt with, as a way of proving that despite being a divorced

---

1 The European standard for letter-sized paper.

woman she was still a responsible mother and 'to show that Kevin did have a male role model in his life in the form of this counsellor.' She also brought her brother with her to parent–teacher interviews because 'I wanted to show them that, while I was divorced, I was not alone.' This reflects an understanding that a man – either in the guise of a professional or as a family member – might provide professional or emotional authority. Moreover, it reflects an internalized understanding that professionals would 'naturally' understand a male 'presence' as a positive force in her son's life.

Even women whose families do reflect the idealized male-headed, nuclear form understand that it is occasionally necessary to shore up their legitimacy with professionals through conscious display. Pat, a wealthy, educated Canadian woman explained: 'I only ask [my husband] to come to meetings where I know it's really gonna count that the father is there ... So that would be another strategy that I would use. I would use my husband as an authority figure when I needed backup. And he played that role very well. Yeah, and it showed that we were united.' This can be seen not only as a way for Pat to present herself as 'normal'; it also reflects her understanding of gendered power in the family. Bringing a husband or brother along lets those in authority know that a woman has resources – the hope is that this will be read as a message that these women will not be so easily pushed around because there's a man on the scene to provide both legitimacy and protection.

Pat and Glenda brought their husband and brother along to critical meetings. Moira, in the United Kingdom, brought along a friend of the family who was a special education needs coordinator. Sheila brought along a friend who is both a colleague and a psychologist. Penelope brought along her mother, who holds a master's degree in social work. Penelope explained her reasons for needing support in the following way: 'I got so frustrated I actually started to ask my Mom to come to the interviews with me so I'd have a witness. I'd say to Mom, "I'm so sick and tired of leaving these interviews believing that I'm the worst mother in the world. At least, being told – subtly – that I wasn't doing my job as a mom." You know, "We've got a problem" and then, that my job as a mother was to ensure that my child would bring his agenda home – like it was always my job to handle the agenda!' These women understood that they needed additional gendered, educational, and professional capital to shore up their legitimacy and to balance the scales of power in these encounters with professionals. In addition, they wanted someone to act as a witness to what happened behind closed doors.

Bearing Witness

Bearing witness in one way or another was a pervasive activity for all the women in the study. Mothers' understanding of themselves as scrutinized not only led them to find ways to represent themselves and their families in a positive light; it also led them to attempt to return the gaze of psy sector scrutiny. One way of 'watching the watchers' for these mothers took the form of meticulous record keeping. When I interviewed mothers in both countries, almost all of them brought along stacks or boxes of files, report cards, papers, assessments, information sheets, letters – anything and everything that had been written about their child and their family. In the interviews, these often served as visual cues for women to recall critical incidents, but they also illuminated discrepancies between what was written and what the women recalled occurring. Women reported using these records frequently in interactions with professionals as a way of keeping track, repudiating discrepancies, and attempting to hold professionals to promises made.

In addition to fighting 'files with files,' these women participated in other ways to switch the direction of the scrutinizing gaze. Many of us tend to think of volunteering as a way of contributing to public and community betterment, and often school volunteering is framed in public educational discourse as an opportunity for parents to 'partner' in their children's educational experiences. While the mothers in this study did volunteer for those reasons, they also expressed a second and often more compelling reason for volunteer activities. Veronica, a Canadian mother of four who lives in a working-class neighbourhood, explained: 'I've had such a hard time with the school, such a hard time, uhm, I didn't even wanna go into the school to volunteer, but I thought, "You know, I need to be there. I need to see how my kids are doing at school." Part of being a volunteer is that I need to see how much of a hard time these teachers are giving my children.'

This perception of needing to keep an eye on the school so that kids will not be abused was pervasive for these mothers, and often the women's fears were borne out. In Canada, Glenda described coming into Kevin's class to volunteer and observing the teacher pull him across the classroom by the arm while verbally disciplining him very loudly in the presence of his classmates. Another Canadian mother, Amanda, spoke about coming in and finding her child's desk enclosed with cardboard, pressed up against a blackboard positioned at the front of the class in such a way that his back was to the rest of the room. In Britain, Corrine discovered that math period, her son's weakest subject, was the time when he was pulled out of the classroom to attend a special needs social skills class. Penelope discovered that the classroom aide she had struggled so hard to obtain local education authority funding for spent most of her time in the school office photocopying papers for the classroom teacher. Each of these women used this information, sometimes to confront authorities, but often simply as a way to fill out their own perceptions of what was 'really' going on at the school.

The volunteering arrangements of mothers in this study served another purpose besides providing mothers with insight into their children's days. For women in both Canada and the United Kingdom, volunteer activities, whether in the classroom, in the school office, on school committees, or in the parents' association, were a way to show that mothers were active and cooperative participants in the educational, medical, and psychiatric complex. Lucille, the Canadian mother of a sixteen-year-old boy, explained her decade-long volunteer career in the schools this way: 'My presence in the school was so that I would be able to talk to the teachers and they would know that David had a parent who was extremely concerned and willing to do anything – anything – and just tell me, and I will be there, and this is what I am doing, and let's work together.' For Lucille volunteering became a way to indicate to the world not only that her son's mother was a good person, and willing to pitch in, but also that David was supported, and someone whose family was there for him in all ways. In other words, despite David's problems, this was a good boy, from a good family. Thus, it was hoped, this was a child and family deserving of consideration and respect.

Unfortunately, consideration and respect were not always afforded mothers, even when they made significant contributions to the general good of the school and community. Veronica, who volunteered in the classroom, in the school library, and on the parents' council, exemplifies this. In her son's school, parents and staff mingle freely in the staff room. However, Veronica says she finds herself ostracized there, noting, 'When I go to the lounge, people – teachers and parents – talk about me and my son's behaviour openly. Nobody talks to me there, but I keep going anyway – I have to.'

Lucille was active in the school council, a 'room mother,' and a volunteer helper in the office who worked hard as a way to show her support of her child. When David entered Grade 4, her school suggested he should have yet another assessment. Finally balking, Lucille refused, saying, 'Look, we've had assessments. We've got assessments out of our ying-yang. Look at the assessments! Can't we have individualized help, an aide, someone to help him in story writing? Something concrete?' A few weeks later, the child's classroom teacher called Lucille, yelling, telling her she 'can't believe that I am so selfish that I would deny my child the right to be assessed, because of my unwillingness to accept his problems.' Lucille makes a nice connection between the inefficiency of volunteering as an insurance policy against being harshly judged as a mother, or against her child being poorly served, saying 'this was right out of the blue – after me doing – like, at the school, all the time.' Apparently, it does not matter how much effort mothers make to evidence their care and commitment; when they fail to comply they still risk being perceived as bad mothers.

Although these mothers worked particularly hard in an attempt to provide protection and advocacy for their children, and to show themselves as participants in their children's educational and community experiences, they were not entirely successful in achieving either of these goals. Nonetheless, despite the relatively low success of these strategies, few of the mothers interviewed had given up trying, because as Veronica said, they *have* to.

Policy Work and Advocacy

As noted earlier in this book, most of the mothers I interviewed in both Canada and the United Kingdom claimed that their occupational commitment had been profoundly affected as a result of their children's disability: this is not to say that the actual care of these children demanded that mothers stay at home. Rather, mothers either opted for contract or part-time work, or gave up their paid employment altogether, in order to become 'full-time advocates,' a term some of the mothers used to describe their current occupation.

This kind of advocacy did not always immediately involve agencies or institutions that dealt directly with the mothers' children. At least half of the mothers had engaged in some sort of committee or policy work at the school board or community health board level, in a support or parents' rights group capacity, or sometimes at a governmental level.

Explaining that she had tired of doing volunteer work without much effect in her son's classrooms, Veronica, the Canadian mother of four boys, explained that she now volunteers at the school board level: 'So, politically. I'm doing this politically ... I've put up my hand and volunteered. They're doing a new booklet from the board on parents' rights ... I've learned all kinds of things that my school shouldn't have done to me and my child. And a lot of the input in that booklet is mine.'

Pat, a Canadian woman whose daughter Chloe was assessed by no less than six different individuals before finally receiving a diagnosis and a treatment that worked for her, was so frustrated with having to begin anew with each professional encountered, telling and retelling her story, undergoing family and child assessment again and again, that she said: 'I did quit my job two years ago – it was just too much. Now I've moved from educational advocacy to mental health advocacy. So I actually am on the mental health committee for the city, representing families and children – and I'm actually the only person on these committees who has actually received any of these services. It's very interesting, the things that have revealed themselves.' In some ways, this strategy is a bit of an end-run. Mothers get involved in volunteering at the administrative or community level not only because they feel they have experience and insight to offer, but also because they hope to effect change in service delivery at the individual level by changing policy at the administrative or community level.

When asked how much time these activities take up, women will admit that it does take a toll on their ability not only to work at their desired capacity, but on their marriages, and on the lives of their other children. Nonetheless, these efforts remain worthwhile for these women, if not in terms of an immediate pay-off for them or their children, then, as a way to contribute something positive in hopes that it might help others. As Pat said, 'One of my personal objectives on this committee is that – with someone as competent as I am and with the skills that I have and the non-fear of professionals that I have, and the resources ... If I find days that I want to give up – my goodness, what are other people feeling? And one of my objectives is to see if we cannot have a real effort at patient – and family – advocacy.' For Pat, as for other women in the study, community advocacy and policy work represent a hope that things can be made better for all parents who encounter the ambiguity of AD(H)D diagnosis and treatment.

Picking up the Slack

Q. How much homework should my child be doing?
A. Division 1 (Grades 1–3): parents and teachers should encourage children to read each evening. No formal assignments should be made,

but from 5–10 minutes of systematic study per night is recommended
Division 2 (Grades 4–6): Formal homework assignments may be given
on occasion. They should be within the half-hour range.

Calgary Board of Education
'A Guide to the Rights and Responsibilities of Parents'

It seems that many people, including teachers, special needs coordinators, family members, and the lay public, are under the impression that
'proper' medication will fix the problems of AD(H)D children. In practice, however, once a child has been diagnosed as having AD(H)D and
has been prescribed an appropriate protocol of medication, the work of
AD(H)D management begins. Children with the disorder require specific teaching strategies to keep distractions at a minimum, to help them
learn organizational skills, and to ensure that they have been communi-
cated with completely by the classroom teacher. In addition, they typically need to learn positive social interaction, having been bullied and
ostracized for years, and they often have huge deficits in their learning
because they literally have not been fully present for large chunks of
their early education. Teachers particularly can assume that a child who
is on medication, and whose performance still does not improve mark-
edly, is a behavioural problem, an intellectual problem, or that the
problem really was located in family pathology after all. After medication has begun is often when real school–parent conflict begins.

Homework was an oppressive and pervasive problem for the mothers in both sites of this study. Mothers in both countries reported that,
because their children were not grasping materials taught during the
daytime, they regularly engaged in an average of two to three hours of
homework; in some cases, this homework schedule occurred every
school night. The children in this study were, on average, nine years old
at the time of the study, and had been diagnosed for two years; the
amount of homework these mothers reported doing is certainly not
typical of what one might expect for children in Grades 2 to 4. Mothers
reported that attending clubs, extracurricular activities, evening play-
time with friends, television, or just general relaxation were not part of
these children's lives during the school year. Further, mothers described
long hours of arguments, frustration, and tears – both from the child
and from the mother – as they struggled to complete school work each
night.

All of the mothers, in both Canada and England, reported emphati-
cally that homework books and/or student agendas, which are ostensi-

bly positioned in educational discourse as vehicles of communication and partnership, instead were a central and painful aspect of their interactions with their children's teachers. Rather than opening up avenues of understanding, the agendas became points of professional penetration into mothers' homes and private relationships with their children. Further, these agendas were clearly understood by mothers as evidence that educators did not see them as partners, but as individuals who (like their children) were required to satisfy the teacher's requirements. Finally, mothers understood these communiqués not as routes by which to achieve a joint understanding with teachers of their children's problems, but as yet another instance wherein they and their children were perceived by teachers to be inadequate.

As noted above, it seems educators can assume that Ritalin alone should be adequate to remedy the deficits in learning, social skills, and behaviour that children who cannot attend have developed. The result is that AD(H)D children who are either not properly diagnosed, or who are treated with medication alone, can end up being perceived by educators as bad or stupid. Daphne's daughter Melanie was one of the children in the latter category. Prior to her diagnosis at eleven years of age, teachers, special educators, and psychologists had tested her as having an extremely low IQ and as lacking the ability to learn. She had been placed in the regular classroom for options, but for core courses she was put into a special classroom. At home, when Daphne worked with Melanie one-on-one, Melanie seemed to read at above-grade levels and was indeed teachable. When Daphne tried to broach this with the classroom teacher, she says, 'The teacher won't talk to me – when I walk into the classroom the teacher rolls her eyes and says, "What do you want now?"' Unwilling to give up on her child or accept the prognosis the specialists offered, Daphne taught Melanie after school for three years. She explained the lengths she went to: 'So, I had a routine on Fridays and I would go into the classroom and Melanie and I would tidy her desk – to be sure that she could find stuff, you know, and what was for homework, and if she had all her books. Well, Melanie had no homework for anything. So I had to tie up with a mother who would tell me what her son had learned that week, give me the information, and I was doing home schooling with Melanie. I was teaching Melanie the stuff that they were learning at school, after school. Because she wouldn't teach her in the classroom.'

Rather than be appreciated, however, for the efforts she made on behalf of her child, Daphne was censured by the professionals who dealt with her, because, as she says, 'I was a pushy mother, pushing her – not accepting the fact that I had a disabled child, pushing her beyond her abilities.' Like so many of the mothers and their efforts, there was little professional praise or appreciation for what in many ways is 'more than good mothering.'

If the mothers were not appreciated for their efforts, then, one wonders why these women would persist in going to such great lengths to compensate for educational shortfalls. Here, British mother Diane offered some insight: 'Well, I was worried for his future. And I cried over it. I was worried about what he might become. He couldn't concentrate. He'd got no education – half the time he was in the headmaster's office, or out of school. He brought home so much work that I knew he was getting nothing done in the school. And each year it seemed the gap between him and his peers got that much wider. I felt I had to make up, as best I could, for what he was missing.'

As noted earlier, poststructural theorists have speculated that mothers, over the past two centuries, have slowly been incorporated into 'partnerships' with professionals in the moral and social regulation of their children (Badinter, 1981; Donzelot, 1997; Rose, 1990). Diane's point provides a more nuanced response to poststructural notions of mothers as more or less willing handmaids to helping professionals. In Diane's narrative, risk operates as a disciplining force: for Diane, as so many others in the study, to give up 'team play' with schools, teachers, doctors, and counsellors, meant to give up on their children as well.

Strategic Diffidence

Although most of the women in both sites ultimately came to have some sort of a showdown with their child's teacher, family physician, psychologist, or pediatrician, this confrontation was preceded by a long, creative process of trying to make things work, attempting to cooperate, or presenting oneself as a part of the solution rather than part of the problem. One strategy used by mothers is what I term *strategic diffidence*. Even though mothers did feel they had knowledge and expertise to offer professionals about their children, they found ways of doing this that were not threatening to professionals. Veronica showed an example of this: 'I asked the teacher, "Did you know there's an evaluation from his prior teacher, and an evaluation by a psychologist on his file? About his learning styles and how you can enable him to learn?" Because I didn't say, "How you're supposed to teach him" –

because when I had done that his first year teacher – male – was, "Oh no. I don't need to read that. I'm a teacher. I *know* how teach. I don't need to read that." So I learned to approach things differently.'

The interaction Veronica described came on the heels of a parent–teacher meeting in which she discovered, to her dismay, that the teacher had not bothered to read her son's hard-won evaluation. Although furious, she knew better than to alienate someone so close to her child. Her experience and response mirrors that of most of the other mothers in the study. Even though they may have felt rage at being judged, frustration at the seeming ineptitude of professionals or the fragmentation of services and information they encountered, and concern on behalf of their children, these mothers seemed to know that they had to at least look like they were on-side with professionals if they hoped to get things done for their kids.

Further, as Pat, reflecting the views of other mothers, noted, 'I do some schmoozing with this – *I have to* – I don't wanna get too confrontational because at the end of the day, they can take it out on Chloe.' Whether in the form of a classroom teacher who can make or break a child's educational experience, a helping professional who can withhold an appropriate referral, or an administrator who can refuse to approve funding for services, the power wielded by professionals kept most mothers, at least temporarily, well behaved.

Lack of Cooperation – Sweating the Small Stuff

The willingness to appear deferential and compliant in hopes that things will continue to move in a positive direction sometimes breaks down. While most mothers tried to cajole or please, there were inevitably times in the process when a line was drawn. Teresa, the Canadian mother of two boys, knew from the outset better than to play by the rules. In discussing her child's first parent–teacher interview in Grade 1, she said, 'They always recommend that you take the kids, but I never did. I do not believe in this – it's a load of hooey as far as I'm concerned. I don't think that this a place for the kids, because, number one, they're gonna tell you the good and the bad about the kids, and the kids don't need to hear the bad. All they really need to hear is how well they're doing in school. But teachers don't use that opportunity. So I don't bring my kids. Period.' For Teresa, the desire to protect her child from a negative experience overrode any urge to cooperate on this issue. Despite an institutional rhetoric of parent–teacher interviews as an opportunity for parents and teachers to find ways to support children, Teresa's hunches about the 'true' nature of the meeting proved correct: that first meeting initiated a long history of punishing parent–teacher interactions.

In England, one of the first phases of assessment seems typically to involve a recommendation of family therapy, reflecting the more explicitly stated British cultural belief that AD(H)D is first and foremost a behavioural problem and an apparent understanding that psychiatric disorders in general stem from family of origin issues. Penelope explains how she resisted professional scrutiny: 'And this psychiatrist – man – had said that he wanted to see us as a family. And we objected to that because we didn't want to be speaking negatively about Morris in front of him. We certainly didn't want to be talking about Morris with his sister there, so we didn't bring her.' Although Penelope did manage to refuse to bring her daughter to these sessions, she was not able to refuse entirely. In the end, she relented to the psychiatrists' insistence on their son's presence, because 'The alternative was – that either we refused to play it their way, in which case we would make no progress whatsoever – because we'd had to wait months. Or, we bent to their way of doing it. So we bent to their way of doing it. But, we did so unhappily.'

Unhappy or not, Penelope's acquiescence was made in light of hard alternatives, and the belief that after a long, difficult struggle to obtain services, she needed to maintain a relationship with the therapist regardless of how inappropriate his demands might seem. In part, this reflects maternal concerns for the immediate outcome: if one does not play according to the rules, one will not continue to be considered part of the team, and the encounter will go badly from the start. A more long-range concern is that if one does not cooperate, the proper referral to the next rung on the ladder will not be made. Finally, if one does not cooperate with professionals, there is always the risk that the underlying suspicion – that the troubled child's problems stem from family pathology – will be shored up because the mother has shown herself from the outset to be non-compliant in dealing with helping professionals.

Being branded a 'bad mother' or an 'overachieving mother,' or a 'hostile mother' was a fear that many of these women shared. This was not so much because of the mothers' self-image, but because they understood that their actions might produce negative fallout for their children in the form of reduced services, refusals to refer children to other professionals, or negative reports being passed on to other professionals.

Bringing in the Big Guns

In many ways, the struggles that mothers engaged in with professionals were what Michel Foucault has named 'truth games.' In games of truth, claims are made to legitimacy through the use of language and a reliance on common understandings of what is 'true' (Foucault, 1984: 74). By bringing in the big guns (other professionals, books, articles), mothers in this study deployed truth games about AD(H)D and its 'proper' treatment by calling on the superior knowledge claims of AD(H)D specialists and educational policy-makers. In doing this, mothers shored up their own claims to knowing their child's needs best. Thus, maternal and superior professionals' knowledge claims about the 'reality' of the disorder and the needs of the child were used in an attempt to bring teachers, special educators, and general physicians to an acceptance of a certain 'truth' about AD(H)D.

Most of the mothers in this study provided teachers and psychologists with written reports, articles from professional journals, materials copied off the Internet and parenting magazines, or suggestion sheets provided by other professionals. Perhaps in response to a perception that these materials were not always received happily or used effectively by teachers and special educators, almost a third of the mothers in the study actually paid specialists working in AD(H)D to come into the school to provide information on their children. Glenda explained: 'I brought a psychologist into the school when Kevin was in Grade 2. I paid for that. Ninety bucks for him to come to the school – just for a meeting with the teacher and the principal and everybody – to go over strategies how to deal with this child. To teach them how to teach him.' Even with the cachet of a professional designation and a specialty practice based in AD(H)D strategies, however, it is not always certain that other professionals take up the knowledge of these 'big guns.' Veronica said, 'The special education teacher is very ineffective, so I've just learned that I need to bring people in. I've brought in an ADD consultant several times – there have been several meetings with admin and teachers, but they don't seem to be using her. They treat her respectfully, but not much happens.'

Thus, even bringing in educators and paying for it oneself is a truth game with limited success. In the end, it seems that playing by the rules, educating the educators, being a team member, presenting oneself as a good and deserving mother and child, and contributing through volunteer hours are strategies with serious limits for mothers.

Refusing to Play

Of the thirty-four mothers I spoke with, two were home-schooling, two had children who were finished formal schooling (although neither had managed to graduate and both were under eighteen years of age), and six in England and seven in Canada had ultimately thrown in the towel and moved their children out of mainstream schools into specialized, segregated settings.

The tactic of giving up or refusing to play is a route that these mothers took only after their efforts at conciliation, education, and advocacy had resulted in what they perceived to be inadequate and often punitive situations for their children. For example, Jenny is a Canadian mother who volunteered for 'playground duty' at her son Mark's school as a way to try to keep the lid on the bullying and isolation he was suffering at the hands of other children. Jenny said that she used to think of herself as a 'partner' in her child's education, along with her son's teachers and the school administration. She had tried repeatedly to engage the principal and teacher in solving the problem, adopting a conciliatory approach in hopes of gaining their support. After one particularly cruel incident, however, in which a hate note was dropped into the family's mailbox on Mark's birthday, Jenny reached the end of her patience. She confronted her 'partners' by storming the staff lunchroom: 'And I went in and I didn't even knock. And one of the teachers looked up, and I said, "You know who I am." And I was furious. And I said, "Now. This has gone on long enough. Look at this letter." I looked at the teacher and said, "You know who wrote this because you know the kids' writing. I don't, because it's not signed. You find out who wrote this. And you make sure that their parents get a copy of this, and you tell them that this was delivered to my child, in his home, on his birthday. And I want to know what happens. You can't sweep this under the carpet. This is it."' When the school failed to meet her halfway, ignoring even this confrontation, Jenny understood that her 'partnership' was little more than an illusion. Dissatisfied with their response, she switched her child to another school in the public system, while at the same time setting the wheels in motion for a switch to a private school. Within three months, Jenny and her family had moved over 1,000 miles and changed the father's job so that they could be close to a school that specifically serves children with attentional problems. Jenny is adamant that her son will never again attend public school.

Pat provides another example of refusal after a particularly difficult incident. She described having an epiphany after Chloe, in Grade 5, had been removed from school as a result of her emotional problems:

> As we were struggling through this, we asked, 'What is the purpose of education?' And I'm not sure it's to always be in a classroom, or to learn a particular curriculum. I am sure for my situation that education for my ADD child means to go through a socialization process that will hopefully keep her intact in order for her to become an adult – where diversity is more acceptable.
>
> So when people ask why she isn't in classrooms, I say, 'I don't care if she's in a classroom. I don't care what kind of marks she gets. I want her to practise being in the community – being human.' In the end, you get down to basics ... You say, 'this is the bottom line – I want to try not to do damage.'

This decision, about what counts in her life, and how little that meshes with the goals of educators, professionals, and community members, has eased things tremendously for Pat's entire family, as Chloe has been recently home-schooled by a group of private tutors. For Pat, the primary goal is to keep her daughter from harm, to see to it that she survives childhood, and to run interference for her when she thinks it will be in her child's best interest. Being perceived as a 'good mother,' playing on the professional team, and complying with institutional and community standards that do not work for her child take a far distant second place.[2]

---

2 The choices made by these mothers – to confront authority, to withdraw the child from the public system, to cease 'playing' on the team – are difficult ones, and carry with them not only risks that they are perhaps not the 'right' thing to do for the child, but also that the mother who makes such a choice will be perceived as a bad or inadequate mother. Indeed, one of the reviewers who read this book in manuscript asked that a comment be made here about bad choices / bad mothering and the very real possibility that these mothers may have added to their problems by not playing along. My sense is that, while mothers' choices may not have always been ideal, they were typically motivated by mothers' desires to protect their children. Further, the choices made by these women came only at the end of a long series of more 'acceptable' maternal attempts to build bridges, provide information, and resolve problems in more collaborative ways.

Resistance and Risk

Following Foucault, rather than assume a unilateral direction of power that might emanate from physicians, educators, and psychological professionals and institutions, I wanted to examine the ways the mothers exercised power in dealing with AD(H)D. In so doing, I considered the notion of what James Scott (1985) has termed 'weapons of the weak' as a way of understanding maternal strategies of resistance related to the stigmatization and surveillance attached to AD(H)D. For Scott, weapons of the weak employ indirect rather than confrontational strategies; they are typically slow, stubborn, and quiet means of resistance. I found that mothers utilized these types of strategies, as for example, in the case of Veronica's refusal to continue with homework support, or in the countless stories mothers told of being rude to teachers, of being aggressive with physicians, of refusing some parts of a child's treatment, or of insisting on keeping at least some family members from attending therapy.

As Peter McLaren (1985) noted, the resistance efforts of disaffected and subordinated actors are typically enacted in ways that are tacit, informal, and unwitting. Indeed, these mothers did often respond to professionals in these ways. Particularly in their early encounters with professionals, mothers' efforts to restate the truth, to draw boundaries around intervention and judgment, and to lay claim to services and information on their own terms occurred in an ad hoc way. These early resistance strategies typically occurred in an immediate response to breaches in mothers' trust in professional knowledge and compassion or in response to a dawning sense that they and their children were being judged inappropriately. These actions by mothers were reactive rather than proactive, spontaneous rather than planned, and typically enacted in private rather than through public means. Only after considerable conflict did mothers move to more public and considered action, such as sitting on policy-making committees or lobbying with schools and boards, or ultimately, refusal. Regardless of the strategies employed or the professional practices responded to, maternal strategies were enacted within highly charged discourses of danger and risk that mediated these women's abilities and willingness to operate freely.

One set of risks women faced was that of being perceived as less than good mothers. Mothers understood perfectly that they were judged, scrutinized, and examined in the public and professional gaze when their children behaved in ways that were not perceived as 'normal,' and indeed these women made conscious efforts to present a 'normal' face. Further, they described tailoring their responses by softening and feminizing their voices and actions, in a sense reflecting an understanding that gentleness, deference, and warmth (i.e., 'normal' feminine and maternal practices) would be more likely to keep professionals on-side.

Another risk that mothers faced was that, by speaking out or refusing further cooperation with professionals, mothers actually might have made their children more vulnerable. All of the mothers I spoke with expressed concern that their struggles had perhaps led professionals to see the child and its family as troubled and undeserving not only of extra services related to the child's disorder, but of the bare minimum afforded to others less troublesome. This was a particularly strong concern for mothers in their interactions with teachers and school administrators – mothers expressed very real concerns that services would be withheld and that their children would be seen as more troublesome than ever. This fear of increasing the child's vulnerability often tempered maternal resistance.

On the other hand, the overwhelming reason given for maternal efforts was a desire to protect and care for their children. These women were watching their children struggle, and it was this, more than wanting to look like good mothers, that motivated them. As British mother Corrine said, 'I knew that Aaron wasn't a bad boy, because at home I had seen how loving and really how lovely he could be. And as time wore on, I could see that side of him quite simply fading away. It was that hope that I could salvage the good part of him that kept me going.' Thus, both challenging *and* cooperating with medical, psychiatric, and educational professionals was for this and other women, motivated by fear for the child's well-being. One fear was that, by soliciting professional help, and by keeping the maternal–professional 'partnerships' alive, these children could also be kept whole and out of harm's way.

For other mothers, the fears and risks of confronting or abandoning maternal–professional interactions over the children were related to discourses of danger and risk attached to AD(H)D in both professional and lay literature. As is so often the case, the claims within professional and lay discourses related to the dangers and risks of AD(H)D are neither clear nor comforting for mothers and their children. As noted earlier, there is considerable clinical evidence that AD(H)D is not a predictor of alcohol or drug abuse (Boyle and Offord, 1991; Boyle et al., 1992; Halikas et al., 1990; Shuckit et al., 1987). Likewise, research does not clearly support a causal link between AD(H)D and delinquency and aggression (Frederick and Olmi, 1994; Farrington, 1989). Despite these ambiguous research findings, helping professional and lay literature relating to ADHD is filled with claims that ADHD children (particularly those who are inappropriately treated) are at risk for poor relationships, criminal activities, truancy, theft, unemployment, isolation, and alcohol and drug problems (Adams, 1998; Brooks, 1994; Choate, no date; CHADD, 1995; Johnston, 1997; Minde, 1987).

When mothers' resistance is enacted within a discursive field of risk and danger attached to non-compliance, these women's commitment to the well-being of their children places severe limits on the resistance they can and will engage in. The 'new prudentialism' that underscores much of present-day risk discourse devolves responsibility for risk and danger from public institutions and policies to the individual and the family, who are now held liable 'for their own risks – of physical and mental ill health, of unemployment, of poverty in old age, of poor educational performance' (Lupton, 1999: 99). In such a discursive climate, mothers are left with few options of refusal, as they and the child itself, rather than schools, doctors, and psychiatrists, ultimately will bear the burden of fault attached to the child's problems. Further, in this discursive field, educational, medical, and psychiatric professional discourse hold in their hands a stacked deck: there are few counternarratives women can take up that promise a successful, employable, and socially integrated child in the way that psychiatry, education, and medicine claim to.

On the other hand, mothers' actions were not undertaken only in response to discourse about risk and danger relating to their children and their futures. As Rosalind explained, when I asked her whether, from her readings on the topic, she had a sense that if she did not get him the ADHD label and treatment that her son Robbie would face increasing difficulties:

Things were *going* very badly. Uh, he – for example, he was becoming more and more socially excluded. When Robbie had a birthday, he would have – twelve children round for a party. And if he got one return every year, that was quite something.

We would have lots of children round for tea and to play with him. Once. And they'd never come back. If he got an invitation, that was unusual.

And in school, his 'friends' would use him as a scapegoat ... If anything happened, the children would blame him automatically, because often it *was* him. And if it wasn't, he was a very credible scapegoat.

Rosalind's comments illustrate how the potential for risk is not only a discursive threat about a possible or imagined future, but is a real worry related to real experiences.

Indeed, not only were children in this study perceived by mothers to be 'really' at risk for problems, but many of the children actually were endangered as a result of their experiences of difference. Pat described her daughter at age seven as a child 'covered in sores' that she herself had created through picking at her skin. Rick, whose mother, Helen, is a part-time nurse, had to spend three weeks in the psychiatric ward of the Calgary Children's Hospital at age nine, under a suicide watch. On the day of our interview in England, Madeleine described her sixteen-year-old son Nick as follows:

> Nick stayed out last night. He came home this morning with plasters on his wrist. Then he went on to tell me how he had lost it last night – he had been drinking, and all his emotions came flooding out. He says that he is heartless, but he is not. He is trying to be someone that he is not. He got himself in such a state that he slashed his wrists. His girlfriend had to stop him from going to the canal as he said he wanted to walk and be by himself.
>
> He wants to get a job, but feels he can't as he has no self-confidence in himself or his ability to do a job. He feels that he is on his own in everything he does, and he has not got any real true friends.
>
> A few days ago we were having a conversation about drugs, and I feel that my son is self-medicating – to be honest, I *know* he is self-medicating. I don't give him much money at all – I am careful of what I give him, but I know his friends supply him. I honestly don't know what to do. What can I do?

For Madeleine, the spectre of risk is real: her son has attempted suicide, he is using recreational drugs, he cannot find an educational placement any longer, and he is unemployable.

Madeleine's son was almost fourteen when Madeleine was finally (and after experiences that were discouraging to say the least) able to locate an ADHD-friendly pediatrician. Once Nick was finally diagnosed, he received virtually no medical, psychological, or educational supports for his special needs from the NHS or the school, and was in fact excluded for significant periods at several points in his education – he has completed only ten years of formal schooling. Nonetheless, even though professional expertise has provided Madeleine and Nick with precious little meaningful assistance, Nick's problems are so overwhelming that Madeleine feels she cannot abandon hope of finding some help from professionals. She and Nick were both scheduled to – yet again – begin family counselling at the time of our visit.

Mediating Factors in Resistance

It is important to note that not all the mothers in this study shared equal resources to bring to their struggles for assessment, services, and treatment of their AD(H)D-identified children. The mothers who home-schooled, for example, were able to do so because of family incomes that permitted them to stay at home and to purchase educational consultants to supplement their own teaching of the kids. Likewise, most of the women who volunteered in classroom activities were typically able to do so because the family did not rely on their paid employment to survive. Mothers who volunteered at the school board, community committee, and policy levels brought considerable cultural capital to these activities; they had educational and social class positions that provided them entrée into these milieus. The mothers who took their children out of the public school system also had, in most cases, significant financial resources that permitted them to pay the tuition for private schooling. The economic inequity of mothers' ability to resist was nicely summed up in Pat's earlier comments about her reasons for lobbying at the policy level. However, her beliefs that other, less-privileged mothers will necessarily encounter even more difficulties in navigating and negotiating the terrain of professional practice relating to AD(H)D are worth examining.

Pat's assumptions echo many researchers who surmise that middle- and upper-class women are more able than poor or marginalized women to resist inscription by professionals as incompetent or bad mothers (Abramowitz, 1996; Arnup, 1995; Baines et al., 1991; Hooper, 1992; Knowles, 1996). It is more than economic capabilities, however, that permit some women to resist better than others. Several of the mothers in this study who came from less privileged backgrounds were surprisingly resourceful in their dealings with professional power. For example, Veronica, whose roots are firmly working class, was able to influence policy through her lobbying for, and contributing to, a parent handbook produced by the Calgary Board of Education. Samantha, who works as a house cleaner and with her unskilled labourer husband raises four children, has managed despite straitened circumstances to gain a subsidized position for her son in a Calgary private school for children with special needs. In England, Gloria, who is herself on full disability assistance, and whose husband works as a parking attendant, has two children who are presently attending full-time boarding schools for children with special needs, with the local LEA picking up the costs.

One possible explanation for this is perhaps the ability of these mothers to draw not on economic but cultural capital to support their resistance efforts. As noted earlier, cultural capital consists not only of material and class resources, but also of available time, information about systems, and a sense of entitlement and assertiveness (Reay, 1998). Gloria, for example, because of her stay-at-home status and her familiarity with systems relating to disability entitlements in Britain, brought many of these cultural capital strengths to bear in her struggle with educational authorities. However, Gloria, Samantha, and Veronica all mentioned one other asset in their ability to deal with professional authorities over their children – scepticism. Veronica explained her ability to deal effectively with authorities this way:

> My Mom is schizophrenic, and I looked after her from the time I was   ·
> thirteen, so I learned early that you can't just take what they say at face
> value. I know what bullshit looks like. It's all about politics. You have to
> fight them on their own ground.
>
>   Because, they're always forcing their rules in your face. So I phone the
> board, and I find out exactly whether what they tell me at the school is
> right or not. And often it's bullshit. Complete bullshit.

Veronica's early experiences with her mother, and also her early experiences with the school, led her to doubt the motives of educators who pay only lip service to mother–professional partnership. She described how she responded when her son's Grade 2 teacher sent home a huge booklet of work that needed to be done:

> I phoned the school board, and they told me the regulation, and I said, 'Oh,
> I need a copy of that.' But I didn't ask them directly – because if the school
> board sends it to me, then the school's gonna hear about it, and they'll
> phone me up and give me a hard time. So I had my friend get it to her
> house, and I got a copy of it. It's a public document, but I wanted to be
> careful.
>
>   And then what I did, was I quoted the regulation. I told them, according
> to this regulation you're not to assign – and I copied the regulation out! – I

said, you're not allowed to assign formal homework, and this is formal homework!

This response – of doubting the teacher, of anonymously obtaining the information, and then getting her friend to actually receive the materials – was Veronica's *first* reaction. Unlike many other, more 'privileged' mothers in this study, she did not need to learn through bitter experience that professionals were not to be trusted. Unlike most of the other mothers in both Canada and England, Veronica 'knew' from the outset that what teachers asked parents to do in terms of picking up the slack and taking on responsibility for homework was neither appropriate nor acceptable. As she succinctly stated, 'Women who do this, who take this homework thing on – they enable the schools. They enable them to get away with not doing their job.' And, quite sheepishly, I have to admit that she's right.[3]

Conclusion

A final aspect of resistance that demands consideration is the relative 'success' of all of these mothers' strategies of resistance. Perhaps home schooling or moving a child to specialized educational setting might be seen as 'winning' against psy sector and educational authorities. However, these 'victories' came at great costs to family members, mothers, and to the children themselves. Penelope's son attends a special boarding school in England, and Sheila's daughter attends a segregated day school in Canada; each noted that although the child's educational needs are now seemingly being met, social needs are a serious concern because of the segregated setting. Glenda, whose son is now home-schooled, shares the same concerns. Rosalind, whose son attends a regular school in the community, acknowledges that she is not sure if he will manage to make it through to graduation; as she notes, it gets harder for him each year to keep up academically, socially, and emotionally.

Feminists have noted that postmodernism and poststructural approaches to research efface the gendered subject positions of women (Benhabib, 1995; Hartsock, 1990). In undertaking this study, I examined the ways that women can appropriate language, knowledge, and dis-

3 It is sometimes humbling, and even embarrassing, to interview other people about experiences that one has personal knowledge of. On hearing Veronica's narrative, I felt humbled that I had not seen earlier that school work was a teacher's, not a mother's, responsibility.

course and use them strategically in their struggles for recognition and legitimacy. I believe the discussion in this chapter on resistance and risk illuminates the creativity mothers engage in when advocating for their children; I also believe it illustrates the limits of those strategies of resistance that mothers use, thus complicating poststructural notions of power as circulating and available to all subjects. In the end, although mothers understand well enough what the rules and moves are in the game, they also know that their chances of 'winning' are profoundly constrained by power that not only circulates and can be appropriated by all subjects, but that is situated in institutions and practices that are able to withstand resistance and wield material power in ways that mothers cannot.

Finally, mothers are constrained in resisting by their concern for their children. Thus, even though professionals may provide flawed assistance, or even cause additional burdens for mothers and their children, these mothers were in many ways held ransom by a belief that, if they wanted to help their children, they must keep professionals on-side. An example of this ambivalent relationship between cooperation with authorities, refusal, and concern for the child is evidenced in Helen's narrative over homework. Most of the mothers in the study – both in Canada and Britain – did not take up Veronica's position of refusal regarding homework or regarding their roles as helpers to the school. Helen, for example, told a story that illustrates quite poignantly the willingness of mothers to take on the helper role:

> We're doing all this homework and at the end of Grade 5 they were doing some sort of project, which I had helped all year long with – you know, they had done two or three different papers. And I had done the research and helped him. And this last one I didn't know they were doing. Or I had come up with part of it, but there was one part of it that they had to go to the library to do – or something. And I didn't know anything about it.
>
> And they had the nerve to give him a zero! Well, to say the least, I hit the roof! When I had been spending hours every night. And the teachers knew I was spending hours every night with him – to get him to do this work. You know – to scribe, to do whatever I needed to do for him. And they let the librarian give him zero because I didn't know exactly what was going on!

In Helen's story, it is possible to see that some mothers cooperate with professionals or support their practices as a result of stereotyped notions that position the ideal woman as helpful and maternal. Helen's narrative indicates that in some ways, she sees that it is 'naturally' her job to get the child's work done – for the benefit of his school record, for the benefit of the teacher, and because that is simply what mothers are supposed to do. Still, this work stems from more than a desire simply to *be seen* as a good woman – rather, it is a desire to *be* a good woman and a good mother. When I asked her whether she had considered it to be her job to make sure he got his work done for the school, Helen replied, 'Sure it was! Because they weren't making sure he got it. Nobody else was doing it! And he deserved better!' In Helen's reply, I believe, we can discern more concern for her son's learning than a desire to please a teacher. In Helen's reply, and in mothers' willingness to resist, or to risk resistance, there is always the one thing that can hold mothers hostage, and keep them going – not fear, not keeping up appearances, but love.

Conclusion

Why Mothers – Reprise

My focus on maternal narratives has been, in part, a response to professional, lay, and academic claims that mothering a child with attention deficit disorder, with or without hyperactivity AD(H)D, is difficult and stressful in and of itself (cf. Atkins, 2000; Berry, 2000; Chisholm, 1996; Foss, 1999; Frederick and Olmi, 1994; Lacharité and Piché, 1992; Londsdorf, 1991; Minde, 1987; Rees, 1998c). In these discursive claims, the AD(H)D child is described as a burden and a worry, while the mothers and families of AD(H)D children are depicted as places of pathology and inadequacy. Additionally, these texts shore up the position of helping professionals as knowledgeable saviours who can and do offer relief and support to overburdened and underresourced parents.

I believe that asking mothers to speak for themselves about what they know and about what they experience in this culture provides a rich view of the operations of power, policy, discourse, and knowledge relating to AD(H)D. Hearing these mothers' stories provides a counternarrative to these pathologizing claims about AD(H)D, mothers and children, difference, and care. Indeed, these mothers' stories offer a direct challenge to commonly held notions of mothers as needy, of children as troubled, and of professionals as knowing helpers.

Although it is true that a number of mothers, particularly those in England, reported that their children were enigmatic and difficult to manage during the early years, for a larger proportion of the mothers, the most pervasive stressors came from sources outside the child and outside the home. Some of the stressors attached to parenting a child who is different arose within the community and the extended family, particularly for mothers in England. However, for *all* of the mothers in the study, in both Canada and Britain, discourse about AD(H)D, policies relating to difference, and especially the practices of helping professionals (educators, medical personnel, and psy sector workers) themselves posed the most significant burden in mothers' parenting dilemmas.

Mothers' stories about their encounters with texts and discourse relating to AD(H)D truth claims, about their challenges in negotiating systems and institutions, and about their interactions with professionals in the fields of medicine, psy sectors, and education, have illustrated several things. First, they illustrate how questionable the assistance of 'helping professionals' was for these mothers and their children. Second, they cast light on the difficulties mothers face when confronted with lay and professional 'knowledge' that is contentious and often misleading. Third, they provide some insight into the resourcefulness and intelligence that these mothers brought to their struggles for their children's well-being. Finally, they show how professional intransigence, incompetence, and judgmentalism in some cases actually created what can be framed as 'iatrogenic' difficulties for mothers. In these instances, mothers and families became labelled as crazy, uncooperative, difficult, pathological, and undeserving – in short, in many mothers' stories, the 'cure' was as bad, or worse, than the AD(H)D itself.

Mothers' Standpoint Revisited

Another reason I chose to focus on maternal narratives relates to Jim Thomas's (1993) comment, quoted earlier, that cultures have the ability to make 'life unnecessarily more nasty, brutish, and short for some people' (1993: 33). I felt it was central to the problem of AD(H)D to speak with mothers precisely because of their situation of vulnerability. As decision-makers whose choices are *limited by* the policies and funding practices; as moral agents who are held responsible *within* the discursive culture; and as relatively subordinate knowledge brokers who must act as interlocutors *between* the professionals, mothers are in a particularly painful position in the discursive culture of AD(H)D.

The stories that mothers have to tell about living in this position provide us with compelling evidence that the debates about AD(H)D, about Ritalin, about mother-blame, and about normalization are not necessarily as straightforward as various claims-makers would have it. Instead, I believe that speaking with mothers casts suspicion on circulating claims about the overreadiness of mothers to seek a psychiatric label for children who present parenting difficulties, about the 'easiness' of relying on medication rather than proper parenting, about the superiority of professional knowledge over maternal insight, and about the pathological nature of mothers whose children are different. Mothers' narratives illuminate the good intentions and insights of these women as they struggle to understand their children, to integrate them into their schools and communities, and to guide them with relative safety into adulthood. In short, when mothers tell us about their struggles, they demonstrate that these struggles are both heroic and guided by compassion. Finally, even in their confusion, anger, frustration, sorrow, and – yes – mistakes, these are mothers whose goal is to do the right thing *despite* the competing discourses, institutional orders, and discursive practices that comprise the culture of AD(H)D.

Nonetheless, while my focus on maternal narratives has been a relatively appropriate and productive point of penetration into the circulating discursive culture of AD(H)D, the choice in taking this approach has not been without contention. During my doctoral studies I was one of some twenty doctoral candidates at my university to receive an award in acknowledgment of doctoral research. At the reception for award winners and their supervisors, held in the university's prestigious faculty club, the recipients spoke for a few moments on their research topics, to the response of warm applause and supportive comments from our academic colleagues. When I stood up and gave my talk, however, another student's supervisor rose from the back row and, in belligerent tones, asked why the project did not include fathers and why, for that matter, did all 'these kinds of studies' systematically omit the travails of men. I explained my reasons – that the culture of mother-blame, and the pre-eminent role of mothers as interlocutors and caregivers made mothers a logical and fertile focus. I also suggested that perhaps a focus on fathers' experiences relating to their AD(H)D children would be a fruitful suggestion for a different research project.

Although this particular gentleman would have none of my rationale, I restate my assertion here. For the purposes of this study, I believe that a focus on maternal struggles has been the most important and fruitful point of penetration for an examination of the gender issues, power relations, and inscriptions of pathology on the family that relate to AD(H)D. Nonetheless, I also acknowledge the need for further studies into the relationship between mothers and fathers, particularly one that would include parents who are both together and separated, as a way to examine the intrafamilial, intergender, and private and public intersections that *parents* experience in dealing with a child who is troubled. An examination of the experiences of fathers alone as they intersect with public institutions, discursive practice, and gender normativity could be very interesting. In the latter study, it would be particularly interesting to speak with fathers who are both within a partnership and with fathers who parent on their own to explore the ways that fully responsible fathering might replicate or differ from fathering within a partnership and from mothering in terms of normative orders relating to blame, risk, and resistance.

Perhaps more importantly, however, I believe that the stories of children who are identified as different need to be told. While mothers in this study were able to speak as loving and concerned caregivers about the pain, isolation, and frustrations they saw their children endure, their insights into the daily schoolroom and playground experiences of their children were, of necessity, limited. Either through a direct engagement with children through interviews, or through observations of children within *their* culture of AD(H)D, children themselves could tell us important things about the experiences of growing up with stigma and about their struggles to be in the world. Children could also provide us with a view of AD(H)D that might demystify circulating discourses about AD(H)D children as bad, unruly, less than competent, 'abnormal,' and necessarily at risk.

Discourse as Culture

In the introductory and methods chapters, I set out an argument that mothers' decision-making and caregiving of children who are identified with attention deficit (hyperactivity) disorder is acted out within the frame of a discursive culture of AD(H)D that is both multifaceted and highly contested. In such a discursive culture, I included professional and lay texts, media representations, and professional discursive practices as each of these relate to difference, the family, good mothering, the pro's and con's of medicalizing and psychiatrizing children, normalization, interprofessional hegemonic struggles, public versus private education and med/psy services, and the superiority of professional versus maternal knowledge and/or truth claims. I also argued that a wide range of medical, psy sector, and educational professionals as well as alternative therapy providers and laypersons generate the discursive materials that comprise this culture of AD(H)D. Thus, the discursive culture in which mothers must understand and decide about AD(H)D is both diverse and diffuse.

Rather, however, than provide a direct analysis of the wide-ranging and varied discursive fields relating to AD(H)D, I have instead situated a small group of women's personal narratives about their children's difference, identification, and treatment against the backdrop of this varied and pervasive AD(H)D discourse and practice. Thus, because the focus of this study was on the mothers' experiences as enacted within the discursive culture of AD(H)D, my analysis of the discursive culture itself has not been perhaps as thorough as it might have been had the focus of this study been otherwise. As it stands, I have created a pastiche of texts and reports of practices, from a variety of sources, to act as the background for mothers' narratives.

Although I worry that this might have resulted in a less than adequate representation and analysis of the actual discursive fields and practices related to AD(H)D, my intention has not been to provide answers one way or another about the rightness of any discursive approach to the problem of AD(H)D or Ritalin. Rather, I have provided enough analysis to give the reader a sense of the contradictions, shortcomings, and pejorative aspects of the varied discourses that relate to the problem of mothering a child who is identified with AD(H)D. I do this to highlight the dilemmas that mothers face in attempting to know and do the 'right' things while trying to care for their children and to illustrate the ways that these discourses are problematic not only for the children involved, but for the mothers themselves.

However, additional studies relating to AD(H)D might fruitfully explore a direct examination of the textual and discursive culture that relates to AD(H)D. It would be important if such a study could further outline the lay and professional lack of consensus about the disorder and its treatment, the pervasive interprofessional miscommunication and even acrimony over handling AD(H)D, and the knowledge and power games attached to AD(H)D at both an interprofessional level and at the level of public policy and funding.

A second concern that I have struggled with in conducting this research hinges on my choice to examine mothers' interactions with discourse and practice in ways that are attenuated rather than direct. An effective approach to understanding the interactions of human actors with discursive practices has been to make a direct connection between subjectivity and culture, basing the research analysis on comments made by participants while viewing television programming (Fiske, 1998) or reading popular magazines (Currie, 1999). The strength of these approaches is that direct connections between discourse, perceptions, and subjectivity can be made, based on observations and questioning. Because, however, so much of the discourse that relates to mothering a troubled child occurs in private spaces such as doctors' offices, classrooms, counselling sessions, and school head or principals' offices, direct and immediate observations of mothers' encounters with all aspects of the discursive culture of AD(H)D were not possible. Additionally, mothers come into contact with lay and professional discourse from such a wide variety of sources (e.g., report cards, parenting literature, newspapers and television, counselling, and educational professional texts) that selecting 'typical' texts for direct observation, particularly when comparing two cultural contexts, would be nearly impossible.

Thus, this study compromises connecting mothers and discourse in attenuated ways. Mothers commented on information about AD(H)D and Ritalin that they have read, and I speculated on what those texts meant in their decision-making processes as a way to connect discourse and agency. Mothers also commented on discourse about mother-blame, risk, and difference, and I also speculated on what those texts meant in terms of mothers' subjectivity as expressed by the women's private beliefs and public responses to their children's problems. In terms of agency and subjectivity, the evidence for these connections to discourse was not based on immediate observation of mothers' readings of discursive materials. However, the collage of interactions and responses reported in this book has demonstrated convincing connections between discursive structure, human agency, and subjectivity.

A final concern stems from my focus on maternal experiences within the diffuse and diverse culture surrounding motherhood and AD(H)D. The resulting analysis has not been a study of the sociology of medicine, medicalization, gender, education, or psychology. Instead, the focus on a culture of difference has resulted in a hybrid study of each of these sociological subdisciplines. While perhaps frustrating for readers wishing for a more detailed or specific analysis of each of these aspects of the problem, maternal narratives provided a crucial suture for each of the various disciplines. As such, this nexus provides insight into how each discipline impinges on the other and how varied aspects of the 'social' impinge on the 'private' experiences of human actors.

That being said, as the data collection and analysis for this study drew to a close, I became convinced that, with AD(H)D, the primary professional–maternal site of conflict over knowledge, power, and care occurred within the school. Again, and again, mothers described how various educators used a wide range of disciplinary practices, such as expert knowledge (Foucault, 1984), danger and risk (Douglas, 1966, 1992; Lupton, 1999), and constructions of normality (Donzelot, 1997; Rose, 1985) to engender maternal compliance and to lay claim to the 'truth' about AD(H)D and about children who are different. Further, a small number of the mothers in the study were themselves educators. I was struck by how these women, as mothers, felt stigmatized, ignored, and pathologized in their dealings with educators; conversely, as professionals, they spoke of their AD(H)D students as a burden, the families as non-compliant, and their workplaces as unsupportive in dealing with children who are difficult and/or different. Further, while this study provides a thorough and illuminating look into the discursive constraints that mothers and children encounter, the chapter on resistance and risk allows us to understand that discursive practices produce real effects, and thus begins to illustrate the advantages that a more materialist analysis might bring to the study of difference. These insights lead me to believe that an ethnographic examination of educational practices relating to the problem of AD(H)D is critical for future studies.

Theoretical Contributions

What are the theoretical strengths of this project? Feminist accounts of motherhood have changed the ways that we think about the naturalness of motherhood. They have also called into question the notion that mothers (freely) choose to mother, mother according to their (unproblematized) inner guide, and that motherhood operates outside of the interests of the state. Finally, they have provided a beginning account of how motherhood itself contributed to the reproduction of the division of labour embedded in nuclear family forms by contributing to the gendered socialization of children. Unfortunately, however, the vast majority of these feminist analyses adhere to a Freudian notion of child development: they stop at the end of the preschool years and, in fact, centre most squarely on issues of pregnancy, childbirth, and infant bonding. As such, the medical intersections that much feminist writing about motherhood examines focus only on mothers as objects of medicalization and intervention, with a particular focus on obstetrics and pediatric medicine. My study, by examining the experiences of motherhood into children's school years, brings the arena of mothering into a nexus of institutional presence that has been previously underexplored in feminist literature: that of the school as interlocutor for the disciplines of education, child medicine, educational psychology, and psychiatry.

The study also initiates a critical examination of the practices of mothers themselves, moving the discussion away from mothers as simply *done to*, to mothers as actively *doing*. Some feminist writers (cf. Findlay and Miller, 1994) and poststructural theorists of the family (cf. Badinter, 1981; Donzelot, 1997) have noted the role of mothers as both objects of social control and as active and sometimes willing agents in administering or passing on that control to the members of their families. Nonetheless, these analyses do not fully examine how these experiences are negotiated, the dilemmas attached to the choices involved in the experiences, or the ways that power is both experienced and appropriated by mothers at the micro-interactional level.

Likewise, critical writings in education tend to examine the negative aspects of the exercise of power inherent in schooling practices as a critique from within. In critical pedagogy, issues of class reproduction and moral education in the classroom have been examined and have problematized our innocent beliefs about public education as a way to achieve social equality. These examinations, however, typically operate as a critique of institutional practices at a macro-level, without examining how those practices are experienced by teachers[1] and, even less often, by children. Even more rarely do they critically consider the relationship between educators and parents (or mothers), who may have shared goals but differing perspectives, strategies, and access to power or the penetration of schools as disciplinary institutions into the 'private' realm of the family. This study examined precisely this problem and thus opens a relatively unexplored vein of educational criticism.

Critical treatments of medicine, psychiatry, and psychology have been more successful in integrating poststructural notions of human subjectivity: there is a lot of work that does examine the ways that power circulates, the ways that disciplines act to classify and categorize

---

1 For an example of educational criticism that does examine the gendered nature of teaching, its ambiguities for women who have little institutional power, who enter into teaching with a wish to help, but who often find themselves acting as – relatively powerless – agents of control, see Grumet, 1988.

ever-finer gradations of the 'abnormal,' and the ways that lives become micro-managed through interactions with a broader array of disciplinary practices. Nonetheless, there are few examples of poststructural analysis that examine these interactions from the perspectives of patients or subjects of the medical gaze; rather, these studies tend to be historical treatises or purely textual discourse analyses. By asking mothers themselves about how they encounter, understand, interpret, and resist or comply with these discursive practices and historical effects, this study has provided us with important empirical insight into the workings of power and the connections between knowledge, discourse, and subjectivity.

Finally, an empirical bridge between meso-level poststructural discourse analysis and micro-level feminist standpoint theory has been fruitful. In the first instance, it complicated traditional feminist theories of domination and empowerment, wherein power is usually seen as specifically located, patriarchal, and oppressive, and where knowledge is formulated as emancipatory and empowering (Allen, 1990). In the second instance, mothers' narratives have enriched and enhanced traditional poststructural notions of the ways that power is circulated and taken up by drawing our attention to the limits imposed by women's material and gendered positions.

Epilogue

The year I gave up, the year I refused to play on the 'team' any longer, was the year we began to get our daughter back. Despite our trepidation over what she might miss from not attending a community school, despite my misgivings about the legitimacy of her diagnosis, despite the worry that this would just be one more false alley along which to become further lost, Hilary went to the school for children with special needs.

I remember the first parent–teacher meeting at that school like it was yesterday. The teacher sat across from us, eyes open, and told us 'Hilary is not keeping up with her homework.'

My heart sank.

I thought, 'Of course she isn't. She's given up. She's learned that her homework produces results that are inadequate or wrong. She's learned that to ask for help results in tears and arguments. She's learned instead to tell us, "No, I have no work to do tonight."'

I thought, 'I know where this conversation is going – I've been here before.'

But this time, the teacher did not ask me about the problems at home, or suggest we have Hilary's medication levels checked, or ask me what I was going to do about it. Instead, she said, 'So what I'm thinking is this. I'm thinking that you need to be taken off homework detail. I think this needs to belong to Hilary and to me. I'm cutting you off.'

It was a simple plan, and one that we all worked on together. Hilary either did her homework, or she stayed after school to catch up. And if she stayed after school, we were to devise some kind of 'consequence' to compensate for the fact that we had to pick her up rather than have her come home on the bus. The teacher facilitated these arrangements. *Facilitated* them.

I am chagrined to admit how hard it was for me to let that homework routine go. I have had to think long and hard about that one. Was my own sense of maternal worth so tied up in producing a good child and looking like a good mother and a good family that I was willing to sacrifice our quality of life just to appease the school? Was I such a polite, compliant, middle-class woman that the thought of truly resisting simply escaped me? Was I so subject to the idea that, if my daughter did not do what her teacher expected, the only avenue remaining to her would be failure, alienation, and a life of pain?

To be honest, I am still not sure. I do know that letting go and letting the teacher own this problem was a terrible struggle for me. Not that I loved the family's daily battles over homework or that I believed it was my job to teach Hilary. For me, letting that homework routine go meant surrendering control, releasing our daughter to the world, and to herself. The process was both exhilarating and terrifying.

It took almost a year, but – by God – she did it. With her teacher's guidance, Hilary took responsibility for her own learning, in school and at home. She has continued to do so for the past five years.

Six months after starting at the special school, Hilary managed another thing we had never dared hope for. She became the best friend of someone in her classroom. This was a first – while Hilary has always had friends, until this child, they had always been friends she made outside of school. Inside school, there had only been derision, stigma, shame, and loneliness.

I cannot tell you how much joy it gave me to pick up the phone and hear someone on the other end ask to speak with Hilary. Every night. Sometimes two or three times a night. It was wonderful.

I also have to admit how frightened I was for her – to see her vulnerable to another child. I remained vigilant – holding my breath while listening to my daughter's end of the phone conversations – looking for clues of hurt, of abuse, of marginalization. I'm ashamed to confess that I also let those suspicions colour the way I treated my daughter's friend; I anticipated the scorpion's sting and withheld both my trust and my gratitude. By way of excuse, all I can say is that watching Hilary endure all those hurts had made me careful and – yes – smaller.

When Hilary first began at the special school, I sought a Ritalin-free trial. I figured that now that she was in a 'proper' school, she would no longer need to be medicated. The school, miraculously, was willing, and all three of us – teacher, parent, and child – monitored the situation to see whether indeed good teaching in an appropriate educational setting might replace undesired medication.

Being either a very slow learner or an incurable sceptic, I have repeated this request and the ensuing experiment each year since. Last year, after only a couple of days, Hilary put a stop to it, and said she needed the medication to help her concentrate.

Hilary continues to use her medication – as she always has – to help her with schoolwork only. She has never taken it on weekends or during vacations. There is still a small part of me that feels uncomfortable with this – that worries whether the medication is a crutch, or that perhaps the demands of school are not a 'natural' part of life, or that we medicate our daughter to facilitate a cruel and demanding educational system.

I suppose somewhere deep down, I believe that once she's finished with formal schooling she will be able to let the medication go. However, I also realize that the choice will be hers and that, in the end, things are not turning out too badly for her, medication or not.

I'm okay with it. And that's pretty damned good, all things considered.

They say you should never look a gorilla in the eye – gorillas perceive a direct gaze as a challenge, and they will either attack or run away. Speaking with Hilary used to be like that. The only times we could talk were in the car or while watching television. Anything else was too threatening; she'd just shut down or shut me down.

Since getting our daughter back, however – and I really do think of it in this way – I know again how blue and clear her eyes are, how open her face, how kind and intelligent her insights are. Since Hilary came back, she looks me – and the world – in the eye, neither flinching nor fighting.

It has been a long trip, from that winter morning at the bus stop, through innumerable doctors, specialists, teachers, camps, workshops, and tutors, through tears, and rage, and – always – worry. But I think we're clear now. I think we're safe.

So why do I tell these things? Is it merely to satisfy the sympathetic reader's curiosity? To offer proof that it wasn't really my fault after all? To claim that, while bad schools systematically undermine children's abilities to learn and to live, good schools can, and do, help them to become whole again?

Yes, in part. But also, I tell these things as a way of explaining how it became possible for me to write this book and not go mad with grief, or lie about what I heard, or both. I tell all this also as a way of explaining what I had to learn about myself in order to stay with these women's stories.

One of the hardest things was learning that I wasn't so smart after all. Sure, I expected to hear women tell me the things I already knew, but it was the things that I did not know that really shook me. Like, that I had been a fool in complying with the school's demands for homework at my daughter's tender age. Like, that other mothers refused Ritalin, or insisted on their children staying in the regular classroom, even though they were provided assurances similar to those that I had grudgingly accepted.

I suppose it is always hard for a woman who thinks of herself as resourceful, defiant, and strong to find out that she has actually behaved in ways that were unimaginative, compliant, and frightened. It was for me. Then again, if I had refused to learn these things from the women whose stories I sought, I would not have been true to my aim of understanding how women in their complexity and their diversity mother children who are different, troubled, and labelled AD(H)D.

I also tell the story of Hilary's return as a way to explain how, because Hilary is safe today, I was able to sit through women's stories and not be preoccupied with my own. I could listen, and hear, rather than have my own worries and anguish drown out the voices of the women I asked to tell me about their lives.

Even so, the fact of being the mother of an ADD child, and the fact of having got through the hard times with her, worked in sometimes contradictory ways during my interviews. On the one hand, I believe my insider knowledge provided me with some compassion for and insight into the lives of the women and children whose narratives were shared. On the other, I have to admit that one of the hardest aspects of listening, hearing, and having my own knowledge about the struggle was the challenge of holding my counsel. Women who I spoke with told me such hard stories of pain in their homes, of seeing terrible things happen to their children, of worry that eroded all joy out of their lives. Sometimes, they asked me what to do.

I struggled with this. I still do. A part of me – the woman sitting and listening at the kitchen table who had shared the same troubles – wanted to tell women to run, not walk, to their nearest specialist school and to never look back. The researcher part of me wanted to avoid saying anything for fear of crossing the boundaries of appropriateness and for fear of being taken too seriously as a source of information because of my university research affiliation. But mostly I wanted to avoid giving advice because, even after living this for eight years and researching it for five, I honestly still cannot decide on an overarching 'truth' about AD(H)D, Ritalin, public versus private schooling, or what must be done.

In the end, I wish I had been courageous enough to tell this to the women who asked: If you believe that the people who are caring for your children necessarily have your child or your family's best interests at heart, you need to reconsider your position. If you think that professional insights about your child's behaviours and treatment are necessarily to be trusted, you probably are in for some disappointments. And sadly, if you think that you are a part of the team when it comes to your child's education and mental health, you are probably wrong.

What I have done is to fulfil my promise to write this book. And my hope, in doing so, is to tell a new truth about mothering, about professional claims to expertise, about the complexity of care, and about the ambiguity of maternal choice in dealing with the assessment and treatment of AD(H)D.

In the end, I hope that this book does not necessarily *clarify* things with pat answers, but that it instead *complicates* them. I think it is important to debunk the easy assumptions such as that AD(H)D is a problem of teaching, a problem of class sizes, a problem of poor maternal care and discipline, a problem of modern lifestyles, a problem of medicalization, or any number of other things. I think it is important to make those easy assumptions more complex.

Clarity has its place, however, and I hope the book has clarified at least one thing. In writing this book, I hope at the very least to have made clear the profound damage done to mothers and children as a result of precisely those easy assumptions about attention deficit (hyperactivity) disorder.

Appendix 1
ICD-10 (1993) Diagnostic Criteria for Research

DEC Report No. 78: Methylphenidate in Children with Hyperactivity
Produced for the National Health Service

Hyperkinetic Disorders, Diagnostic Criteria

Note: *The research diagnosis of hyperkinetic disorder requires the definite presence of abnormal levels of inattention, hyperactivity, and restlessness, that are pervasive across situations and persistent over time, and that are not caused by other disorders such as autism or affective disorders.*

G.1. *Inattention*

At least six of the following symptoms of inattention have persisted for at least 6 months to a degree that is maladaptive and inconsistent for the developmental level of the child.

1. Often fails to give close attention to details, or makes careless errors in schoolwork, work, or other activities;
2. Often fails to sustain attention in tasks or play activities;
3. Often fails to follow through in instructions or to finish schoolwork, chores or duties in the workplace (not because of oppositional behaviour or failure to understand instructions);
4. Is often impaired in organizing tasks and activities;
5. Often avoids or strongly dislikes tasks, such as homework, that require sustained mental effort;
6. Often loses things necessary for certain tasks or activities, such as school assignments, pencils, books, toys, or tools;

7. Is often easily distracted by external stimuli;
8. Is often forgetful in the course of daily activities.

G.2. *Hyperactivity*

At least three of the following symptoms of hyperactivity have persisted for at least 6 months to a degree that is maladaptive and inconsistent with the developmental level of the child:

1. Often fidgets with hands or feet or squirms on seat;
2. Leaves seat in classroom or in other situations in which remaining seated is expected;
3. Often runs about or climbs excessively in situations in which it is inappropriate (in adolescents or adults, only feelings of restlessness may be present);
4. Is often unduly noisy in playing or has difficulty in engaging quietly in activities;
5. Exhibits a persistent pattern of excessive motor activity that is not substantially modified by social context or demands.

G.3. *Impulsivity*

At least one of the following symptoms of impulsivity has persisted for at least 6 months to a degree that is maladaptive and inconsistent with the developmental level of the child:

1. Often blurts out answers before questions have been completed;
2. Often fails to wait in lines or await turns in games or group situations;
3. Often interrupts or intrudes on others (e.g., butts into others' conversations or games);
4. Often talks excessively without appropriate response to social constraints.

G.4. Onset of the disorder is no later than the age of 7 years

G.5. *Pervasiveness*

The criteria should be met for more than a single situation, e.g., the combination of inattention, impulsivity, and hyperactivity should be present both at home and at school, or at home and another setting where children are observed, such as a clinic. (Evidence for combined situationality will ordinarily require information from more than one source; parents' concerns about classroom behaviour, for instance, are unlikely to be sufficient.)

G.6. The symptoms in G1–G3 cause clinically significant distress or impairment in social, academic, or occupational functioning.

G.7. The disorder does not meet the criteria for pervasive developmental disorder, manic episode, depressive episode, or anxiety disorders.

From the International Classification of Diseases (10th ed.) by the World Health Organization, 1993, Geneva. Copyright 1993 by the World Health Organization (Gilmore, 1998).

Appendix 2
DSM IV (1994) Criteria for AD(H)D

DEC Report No. 78: Methylphenidate in Children with Hyperactivity
Produced for the National Health Service

Attention-Deficit / Hyperactivity Disorder, Diagnostic Criteria

A. Either (1) or (2).

(1) Six (or more) of the following symptoms of Inattention have persisted for 6 months to a degree that is maladaptive and inconsistent
with developmental level:

Inattention

a. Often fails to give close attention to details or makes careless mistakes in schoolwork, work, or other activities;
b. Often has difficulty sustaining attention in tasks or play activities;
c. Often does not seem to listen when spoken to directly;
d. Often does not follow through on instructions and fails to finish
   schoolwork, chores, or duties in the workplace (not due to
   oppositional behavior or failure to understand instructions);
e. Often has difficulty organizing tasks and activities;
f. Often avoids, dislikes, or is reluctant to engage in tasks that require
   sustained mental effort (such as schoolwork or homework);
g. Often loses things necessary for tasks or activities (e.g., toys, school
   assignments, pencils, books, or tools);
h. Is often easily distracted by extraneous stimuli;
i. Is often forgetful in daily activities.

(2) Six (or more) of the following symptoms of Inattention have persisted for 6 months to a degree that is maladaptive and inconsistent with developmental level:

Hyperactivity

a. Often fidgets with hands or feet or squirms in seat;
b. Often leaves seat in classroom or in other situations in which remaining seated is expected;
c. Often runs about or climbs excessively in situations in which it is inappropriate (in adolescents or adults, may be limited to subjective feelings of restlessness);
d. Often has difficulty playing or engaging in leisure activities quietly;
e. Is often 'on the go' or often acts as if 'driven by a motor';
f. Often talks excessively.

Impulsivity

g. Often blurts out answers before questions have been completed;
h. Often has difficulty awaiting in turn;
i. Often interrupts or intrudes on others (e.g., butts into conversations or games).

B. Some hyperactive–impulsive or inattentive symptoms that caused impairment before age 7 years.

C. Some impairment from the symptoms is present in two or more settings (e.g., at school, work, and at home).

D. There must be clear evidence of clinically significant impairment in social, academic, or occupational functioning.

E. Does not occur exclusively during the course of a Pervasive Developmental Disorder, Schizophrenia or other Psychotic Disorder, or a Personality Disorder.

From the American Psychiatric Association's 1994 *Diagnostic and Statistical Manual of Mental Disorders*, 4th ed. (DSM IV) (Gilmore, 1998).

Appendix 3
Brief Biographical Details of Participants

Canadian Women and Their Children

Amanda is white, twenty-seven years old, and the mother of five children. She is divorced, living on her own, and cares for her children without support from her ex-husband. She is poor, living on social assistance. Her son, **Michael**, is eight years old and has been diagnosed since he was in kindergarten at age five and a half. He takes Ritalin, is involved in play therapy, and has been coded as mild-to-moderately disabled through the Calgary Board of Education. Amanda participates in a state-funded support group for mothers of children with ADD. The focus of the group is one of advocacy for the family with school and medical officials, although a great deal of informal therapy and intervention is involved in the group meetings and in home visits by the social worker who runs the group. None of Michael's other siblings have been diagnosed with ADD.

Belinda is a white, professional woman, forty-six years old, married with three children. The father is an engineer, and although Belinda has a Master's degree in a helping profession, she is at home full-time, because of family demands. Her nine-year-old son **Adam** has been diagnosed since he was six, and the only treatment being used at present is 'love and understanding.' Adam has used Ritalin briefly, but did not tolerate it well – Belinda works considerably with the school and teachers to get Adam's educational needs met, and Adam also uses a home tutor several evenings a week. Adam's siblings have not experienced attentional or learning difficulties.

Clarissa is Latina, thirty-nine years old, and the mother of **Julio**, who is eleven. Julio was born in Argentina; his parents immigrated to Canada via the United States when he was three years old. Julio takes a wide array of holistic treatments to manage his ADD, including vitamins, a highly regulated diet, herbal treatments, and massage. Julio also attends a special private school for children with learning and attentional difficulties. Clarissa and her husband have one other child, a daughter, who is not diagnosed. The father is a successful businessman. Clarissa, in part because of difficulties with English and in part because of Julio's needs, has never worked outside the home in Canada.

Daphne is white, forty years old, and a professional woman who works part-time in medical research. Her husband is an executive, and the family is upper middle class. Daphne's eleven-year-old daughter, **Melanie**, has been diagnosed with ADD for four years, although she has been investigated for a number of problems since early childhood. Daphne attends a special school for children with learning difficulties, but takes no medication at present for ADD. Melanie has been coded as mild-to-moderately disabled through the Calgary Board of Education. The family lived in England until Melanie was almost four years old, and has been in Canada ever since.

Deanna is married, white, forty-one years old, and the mother of **Ariel**, who is nine. She works part-time as a sales clerk, and her husband works as a labourer. The family is working class. Ariel is adopted and was diagnosed at age six at her mother's request; she takes Dexedrine. Deanna attends a semi-monthly meeting for parents with children diagnosed with ADD. The family has been involved in family therapy, and Ariel has regular meetings with a child psychologist.

Glenda is white, thirty-six years old, and the mother of **Kevin**, who is eleven. Kevin was diagnosed at age eight, through his school. His kindergarten teacher first identified him as problematic. Brenda describes Kevin's treatment today as consisting only of 'pure love.' However, Kevin has taken Ritalin briefly, had just begun to attend a special private school for children with learning and attentional problems at the time of our interview, and has seen a social worker with his mother during Brenda's divorce from Kevin's father. Brenda is remarried to a professional. She was not working at the time of our interview so that she 'could dedicate time to Kevin.' She had worked earlier, however, and intended to return to work once Kevin got settled in his new school. Kevin has one younger brother who is not diagnosed. Kevin has been coded as mild-to-moderately disabled through the Calgary Board of Education.

Helen is white, forty-six years old, and the mother of **Rick**, who is fourteen years old. Rick was diagnosed at six years of age, having been identified by his school as difficult. At present Rick takes Ritalin, attends a special school for children with attentional and learning problems, and sees a child psychologist. Rick has been coded as mild-to-moderately disabled through the Calgary Board of Education. Helen and her husband have been married for seventeen years, and they have two children – Rick and a younger sister who is not diagnosed. The family is middle class; the father is a tradesman and Helen is a nurse. Because of family commitments, Helen is only able to work part-time, although she states she would like eventually to return to full-time work.

Jenny is white, thirty-six years old, and the mother of **Mark**, who is fifteen years old, and who has been diagnosed since he was ten. Jenny is of Chinese descent, is divorced from Mark's father, and remarried to the father of her two other children. The family is upper middle class and has sent all of their children to private schools. For the past year, Mark has been attending a special school for children with learning and attentional problems. Mark also takes Dexedrine 'for Math.' Mark has been coded as mild-to-moderately disabled through the Calgary Board of Education.

Lucille is married, white, forty years old, and the mother of three children. She has a degree in social work, but does very little paid work at present. She has done a great deal of advocacy work on behalf of children with special needs, both at the school level and at the board of education policy level. Lucille's husband is a professional, and the family is middle class. Lucille's son **David** is sixteen years old and has been diagnosed since he was eight, when the school identified him as 'troubled.' He does not take Ritalin, but uses a number of natural treatments (homeopathy, vitamins). He has been coded as mild-to-moderately disabled through the Calgary Board of Education. David has a younger brother who is diagnosed with autism.

Lydia is married, white, fifty-two years old, and a professional woman. Her husband is a journeyman, and the family describes itself as middle class. Lydia's only daughter **Karla** is thirteen years old and has been diagnosed for two years. Karla takes Dexedrine, although she often refuses it. Lydia believes that Karla's diagnosis came 'too late' and that this accounts for her resistance to the medication.

Marlene is white, thirty-five years old, and the mother of **Leanne**, who is thirteen. Leanne has been diagnosed since she was eight years old, and she takes slow-release Ritalin. Marlene attends a state-funded support group for parents with ADD-identified children. Marlene is divorced from Leanne's father and has remarried a man who works as a janitor. The family is working class. Two other, younger siblings do not have difficulties in school or home.

Pat is white, forty-three years old, and the mother of **Chloe**, who is twelve. Chloe has been diagnosed with ADD since she was five years old. Chloe has spent some time in residential psychiatric care; she suffered from anxiety and depression stemming from severe social ostracism and was considered a risk for suicide. At present, she is taking Prozac, and there is some talk or 'reintroducing a stimulant.' She attends a special private school for children with learning and attentional problems, and she has been seen by social workers, psychologists, and child psychiatrists. Chloe has been coded as severely disabled through the Calgary Board of Education, and her tuition at the private school is paid by the board. Pat has an intact, twenty-year marriage. She is upper middle class; the father works as a consultant engineer. At present, Pat does not work, although she possesses a Master's degree. She has tried to work part-time at various points in Chloe's life, but is staying home for the moment. Chloe has one younger sister who experiences no difficulties.

Samantha is white, twenty-five years old, and the mother of **Justin** who is eight. Justin was diagnosed at age five, through his kindergarten teacher. He takes Ritalin twice a day and attends a special school for children with learning and attentional problems. At the suggestion of Justin's diagnostic team, Samantha briefly saw a social worker for support during her divorce. Samantha is divorced and remarried, and has four young children. The family is working class: Samantha works as a house cleaner, and her husband works as a labourer. Justin's biological father is not supportive of Samantha or Justin; Samantha suspects 'he's got it [ADD] too.'

Sheila is divorced, thirty-four years old, and the lone parent of **Sheryl**, who is thirteen. Sheila is a First Nations person who works full-time as a health professional and describes the family as 'working poor.' Her son lives with his father in another city. Sheryl was diagnosed at age eight, through her school. She now attends a special school for children with learning and attentional problems and uses a number of natural supplements to deal with her attentional problems. She has been coded as mild-to-moderately disabled through the Calgary Board of Education.

Sonia is white, forty-two years old, and the mother of **George**, who is ten. Sonia and George's father are both professionals with graduate degrees. The family is upper middle class, with both parents working full-time in the academy. George, a lone child, was sent for assessment by his school, and had just been diagnosed following a two-week double-blind Ritalin trial. At the time of our interview, he had been prescribed Ritalin, but was only to begin taking it the following week.

Teresa is white, forty-six years old, a teacher, and the mother of **Neil**, who is sixteen. Neil was diagnosed at age six through his school, but has never taken Ritalin. Instead, Teresa works together with the school at both a classroom and teacher level and with the administration in terms of policy and planning. Teresa has been married for over twenty years, and has two other children with Neil's father – neither of these children have encountered difficulties. In the last two years, Teresa has returned to teaching on a full-time basis; prior to this, she states she was engaged full-time as 'Neil's advocate.'

Veronica is white, thirty-seven years old, working class, and the mother of four boys. Her twelve-year-old son **Jason** has been diagnosed since he was eight years old, when the school pushed for an assessment. He takes Clonidine and Ritalin and has been coded as mild-to-moderately disabled through the Calgary Board of Education.

Veronica is married to the boys' father, who works in the computer industry. Veronica is very actively involved in working with the schools at the local and board level, and she has been a member of several committees working on special needs policy.

British Women and Their Children

Amy is white, thirty-one years old, married to a pub owner, and is a stay-at-home mother to two children. She is divorced from her children's father, who provides financial support and some shared access. Her six-year-old daughter **Jana** has been diagnosed for a year and is receiving no treatment, educational interventions, or funding assistance. Amy is currently pushing for Jana to be statemented, with little optimism over the outcome.

Becky is a U.S.-born Latina woman living in London. She works as a freelance editor and is separated from her husband, who works in the financial sector. The family is well-to-do, the separation has been amicable, and both parents continue to hold close ties to both South and North America. Becky feels that because of her American background she has been more able to access information (if not necessarily services) than many British women. Becky's son **Anton**, who is almost eight years old, has been diagnosed for two years, so he is much younger than the average diagnosed British child in the study. He is taking Clonidine and Ritalin. Becky runs an on-line support group for parents of children with ADHD.

Cassandra is white, thirty-eight years old, and a nursing student who lives in a working-class neighbourhood outside London. She is divorced and remarried, raising three kids in a blended family. Her fourteen-year-old son, **Matthew**, is diagnosed with ADHD, and he and his stepfather have a relationship that Cassandra characterizes as being 'quite hostile.' Matthew had just been diagnosed at the time of our interview, and he was not yet receiving any treatment, educational intervention, or funding assistance.

Christine is white, thirty-seven years old, and the mother of eight-year-old **Drew**. She is married to a man with one child from a previous marriage, and together they have three children. Christine's husband is a professor, and Christine is a psychoanalyst, as are both her parents. She describes herself as upper middle class. Drew presently takes Ritalin and Amyltriptylene, an antidepressant. He also attends a special school for children with learning and attentional problems, for which he receives state funding, having been 'statemented' through his local educational authority. Christine reports that her psychoanalytic background presented no challenges to her acceptance of ADHD as a psychological, biological problem.

Corrine is white, forty-four years old, and the mother of **Aaron**. She lives in a middle-class neighbourhood in south London and has been married to Aaron's father for twenty-five years. She describes herself as a 'new-age computer consultant' and works from her home, where she also teaches Yoga on a freelance basis. Aaron is Corrine's only child. He is almost eighteen years old, has been diagnosed for the past five years, takes Wellbutrin for depression and works with an ADHD 'coach' to develop his social and 'life' skills. He attends an alternative school, and at the time of our interview was on suspension because of disciplinary problems. He was never statemented while in the public system.

Diane is white, thirty years old, and the mother of thirteen-year-old **Andrew**. She lives on social assistance, and raises three children in a council flat in north London. She is separated from Andrew's father, who provides no support for the children. At the time of our interview, Andrew had been diagnosed for six months, and was taking Ritalin four times daily for ADHD. He has not been statemented, although Diane has been pushing to get the process started.

Dolores is white, thirty-eight years old, in an intact marriage, and is the mother of four children. She is a nurse's aide, and her husband works as a gardener. The family lives in a working-class suburb of London. Their son, **Adrian,** is twelve years old, and he has been diagnosed with ADHD for two years. He takes Ritalin twice daily. Despite his diagnosis and medication, Adrian has not been statemented through his school.

Evelyn is a white, upper-class woman, who is the forty-four-year-old mother of **Harry**. She possesses a graduate law degree from a prestigious university and is in an intact marriage to another lawyer. The family lives in a southern suburb of London. Harry takes Ritalin, and he has received some counselling. Evelyn has worked on an on-and-off basis since Harry was born, but has recently returned to work in a less demanding job than she is qualified for, in order that she can support Harry, who has not been statemented.

Fran is the white, twenty-eight-year-old mother of **Angus**, who is six years old, and a nine-year-old daughter who has juvenile diabetes. Fran is at present unemployed, although she has worked as a travel agent until recently. She states she is unable to work, as Angus is at present excluded from school with ten hours of home tutoring provided by the local educational authority. Fran recently separated from Angus's father, and lives with her new partner, a consultant, in an upscale neighbourhood in Exeter. Angus is neither statemented, nor does he take medication for ADHD. Fran states that going through her daughter's diagnosis and treatment for diabetes has 'really highlighted how little help Angus has received for his problems in comparison.'

Gloria is white, forty-eight years old, and the mother of three children aged eleven to seventeen. Her oldest son and daughter have both been diagnosed with dyspraxia, and Gloria is convinced the oldest son also has ADHD. **Keith**, at eleven years, has been diagnosed with ADHD for four years, takes Ritalin, and attends a special boarding school for children with learning and attentional problems. He receives full funding because he has been statemented and because no appropriate facility exists within his local area. Gloria is herself on disability assistance, and her husband is a labourer. Gloria runs an on-line support group from her home.

Jean is white and a well-to-do, stay-at-home mother of two children, one of whom is fully grown and living away from home. The family lives in a lovely house in the country, and the father is a retired diplomat. Her son, **Stuart**, is thirteen years old and has been diagnosed since he was nine years old. He takes slow-release Ritalin and attends a boarding school for children with learning and attentional problems. He has been statemented.

Kate is white, forty-two years old, and the mother of four, who runs a support group in a rural community outside London. She also works as a 'coach' for children and families dealing with ADHD. She is married to a mechanic and describes herself as middle class. Her twelve-year-old son **Colin** has been diagnosed for four years, and he takes Ritalin, uses a coach, and attends one-on-one counselling.

Madeleine heads a very active support group for parents of children with ADHD in a medium-sized town outside London. She is a black single woman, living on social assistance, and raising four children on her own. Her sixteen-year-old son **Nick** was diagnosed at age thirteen, and he is prescribed Dexedrine. Nick has been excluded from school several times and was at home at the time of our interview. He has not been statemented. Madeleine's ex-partner provides her with virtually no financial or emotional support.

Moira is white and in her late forties. She is married and the adoptive mother of twelve-year-old **Teddy** and his older sister Rita. Moira possesses two graduate degrees and is married to a professional. The family is upper-middle-class and lives in a semi-rural London suburb. Moira has been unable to work, although she would like to. Teddy has been diagnosed for four years, takes Ritalin for ADHD, and attends a special school for children with attentional and learning problems. He has been statemented.

Penelope is twelve-year-old **Morris**'s mother. She is white, a home-maker, married to a professional man, and is raising two children in an upper-middle-class neighbourhood outside of London. At the time of our interview, Morris was just diagnosed, and he was taking Ritalin on a trial basis. Morris attends a special school for children with learning problems; however, he has not been statemented.

Priscilla is white, forty years old, and the mother of fourteen-year-old **David**, who is an only child. She runs an informal support group in her semi-rural community south of London. She is married and stays at home. David was identified at eleven years of age, is taking Ritalin, and at the time of our interview was on a temporary exclusion from school because of behavioural concerns. He is not yet statemented, although the process is under way.

Rosalind is thirty-six years old and the mother of **Robbie** and three other children. She is a white, stay-at-home mother in an intact marriage, and her husband works in upper management in a transport firm. Robbie is thirteen years old and has been diagnosed for five years. He takes Pemoline for his ADHD and attends a private school for children with learning and attentional problems. He has not been statemented, so he receives no special services or accommodations from his local school.

Appendix 4
Interview Guide

Identification

1. Please tell me the story of how you first came to think of your child as different.
2. Who identified your child first as a candidate for ADD assessment?
3. What were your thoughts about that news?
4. Did you agree? Disagree? Why? Why not? How was this resolved?
5. What happened next?

Assessment

6. Please tell me how the diagnostic process occurred.
7. What was your role as a parent during this time?
8. Did you have any challenges in obtaining information about ADD?
9. What kinds of information and assistance did you, or your partner obtain? Please describe how each of you was involved at this point.
10. What kinds of written materials, files, information, or tests were provided to your child during this time? By whom? How involved were you with officials during the process?
11. Did you ever feel like you were sidelined during the assessment process? By whom? How did you manage to resolve this?

Dealing with Professionals

12. Please tell me about any differences of opinion between yourself and any others during the diagnostic process:

- Teacher
- Physician
- Special educator
- Alternative medicine provider (which types)
- Other parents – support group
- Family members
- Spouse or partner

How were these difficulties resolved?

13. Please tell me about any difficulties that you experienced with the following professionals in relation to treatment once diagnosis had been made:

- Teacher
- Physician
- Special educator
- Alternative medicine provider (which types)
- Other parents – support group
- Family members
- Spouse or partner

How were these difficulties resolved?

14. Did you ever refuse any kind of treatment for your child with ADD, or try to? Please tell me about that.
15. Did you ever insist on treatment, or have to struggle to obtain treatment or services for your child? Please tell me about that.
16. Who, in your family, was the primary contact with professionals concerning your child's difficulties? Why do you think that was? What were the pro's and con's of these arrangements?
17. Did you ever experience any feelings of stigma or discomfort relating to your child and the diagnosis? How did these occur?
18. Did you experience any difference of opinion with any of the following when your child was being diagnosed or treated? If so, please tell me about that.

- Immediate family, spouse
- Extended family

- Friends
- Strangers, acquaintances

19. Please tell me how this experience has affected you personally. Try to describe for me some occurrences that have made you feel:

- Angry
- Sad
- Frustrated
- Guilty
- Ambivalent
- Worried
- Scared
- Proud
- Happy
- Cynical

20. Have you ever wondered what your role is, if any, in your child's problems? If so, please describe your concerns.
21. Please tell me what kinds of activities you have been involved in that relate to your child's diagnosis?

- Attended workshops
- Attended meetings with school
- Attended classes on ADD
- Attended support groups
- Volunteered in any capacity at school
- Volunteered in any capacity elsewhere (describe)
- Engaged in advocacy or lobbying work
- Other (describe)

22. What kind of information did you obtain about ADD? From where or whom? Was that information helpful to you? Confusing or harmful? Please explain.
23. What has been the worst part of this experience for you?
24. What has been the best part of it?
25. Do you think the label has been helpful for your child? Your family? Your own peace of mind. Please explain why and/or why not.
26. Is there anything more that you would like to add that we have not covered so far?

Appendix 5
List of Textual Materials Examined

This sample of materials related to AD(H)D is representative of the intersections of public discourse and private experience. For bibliographical details, see References.

Adams, 1998
Adduci, 1991
Anonymous, 1998a, 1998b,
    1998c, 1998d, 1999a, 1999b,
    1999d, 1999e, 2000, no date
Atkins, 2000
Baughman, 1999
Berry, 2000
Bongers, 1997
Bowles, 2000
Breggin, 1991, 1998
Browne, 2000a, 2000b
Calgary Learning Centre (CLC),
    1997a, 1997b
Cheaklos et al., 2000
Children and Adults with Attention Deficit Disorder
    (CHADD), 1995
Chisholm, 1996
Choate, no date
Cohen, 1999
Efamol, 1998
Enrich, 1996

Flynn, 2000
Foss, 1999
Gilmore et al., 1998
Habib, 1998
Hough, 1997
Jenish, 2000
Johnston, 1997
Mack, 2000
Maté, 2000a, 2000b
McConnell, 1997
Merrow, 1995
Minde, 1987
Murphy, and LeVert, 1995
Palmer and Bongers, 1997
Rapp, D.D., 1999
Rees, 1998a, 1998b, 1998c, 1998d
Rees and Dawson, 1998
Schatsky and Yaroshevsky, 1997
Scott, 1987
Sealander et al., 1995
Stordy, no date
Swartz, 1997
Ullman and Ullman, 1996

Appendix 6
Sample Parent Assessment Observation Checklists

6a Attention Deficit Disorder – Parent Questionnaire

We recognize the variability of behaviour in children. Please fill out the following behaviour rating scale based on your observation of this student (sic) over a length of time.

RATING SCALE

Child's Name _____ Age: _____ Grade: _____

Completed by: _____

Observed for the week of (date) *Saturday   Day 8*

Circle the number in the one column which best describes the child

	Not at all	Just a little	Pretty much	Very much
1. Often fidgets or squirms in seat	0	1	2	3
2. Has difficulty remaining seated	0	1	2	3
3. Is easily distracted	0	1	2	3
4. Has difficulty awaiting turn in groups	0	1	2	3
5. Has difficulty following instructions	0	1	2	3
6. Often blurts out answers to questions	0	1	2	3
7. Has difficulty sustaining attention to tasks	0	1	2	3
8. Often shifts from one uncompleted activity to another	0	1	2	3
9. Has difficulty playing quietly	0	1	2	3
10. Often talks excessively	0	1	2	3
11. Often interrupts on others	0	1	2	3
12. Often does not seem to listen	0	1	2	3
13. Often engages in physical (sic) dangerous activities without considering consequences	0	1	2	3

6b Attention Deficit Disorder – Teacher's Questionaire

Child's Full Name: _____

(Note: Original source not legible)

	Before drug	After 1 week	After 2 weeks
1. Works independently			
2. Persists with tasks for reasonable period of time			
3. Completes assigned task with little additional assistance			
4. Follows simple directions accurately			
5. Follows well in the classroom			
6. Functions well in the classroom			
7. Behaves positively with peers/classmates			
8. Verbal communication clear and 'connected'			
9. Non-verbal communication accurate			
10. Understands and complies with group norms and social rules			
11. Skilful in making and sustaining friendships			
12. Extremely overactive (out of seat, 'on the go')			
13. Overreacts			
14. Impulsive (acts or talks without thinking)			
15. Restless (squirms in seat)			
16. Fidgety (hands always busy)			
17. Tries to get others into trouble			
18. Starts fights over nothing			
19. Makes malicious fun of people			
20. Defies authority			
21. Picks on others			
22. Mean or cruel to other children			

For each item of each occasion enter the number 1 through 5 that most closely corresponds to your evaluation of the child's behaviour

Almost never   Almost always

1   2   3   4   5

References

Abramowitz, M. 1996. *Regulating the lives of women: Social welfare policy from Colonial times to the present*. Boston: South End Press.

Adams, S. 1998. 'Supplements and nutrition touted as ADD treatment.' *Calgary Herald*, 6 June, A12.

Adduci, L. 1991. 'My child couldn't pay attention.' *Woman's Day*. 3 Sept., no page no. Distributed with permission by Pro Health.

Alberta Children's Hospital. 1993. 'Attention deficit disorder.' Calgary: Developmental Clinic, Alberta Children's Hospital.

Alberta College of Physicians and Surgeons. 1999. 'Prescription rates in Alberta.'

Alberta Learning. 1997. 'Guide to education for students with special needs.' Edmonton: Government of Alberta.

– 2000a. 'Designated special education private schools.' Edmonton: Government of Alberta.

– 2000b. 'Handbook for the identification and review of students with severe disabilities.' Edmonton: Government of Alberta.

– 2000c. 'Shaping the future for students with special needs: A review of special education in Alberta, final report.' Edmonton: Government of Alberta.

– 2000d. 'School funding rates: 1999/2000 to 2002/2003 school years.' Edmonton: Government of Alberta.

Allan, J. 1996. 'Foucault and special educational needs: A "box of tools" for analysing children's experiences of mainstreaming.' *Disability and Society* 11: 219–33.

Allen, A. 1990. 'Foucault on power: A theory for feminists,' in S.J. Hekman, (ed.), *Feminist interpretations of Michel Foucault*. University Park: Pennsylvania State University Press, 265–82.

Ambert, A.-M. 1992. *The effect of children on parents*. Binghamton, NY: Haworth Press.

American Psychiatric Association. 1994. *Diagnostic and Statistical Manual of Mental Disorders*, 4th ed. Washington, DC: American Psychiatric Association.

Anastopoulos, A.D., R.A. Barkley, and T.L. Shelton. 1997. 'The history and diagnosis of attention-deficit / hyperactivity disorder,' in P. Cooper and K. Ideus (eds.), *Attention deficit hyperactivity disorder: Educational, medical and cultural issues*. Maidstone, Kent: Association of Workers for Children with Emotional and Behavioural Difficulties, 21–7.

Anonymous. 1998a. 'Disruptive or just ill?' BBC News. 6 April. http://news6.thdo.bbc.co.uk/english/uk/newsid_71000/7192b.stm

– 1998b. 'The importance of not being earnest.' BBC News – Health. 6 Nov. http://news6.thdo.bbc.co.uk/english/uk/newsid_717747213.stm

– 1998c. 'Education ban on "cosmetic" expulsions.' BBC News – Education. 16 Jan. http://news6.thdo.bbc.co.uk/english/uk/newsid_131000/131800.stm

– 1998d. 'Suggestions for teachers of students with attention deficit disorder.' Calgary: Horizon Educational Resource Centre.

– 1999a. 'Attention deficit disorder and hyperactivity. Factsheet 5, for parents and teachers.' London: Royal College of Psychiatrists.

– 1999b. 'Drug to control children "overused."' BBC News – Education. 24 May. http://news6.thdo.bbc.co.uk/hi/english/uk/newsid_71469/71296.stm

– 1999c. 'Schools ordered to cut total of pupils selected by ability.' *London Independent*.

– 1999d. 'U.K.: Britain's excluded millions.' BBC News. 7 Sept. http://news6.thdo.bbc.co.uk/hi/english/uk/newsid_71382/71300.stm

– 1999e. 'Wonder drug, or playground curse?' *Guardian*. Manchester, England. 17 Oct., 1.

– 2000. 'More children to get "kiddie cocaine" drug.' *Metro*. London, England. 28 Feb., 12.

– 2001a. 'Encopresis.' MSN Health. 23 Jan. http://content.health.msn.com/content/asset/adam_disease_soiling

– 2001b. 'Excluded pupils dropped from tables.' BBC News – Education. 11 Jan. http://news.bbc.ca.uk/hi/english/education/newsid_112000/112223.stm

– No date. 'Information pamphlet – Calgary Academy neurofeedback program.' Calgary: Calgary Academy.

Apple, M. 1995. *Education and power*. New York and London: Routledge.

Armstrong, D. 1983. *Political anatomy of the body: Medical knowledge in Britain in the twentieth century*. Cambridge: Cambridge University Press.

Armstrong, L. 1993. *And they call it help: The psychiatric policing of America's children*. Reading, Mass.: Addison-Wesley.

Arnup, K. 1994. *Education for motherhood: Advice for mothers in twentieth-century Canada*. Toronto: University of Toronto Press.

– 1995. *Lesbian parenting: Living with pride and prejudice*. Charlottetown, PEI: Gynergy Books.

Asch, A., and M. Fine. 1997. 'Nurturance, sexuality, and women with disabilities: The example of women and literature,' in L.J. Davis (ed.), *The disability studies reader*. New York and London: Routledge, 3–43.

Atkins, L. 2000. 'Is it time for my Prozac, mum?' *Guardian*. 7 March, 8.

Badinter, E. 1981. *The myth of motherhood: An historical view of the maternal instinct*. London: Souvenir Press.

Baines, C., P. Evans, and S. Neysmith. 1991. *Women's caring: Feminist perspectives on social welfare*. Toronto: McClelland and Stewart.

Baker, D., and K. McCall. 1995. 'Parenting stress in parents of children with attention deficit hyperactivity disorder and parents of children with learning disabilities.' *Journal of Child and Family Studies* 31: 57–60.

Ball, S.J. 1990. 'Introducing Monsieur Foucault,' in S.J. Ball (ed.), *Foucault and education: Disciplines and knowledge*. New York and London: Routledge, 1–10.

Barbre, J.W. 1999. 'Meno-boomers and moral guardians: An exploration of the cultural construction of menopause,' in Rose Weitz (ed.), *The politics of women's bodies: Sexuality, appearance and behavior*. New York: Oxford University Press, 242–52.

Batt, S. 1994. *Patient no more: The politics of breast cancer*. Charlottetown: Gynergy books.

Baughman, F.A. 1999. 'Education "disorders" fraud.' *Psychiatry: Betraying and drugging children*. Toronto: Citizens Commission on Human Rights.

Benhabib, S. 1995. 'Feminism and postmodernism,' in L. Nicholson (ed.), *Feminist contentions*. New York and London: Routledge, 17–34.

Bernier, J., and D. Siegel, 1994. 'Attention deficit hyperactivity disorder: A family and ecological systems perspective.' *Families in Society* 753: 142–51.

Berry, C.A., S.E. Shaywitz, and B.A. Shaywitz. 1985. 'Girls with attention deficit disorder: A silent minority? A report on behavioral and cognitive characteristics.' *Pediatrics* 76: 801–9.

Berry, D. 2000. 'Enjoy children's spirit ... Don't suppress it!' Spirited Kids Foundation.

Blum, L. (1993). 'Mothers, babies and breastfeeding in late capitalist America: The shifting contexts of feminist theory.' *Feminist Studies* 2(19): 291–311.

Bodien, P. 2000. 'ADHD article from NICE now up.' SENCO forum mailing list archive. 2 Nov. http//forum/nfgl.gov.uk/majordomo-archives/senco-forum.archive.011/msg(...11/2/2000)

Bongers, A. 1997. 'At attention: Critics worry Ritalin is being used as "sit down and shut up drug" in classrooms.' *Calgary Herald.* 30 June, A14.

Booth, T., M. Ainscow, and A. Dyson. 1998. 'England: Inclusion and exclusion in a competitive system,' in M. Ainscow, T. Booth, and A. Dyson (eds.), *From them to us: An international study of inclusion in education.* London and New York: Routledge, 193–225.

Bowles, D. 2000. 'Ritalin made my son a demon.' SENCO forum mailing list archive. 1 April. http://forum.ngfl.gov.uk/majordomo/archives/senco-forum.archive.011/msg(...4.1.2000)

Boyd, S.C. 1999. *Mothers and illicit drugs: Transcending the myths.* Toronto: University of Toronto Press.

Boyle, M., and D. Offord. 1991. 'Psychiatric disorders and substance abuse in adolescents.' *Canadian Journal of Psychiatry* 36: 699–705.

Boyle, M., D. Offord, Y. Racine, P. Szatmari, J. Fleming, and P. Links. 1992. 'Predicting substance use in later adolescence: Results from the Ontario Child Health Study follow up.' *American Journal of Psychiatry* 149: 761–67.

Breggin, P. 1991. *Toxic psychiatry.* New York: St Martin's Press.

– 1998. *Talking back to Ritalin.* Monroe, Maine: Common Courage Press.

Brooks, R.B. 1994. 'Children at risk: Fostering resilience and hope.' *American Journal of Ortho-Psychiatry* 64: 545–53.

Brown, C., and K. Jasper, 1993. 'Why weight? Why women? Why now?' in C. Brown, and K. Jasper (eds.), *Consuming passions: Feminist approaches to weight preoccupation and eating disorders.* Toronto: Second Story Press, 16–35.

Browne, A. 2000a. 'Children face mind-control drugs.' *Guardian.* 1 March, 1–2.

– 2000b. 'Mind-control drug threat for children.' *Guardian.* 1 Jan. http://www.newsunlimited.co.uk/observer/uk_news/story/0,3879,1411 45,00.html

Burman, E. 1994. *Deconstructing developmental psychology.* London: Routledge.

Butler, J. 1995. 'Contingent foundations,' in L. Nicholson (ed.), *Feminist contentions.* New York and London: Routledge, 35–58.

Butler, S. 1985. *Conspiracy of silence: The trauma of incest.* Volcano, Calif.: Volcano Press.

Calgary Board of Education (CBE) 1997. 'Statement of vision: As trustees dedicated to public education, we share a vision.' Calgary: CBE.

– 1999a. 'Chief superintendent's operating policy: Policy 3003 – special education.' Calgary: CBE.

– 1999b. 'My student and the Calgary Board of Education: A guide to the rights and responsibilities of parents.' Calgary: CBE.

- 1999c. 'Learning environment action plan final report.' Calgary: CBE.
Calgary Learning Centre (CLC) 1997a. *Calgary Learning Centre news.* Calgary: CLC.
- 1997b. 'Welcome to the Calgary Learning Centre.' Calgary: CLC.
Campbell, S.B. 1990. *Behaviour problems in preschool children.* New York: Guilford.
Caplan, P. 1989. *Don't blame mother: Mending the mother–daughter relationship.* New York: Harper and Row.
Castel, R. 1991. 'From dangerousness to risk,' in Graham Burchell, Colin Gordon, and Peter Miller (eds.), *The Foucault effect: Studies in governmentality.* Chicago: University of Chicago Press, 281–98.
Castel, R., F. Castel, and A. Lovell. 1982. *The psychiatric society.* New York: Columbia University Press.
Cheaklos, C., B. Frankel, W. Plummer, and S. Schindehette, 2000. 'Heavy mettle.' *People* 54(18) [30 Oct.]: 56–61.
Chernin, K. 1981. *The obsession: Reflections on the tyranny of slenderness.* New York: Harper and Row.
Children and Adults with Attention Deficit Disorder (CHADD). 1995. 'It's a neurobiological thing.' Calgary: CHADD Canada Inc.
Chisholm, P. 1996. 'The ADD dilemma: Is Ritalin the best way to treat attention deficit disorder?' *Maclean's Magazine*, 11 March, 41–2.
Choate, P. No date. 'Some tough questions about adult and teen ADHD.' Calgary: Peter Choate and Associates.
Cohen, D. 1999. 'Just say no to classroom drugs.' *Globe and Mail.*
Collins Hill, P. 1994. 'Shifting the centre: Race, class and feminist theorizing about motherhood,' in E.N. Glenn, G. Chang, and L.R. Forcey, (eds.), *Mothering: Ideology, experience and agency.* New York: Routledge, 45–66.
Conrad, P. 1976. *Identifying hyperactive children.* Washington, DC: Heath.
- 1992. 'Medicalization and social control.' *Annual Review of Sociology* 18: 209–32.
Conrad, P., and J.W. Schneider. 1980. *Deviance and medicalization: From badness to sickness.* St Louis: C.V. Mosby.
Cooper, P. 1998. 'Introduction: The reality and hyperreality of AD/HD: An educational and cultural analysis,' in P. Cooper and K. Ideus (eds), *Attention deficit hyperactivity disorder: Educational, medical and cultural issues.* Maidstone, Kent: Association of Workers for Children with Emotional and Behavioural Difficulties (AWCEBD), 6–20.
Cooper, P., and K. Ideus. 1998. 'Attention deficit hyperactivity disorder: Trojan horse or gift horse?' in P. Cooper and K. Ideus (eds.), *Attention deficit hyper-*

activity disorder: Educational, medical and cultural issues. Maidstone, Kent: AWCEBD, 123–37.

Cosgrove, P.V.F. 1997. 'Attention deficit hyperactivity disorder: A U.K. review.' *Primary Care Psychiatry* 3: 101–13.

Cotugno, A.J. 1993. 'The diagnosis of attention deficit hyperactivity disorder (ADHD) in community mental health centres: Where and when.' *Psychology in the Schools* 30: 338–44.

Croskery, B. 2000. 'Public presentation: Town hall meeting concerning special education needs. Calgary: BCE.

Currie, D.H. 1999. *Girl talk: Adolescent magazines and their readers.* Toronto: University of Toronto Press.

Daikin, N., and J. Naidoo, 1995. 'Feminist critiques of health promotion,' in R. Bunton, S. Nettleton, and R. Burrows (eds.), *The sociology of health promotion: Critical analyses of consumption, lifestyle and risk.* London: Routledge, 74–91.

Daly, K. 1995. 'Reshaping fatherhood: Finding the models,' in W. Marsiglio, (ed.), *Fatherhood: Contemporary theory, research, and social policy.* Thousand Oaks, Calif.: Sage, 21–40.

Dehli, K. 1996. 'Unfinished business? The dropout goes to work in education policy reports,' in D. Kelly and J. Gaskell (eds.), *Debating dropouts: Critical policy and research perspectives on school leaving.* New York and London: Teachers College Press, 7–29.

Department for Education and Employment (DFEE). 1994a. 'Code of practice on the identification and assessment of special educational needs.' London: Her Majesty's Stationery Office (HMSO).

– 1994b. 'The education (special education) regulations.' London: HMSO.

– 1994c. 'Special educational needs: A guide for parents.' London: HMSO.

– 1994d. 'The use of exclusion.' London: HMSO.

– 1996. 'Statistics in schools.' London: HMSO.

– 1999. 'Circular 15/9: Maintained special schools.' Sherwood Park, Annesley, Nott: DFEE Publications.

Diprose, R. 1994. *The bodies of women.* London: Routledge.

Donzelot, J. 1997 [1979]. *The policing of families.* Baltimore, MD: Johns Hopkins University Press.

Douglas, M. 1966. *Purity and danger: An analysis of concepts of pollution and taboo.* London: Routledge and Kegan Paul.

– 1992. *Risk and blame: Essays in cultural theory.* London: Routledge.

Efamol. 1998. 'Not stupid, not naughty, not lazy.' Burnaby, BC: Flora Manufacturing and Distributing Ltd.

Ehrenreich, B., and D. English. 1978. *For her own good: 150 years of the experts' advice to women.* New York: Anchor Press / Doubleday.

Enrich 1996. 'Attention: ADHD.' : Enrich Newsletter. Corporate handout.

Farrington, D. 1989. 'Early predictors of adolescent aggression and adult violence.' *Violence and Victims* 4: 79–100.

Feingold, B. 1975. *Why your child is hyperactive*. New York: Random House.

Findlay, D., and L. Miller. 1994. 'Medical power and women's bodies,' in B. Singh Bolaria and Rosemary Bolaria (eds), *Women, medicine and health*. Halifax: Fernwood, 115–39.

Fiske, J. 1998. 'Audiencing: Cultural practice and cultural studies,' in N.K. Denzin and Y.S. Lincoln (eds.), *The landscape of qualitative research: Theories and issues*. Thousand Oaks, Calif.: Sage, 359–82.

Flanagan, P. 1998. 'Teen mothers: Countering the myths of dysfunction and developmental disruption,' in C.G. Coll, J.L. Surrey, and K. Weingarten (eds.), *Mothering against the odds: Diverse voices of contemporary mothers*. New York and London: Guilford, 238–54.

Flynn, P. 2000. *Main campaigns: Are too many of our children being drugged?* London: Paul Flynn, MP (U.K.).

Forehand, R., M. Wierson, C. Frame, T. Kemptom, and L. Armistead, 1991. 'Juvenile delinquency entry and persistence: Do attention problems contribute to conduct problems?' *Journal of Behavior Therapy and Experimental Psychiatry* 22: 261–4.

Foss, K. 1999. 'Helping mom and dad help Johnny.' *Globe and Mail*. 20 April, 19–21.

Foucault, M. 1977. 'Intellectuals and power: A conversation between Michel Foucault and Giles Deleuze,' in D. Bouchard (ed.), *Language, counter-memory, practice: Selected essays and interviews by Michel Foucault*. Oxford: Basil Blackwell, 212–31.

– 1980a. 'Two lectures,' in C. Gordon (ed.), *Power/knowledge: Selected interviews and other writings by Michel Foucault, 1972–1977*. New York: Pantheon, 74–108.

– 1980b. 'Truth and power,' in C. Gordon (ed.), *Power/knowledge: Selected interviews and other writings by Michel Foucault, 1972–1977*. New York: Pantheon, 109–33.

– 1984. 'Truth and method,' in P. Rabinow (ed.), *The Foucault reader*. New York: Pantheon, 51–76.

– 1987. 'The ethic of care of the self as a practice of freedom: An interview translated by J.D. Gauthier,' in J. Bernauer and D. Rasmussen (eds.), *The final Foucault*, London: M.I.T. Press, 1–20.

– 1988. 'Technologies of the self: A seminar with Michel Foucault,' in L. Martin, H. Gutman, and P. Hutton (eds.), *Technologies of the self*. Amherst: University of Massachusetts Press, 16–49.

- 1991. 'Questions of method,' in G. Burchell, C. Gordon, and P. Miller (eds.), *The Foucault effect: Studies in governmentality.* London: Harvester Wheatsheaf, 73–86.
- 1995. *Discipline and punish: The birth of the prison.* New York: Vintage.

Fraktman, M.G. 1998. 'Immigrant mothers: What makes them high risk?' in C.G. Coll, J.L. Surrey, and K. Weingarten (eds.), *Mothering against the odds: Diverse voices of contemporary mothers.* New York and London: Guilford, 85–107.

Franklin, B.M. 1994. *From 'backwardness' to 'at-risk': Childhood learning difficulties and the contradictions of school reform.* Albany: State University of New York.

Fraser, N. 1994. 'A genealogy of dependency: Tracing a keyword of the U.S. welfare state.' *Signs: A Journal of Women in Culture and Society* 19: 309–36.
- 1995. 'False antithesis,' in L. Nicholson (ed.), *Feminist contentions.* New York and London: Routledge.

Frederick, B.P., and J.D. Olmi, 1994. 'Children with attention deficit / hyperactivity disorder: A review of the literature on social skills deficits.' *Psychology in the Schools* 31: 200–96.

Gilligan, C. 1983. 'Woman's place in man's life cycle,' in H. Giroux and D. Purpel (eds.), *The hidden curriculum and moral education: Deception or discovery?* Berkeley, Calif.: McCutchan, 209–28.

Gilmore, A., L. Best, and R. Milne. 1998. 'DEC report no. 78: Methylphenidate in children with hyperactivity.' London: National Health Service.

Giroux, H. 1981. 'Introduction: Ideology, culture and the process of schooling.' *Ideology, culture and the process of schooling.* Philadelphia: Temple University Press.

Greenblatt, A. 1994. 'Gender and ethnicity bias in the assessment of attention deficit disorder.' *Social Work in Education* 16: 89–95.

Grumet, M.R. 1988. *Bitter milk: Women and teaching.* Amherst: University of Massachusetts Press.

Habib, M. 1998. 'Learning disorders linked to essential fatty acids.' *Victoria Times-Colonist*, 8 Feb., A5.

Halikas, J., J. Meller, C. Morse, and M. Lyttle. 1990. 'Predicting substance abuse in juvenile offenders: Attention deficit disorder versus aggressivitiy.' *Child Psychiatry and Human Development* 2: 49–55.

Hallahan, D., J. Kauffman, and J. Lloyd. 1996. *Introduction to learning disabilities.* Needham Heights, Mass.: Allyn and Bacon.

Haraway 1991. *Symians, cyborgs and women: The reinvention of nature.* New York and London: Routledge.

Hartsock, N. 1990. 'Foucault on power: A theory for women?' in L. Nicholson (ed.), *Feminism/postmodernism.* New York and London: Routledge, 157–75.

– 1996. 'Postmodernism and political change: Issues for feminist theory,' in S.J. Hekman (ed.), *Feminist interpretations of Michel Foucault*. University Park: Pennsylvania State University Press, 39–55.

Hooper, C.-A. 1992. *Mothers surviving child sexual abuse*. London and New York: Tavistock/Routledge.

Hough, A. 1997. 'Ritalin: Wonder drug or Band-Aid solution?' *Vue Weekly*. Edmonton. 13–19 Nov., 11.

Jackson, P.W. 1983. 'The daily grind,' in H. Giroux and D. Purpel (eds.), *The hidden curriculum and moral education: Deception or discovery?* Berkeley, Calif.: McCutchan, 28–60.

Jenish, D.A. 2000. 'Reclaiming the good life.' *Maclean's Magazine*. 113(20): 54–7.

Johnston, J. 1997. 'ADHD in teenagers.' *Alberta Parent Quarterly*: 10–14.

Kenway, J. 1990. 'Education and the right's discursive politics: Private versus state schooling,' in S.J. Ball (ed.), *Foucault and education: Disciplines and knowledge*. New York, London: Routledge, 167–20b.

Kewley, D.G. 1998. 'Attention deficit (hyperactivity) disorder is under-diagnosed and undertreated in Britain.' *British Medical Journal* 23: 1594–6.

Kiger, G. 1985. 'Economic transformation and the processing of hyperactive school children.' *Mid-American Review of Sociology* 10: 65–85.

Knowles, C. 1996. *Family boundaries: The invention of normality and dangerousness*. Peterborough, Ont.: Broadview Press.

Lacharité, C., and C. Piché, 1992. 'Parental stress in mothers of preschoolers: Validity standard of the parenting stress index in Quebec.' *Santé Mental au Quebec* 172: 183–203.

Lacombe, D. 1994. *Blue politics: Pornography and the law in the age of feminism*. Toronto: University of Toronto Press.

Landsmann, G. 1998. 'Reconstructing motherhood in the age of "perfect" babies: Mothers of infants and toddlers with disabilities.' *Signs: Journal of Women in culture and society* 24(1): 69–99.

Lasch, C. 1977. *Haven in a heartless world*. New York: Basic Books.

Lather, P. 1991. *Getting smart: Feminist research and pedagogy with/in the postmodern*. New York: Routledge.

Leifer, R. 1990. 'Introduction: The medical model as the ideology of the therapeutic state.' *Journal of Mind and Behavior* 11: 247–58.

Litt, J. 2000. *Medicalized motherhood: Perspectives from the lives of African-American and Jewish women*. London: Rutgers University Press.

Londsdorf, B. 1991. 'The effects of expressed emotion: Role strain and parenting mastery on the behavior of children with attention deficit hyperactivity disorder.' Doctoral dissertation.

Lupton, D. 1995. *The imperative of health: Public health and the regulated body.* Thousand Oaks, Calif.: Sage.

– 1999. *Risk.* London and New York: Routledge.

Lupton, D., and L. Barclay. 1997. *Constructing fatherhood: Discourses and experiences.* Thousand Oaks, Calif.: Sage Publications.

Mack, T. 2000. 'I didn't want my son on drugs.' *Independent.* London. 23 March, 2–3.

MacLeod, L. 1987. *Battered but not beaten ... Preventing wife battering in Canada.* Ottawa: Canadian Advisory Council on the Status of Women.

Malacrida, C. 1998. *Mourning the dreams: How parents create meaning from miscarriage, stillbirth and early infant death.* Edmonton: Qual Institute Press.

– 2001. 'Motherhood, resistance and attention deficit disorder: Strategies and limits.' *Canadian Review of Sociology and Anthropology* 38(2): 141–65.

– 2002. 'Alternative therapies and attention deficit disorder: Discourses of maternal responsibility and risk.' *Gender and Society* 16(3) 366–86.

Martin, E. 1992. *The woman in the body: A cultural analysis of reproduction.* Boston, Mass.: Beacon Press.

Maté, G. 2000a. 'Attention please: Doctors must stop thinking of ADD as a disease that can only be controlled with drugs.' *Globe and Mail.* 4 May, A15.

– 2000b. *Scattered: How attention deficit disorder originates and what you can do about it.* New York: E.P. Dutton.

McConnell, H. 1997. 'ADHD just doesn't add up to British Psychological Society.' *Medical Post.*

McCracken, G. 1988. *The long interview.* Newbury Park, Calif.: Sage.

McGee, R., S. Williams, and P.A. Silva, 1987. 'A comparison of girls and boys with teacher-identified problems of attention.' *Journal of the American Academy of Child and Adolescent Psychiatry* 26: 711–17.

McKee, L., and M. O'Brien, 1982. 'The father figure: Some current orientations and historical perspectives,' in L. McKee, and M. O'Brien (eds.), *The father figure.* London and New York: Tavistock, 3–25.

McLaren, P. 1985. 'The ritual dimensions of resistance: Clowning and symbolic inversion.' *Journal of Education* 167: 84–97.

Merrow, R. 1995. 'ADD – a dubious diagnosis?' Learning Matters Inc. http://www.pbs.org/merrow/repository/television/past/-attn.html

Middleton, S. 1997. *Disciplining sexuality: Foucault, life histories and education.* New York: Teachers College Press.

Mills, S. 1997. *Discourse.* London and New York: Routledge.

Minde, K. 1987. 'The child with attention deficit disorder: Medical and psychological treatment.' *Learning Disabilities Magazine.* Calgary: Learning Disabilities Association of Alberta.

Murphy, K.R., and S. LeVert. 1995. *Out of the fog: Treatment options and coping strategies for adult attention deficit disorder*. New York: Skylight Press.

NICE 2000. 'Guidance on the use of methylphenidate for ADHD.' London: National Health Service.

Nelson, F. 1996. *Lesbian motherhood: An exploration of Canadian lesbian families*. Toronto: University of Toronto Press.

Oakley, A. 1984. *The captured womb: A history of the medical care of pregnant women*. Oxford: Basil Blackwell.

Olssen, M. 1999. *Michel Foucault: Materialism and education*. Westport, Conn.: Bergin and Garvey.

Palmer, D., and A. Bongers, 1997. 'Ritalin use in Canada up 35% – and climbing.' *Calgary Herald*. 30 June, A2.

Pfohl, S. 1978. *Predicting dangerousness*. Toronto: Lexington Books.

Popkewitz, T.S. 2000. 'Globalization/regionalization, knowledge and the educational practices: Some notes on comparative strategies for educational research,' in T.S. Popkewitz (ed.), *Educational knowledge: Changing relationships between the state, civil society and the educational community*. Albany, NY: State University of New York, 3–29.

Porter, R. 1987. *A social history of madness: Stories of the insane*. London: Phoenix.

Purpel, D.E. 1988. *The moral and spiritual crisis in education: A curriculum for justice and compassion in education*. South Hadley, Mass.: Bergin and Garvey.

Rapp, D.D. 1999. 'Helping children, not drugging them.' Toronto: Citizens Commission on Human Rights.

Rapp, R. 1999. *Testing women, Testing the fetus: The social impact of amniocentesis in America*. New York and London: Routledge.

Reay, D. 1998. 'Cultural reproduction: Mothers' involvement in their children's primary schooling,' in M. Grenfell, and D. James (eds.), *Bourdieu and education: Acts of practical theory*. London: Falmer Press.

Rees, A. 1998a. 'Drug's success fuels misdiagnosis.' *Calgary Herald*, 13 March, A13.

– 1998b. 'Private school brings hope to ADHD children.' *Calgary Herald*. 12 March, A13.

– 1998c. 'Rise in ADHD cases worrying – Expert.' *Calgary Herald*. 13 March, A13.

– 1998d. 'Teachers key to rising ADHD diagnosis – doctor.' *Calgary Herald*. 10 March, A11.

Rees, A. and C. Dawson, 1998. 'Use of Ritalin under attack: Some parents too quick to seek medication for behavioral disorders, says Calgary doctor.' *Calgary Herald*.

Riessman, C.K. 1993. *Narrative analysis*. Newbury Park, Calif.: Sage.

Roberts, D.E. 1999. 'Mothers who fail to protect their children: Accounting for private and public responsibility,' in J.E. Hanigsberg, and S. Ruddick (eds.), *Mother troubles*. Boston, Mass.: Beacon, 31–49.

Rose, N. 1985. *The psychological complex: Psychology, politics and society in England 1869–1939*. London: Routledge and Kegan Paul.

– 1990. *Governing the soul: The shaping of the private self*. London: Routledge.

Rotundo, A.E. 1987. 'Patriarchs and participants: A historical perspective on fatherhood,' in M. Kaufman (ed.), *Beyond patriarchy: Essays by men on pleasure, power and change*. Toronto and New York: Oxford University Press.

Rowland, R. 1987. 'Technology and motherhood: Reproductive choice reconsidered.' *Signs: Journal of Women in Culture and Society* 12(3): 512–29.

Schatsky, D., and F. Yaroshevsky. 1997. 'Ritalin, Ritalin, who's got the Ritalin?' *Globe and Mail*. 3 Sept., 15.

Schuckit, M.A., S. Sweeney, and L. Huey. 1987. 'Hyperactivity and the risk for alcoholism.' *Journal of Clinical Psychiatry* 40: 275–7.

Scott, J.C. 1985. *Weapons of the weak: Everyday forms of peasant resistance*. London: Yale University Press.

Scott, J.W. 1988. 'Deconstructing equality-versus-difference: Or, the uses of poststructuralist theory for feminism.' *Feminist Studies* 1: 33–50.

Scott, M.E. 1987. 'Attention deficit disorder (ADD).' *ERIC clearinghouse on handicapped and gifted children*. Washington, DC: U.S. Department of Education.

Sealander, K.A., V.L. Scheibert, M.E. Eigenberger, J.K. Flahive, M.T. Hill, and M.J.N. Brumbaugh. 1995. 'Attention-deficit hyperactivity disorder: An overview for elementary school teachers.' *Early Childhood Education* 28: 9–15.

Shorter, E. 1975. *The making of the modern family*. New York: Basic Books.

Sigmon, S.B. 1987. *Radical analysis of special education: Focus on historical development and learning disabilities*. London, New York, and Philadelphia: Falmer Press.

Slee, R. 1994. 'Finding a student voice in school reform: Student disaffection, pathologies of disruption and educational control.' *International Studies in Sociology of Education* 4: 147–72.

Smith, D.E. 1987. *The everyday world as problematic: A feminist sociology*. Toronto: University of Toronto Press.

– 1990. *Texts, facts and femininity: Exploring the relations of ruling*. New York and London: Routledge.

Sparks, E. 1998. 'Against all odds: Resistance and resilience in African American welfare mothers,' in C.G. Coll, J.L. Surrey, and K. Weingarten (eds.), *Mothering against the odds: Diverse voices of contemporary mothers*. New York and London: Guilford, 215–37.

Stordy, J.B. No date. 'Essential fatty acids and learning disorders.' *Printed with the concent [sic] of* Pro Health. No city, no publisher.

Swartz, J. 1997. 'Whither, evening primrose oil?' *Globe and Mail*, 13 Dec., A13.

Szasz, T.S. 1974a. *The myth of mental illness: Foundations of a theory of personal conduct*. New York: Perennial Library, Harper and Row Publishers.

– 1974b. *The myth of psychotherapy: Mental healing as religion, rhetoric and repression*. Garden City, NY: Anchor Press / Doubleday.

Szumowski, E.K., L.J. Ewing, and S.B. Campbell, 1986. 'What happens to "hyperactive" preschoolers?' *Journal of Children in Contemporary Society* 19: 75–88.

Taylor, E. 1997. 'Hyperactivity as a special educational need,' in P. Cooper, and K. Ideus (eds.), *Attention deficit / hyperactivity disorder*. Maidstone, Kent: AWCEBD, 96–107.

Thomas, J. 1993. *Doing critical ethnography*. Thousand Oaks, Calif.: Sage.

Thorne, B. 1992. 'Feminism and the family: Two decades of thought,' in B. Thorne and M. Yalom (eds.), *Rethinking the family: Some feminist questions*. Boston, Mass.: Northeastern University Press, 3–30.

Turner, B. 1997. 'From governmentality to risk: Some reflections on Foucault's contribution to medical sociology,' in A. Petersen and R. Bunton (eds.), *Foucault: Health and medicine*. London: Routledge, vii–xii.

Ullman, J.R., and R. Ullman, 1996. *Ritalin free kids: Safe and effective homeopathic medicine for ADD and other behavioral and learning problems*. Rocklin, Calif.: Prima Publishing.

Vallance, E. 1983. 'Hiding the hidden curriculum: An interpretation of the language of justification in nineteenth-century educational reform,' in H. Giroux and D. Purpel (eds.), *The hidden curriculum: Deception or discovery?* Berkeley, Calif.: McCutchan, 2–27.

Walker, L. 1979. *The battered woman*. New York: Harper and Row.

Weedon, C. 1987. *Feminist practice and poststructuralist theory*. Oxford: Basil Blackwell.

– 1999. *Feminism, theory and the politics of difference*. Oxford: Blackwell.

Woodward, W. 2001. 'Anger over Blair's two-tier school policy.' *Guardian Weekly*. 15–21 Feb., 8.

Young, P. 1997. 'Childhood assessment of attention deficit hyperactivity disorder.' *Alberta Parent Quarterly*, Spring.

Zola, I.K. 1983. *Socio-medical inquiries*. Philadelphia: Temple University Press.

Index